View from the Podium

A Music Teacher's Journey

Edward Judd

D1523311

Creative Music Productions—Madison, WI
ISBN: 978-0-578-55721-2
Library of Congress Control Number: 9780578557212
View from the Podium | Edward Judd
Available formats: eBook | paperback distribution

Dedication

To my mom, whose encouragement, support, and love made this journey possible.

Acknowledgments

There are many that I have depended on through my music teacher journey, my wife, who always helped where she could, and family, my brother David, colleagues, teachers, both those I have mentioned in the book, and those I have not, friends, both personal and professional, etc. Special thanks to Jim LeBaron for technical help, and cover photos

Table of Contents

Prologue

"(When the music ended…) At first, there was silence. Then the applause started and began to grow exponentially. I had the students stand for the applause and then turned around to take a bow. I stood there dumbfounded by what I saw. Most of the audience were standing and applauding, but there were many folks scattered across the audience that were in tears. Many of them were men as well as women, and some of them so inconsolable that they were unable to stand or clap. I had been able to stir the emotions of an audience through music before, but nothing like this."

The idea for this book started on the occasion of the celebration of my 40th year in music education. I wrote a reflection for my spring concert that year that outlined several of what you might call my greatest moments as a music educator. As a result of encouragement from family and friends, this then became the reason I wanted to write this book, so I could share with folks some of these wonderful experiences I have had as a member of this profession.

Some of the names have been changed to protect the innocent and the guilty, although I'm not sure the guilty deserve it. Still, I realize that some folks may remember the events contained in this book different than I do.

In my younger days, I had the same preconceptions that most folks have who are not music educators. As I became exposed to the classroom, I have to admit that I was somewhat surprised by the realities of education, and music education in particular. However, far more interesting than the various attempts by television and the media to portray this profession. Before we start, a few organizational definitions:

NafME – National Association for Music Education – The

,onal professional organization for music teachers. The organization changed its name a few years ago. In the book, it is also referred to by its old name of MENC – Music Educators National Conference

MMEA – Maine Music Educators Association – The Maine affiliate of NafME, serving the music teachers of Maine.

Introduction

A major reason I wanted to write this book, was so that I could share with folks some of the wonderful experiences I have had as a member of this profession. It certainly didn't turn out anywhere near what I expected it would when I began this journey. Besides being blessed with people I have met along the way who were positive and supportive, it also allows me to call people to account who refused to acknowledge the value of what I teach. Music is unique in the curriculum that we teach in the schools. There are very few other classes in which students from both multiple grades, and multiple ability levels are not only all mixed in together, but must all be engaged in a singular activity in which the efforts of the entire group must be channeled to create a work of art. Many of us are aware of the power that music has, and when I can guide students to use that power to make a definitive statement without using words, or to bring audience members to tears (in a good way), then my class is contributing to the growth and well-roundedness of my students. As the National School Boards Association once said, "The purpose of school is not to create biological robots."

However, as I was writing this, I began to see that I was also outlining multiple struggles, both to become a music teacher, and then to provide my students with the best instruction and musical experience that I could. When one is training to become a music teacher, your professors will warn you that you are liable to encounter principals and other administrators that are unsupportive, uninformed, and may even try to limit the growth of your music program. Now that I am in the final stages of my career, I feel fortunate that I now have administrators that are positive and supportive. That

the case. More times than I can count, I have
.d with Superintendents, School Board members,
, and other administrators that: A) talked the talk
ɔuldn't walk the walk; B) were fairly ignorant of what is
ɔessary for a music program to succeed; or C) actively
engaged in practices meant to limit the growth and success of
the music program. In the situation that I now teach in, these
things no longer exist, and that is a blessing, not only to
myself but also to my students.

If you think that this is a story about a hotshot conductor
who allows the world to believe that conducting school kids is
beneath him, I'm sorry to disappoint you. If you think this is
a story about an unbelievably successful music teacher, whose
students go on European tours, or whose band regularly
marches in the Rose Bowl Parade, you've also reached the
wrong place. This story is about a teacher that has had a
number of extraordinary experiences, successes and failures,
and has been able to have a positive impact on his students.
Not too long ago, I was at a fast food restaurant near a school
that I used to teach. The woman who waited on me
recognized me, even though it had been many years since she
was my student. When she told me her name it sounded
vaguely familiar, but I really didn't remember her, it had been
so long. As I was leaving, she said to me "I'll never forget
you. You changed my life." Funny, I don't remember doing
that. I spent most of my time working with kids to help them
be the best musicians they could be and help them attain a
healthy respect for the music they were performing. Being a
teacher that changes kids' lives is certainly a bonus, but I have
encountered former students such as this woman in the fast
food restaurant on a number of occasions.

It's so hard to believe that I've been doing this for more than
40 years. Moreover, I'm really not certain at what point I

would want to stop. A lot of peers my age have already retired, and many of the rest seem to be counting the years. In fact, I remember one music teacher who was counting the years before his retirement when he was in his mid-forties. I was in my mid-twenties at the time and I remember vowing to myself that I would never be that way. If I ever became that, then I would know it would be time to quit. It is perhaps that experience that made me want to continue even to this day. Another influence that may also be responsible is a well-known quote from Pablo Casals, a widely known cello player who performed well into his 90's. Casals is quoted as saying "To retire, is the beginning of death." I kind of identify with this. I can't imagine a time when I won't see students, help them perfect their skills, lead them to "Aha!" moments, even laugh at some of their corny jokes that kids that age are prone to make. Time will tell if I am able to continue, so long as my health holds out. Of course, if you were to ask my wife, she would tell you that I already have one foot in the nursing home, and the other on a banana peel.

But getting back on track. As I said before, I want to share with you some of the wonderful experiences I have had as a music teacher, However, before we get into that, it would be good to examine the question of how I became a music educator and why.

EARLY YEARS

So if someone were to ask me what does it take for a person to become a music teacher, there is no easy answer. Sure, one has to have a certain degree of talent and skill, but a lot of that starts fairly early. In my case, I started my road to music through my mom. She didn't plan on me growing up to be a music teacher when I was 3-years-old of course. She just wanted me to experience what it was like to make music at that age. She would play the piano, and I would sing along. That's how it started. Now a few 3-year-olds can sing simple tunes, although many cannot. They can initiate a singing voice, but they have yet to develop a sense of tonality. Until they understand what a high pitch and low pitch sound like and are able to adjust their singing voices to the correct pitch, they will pretty much sing random notes.

However, it seems that I had the ability at that young age to not only sing the correct pitches, but to sing songs that were more sophisticated than simple nursery rhyme ditties. When I very young, I remember singing songs with my mom as she played the piano. When I was 5, my mom brought me to perform in the local CYO variety show. The CYO, or Catholic Youth Organization had a strong presence in those days, providing catholic teenagers with activities and opportunities to socialize within the scope of the church. Their variety show was a major event in the parish, and the show was always well attended. To perform in the show was both exciting and scary, especially since everyone else who was performing were teenagers, and at that age, it seemed that I was the only kid performing with a bunch of adults. I sang the tune "Peggy O'Neil" and I could sing it fairly well although I would at times be a bit "creative". I could sense when the range of the song went beyond what I could sing. Sometimes the notes were a little too high for me. But I had the sense that if I dropped my voice an octave, I could still continue singing. I, of course, had no idea what I was doing, and was somewhat puzzled when the audience seemed to get a kick out of it. I apparently was doing cute at that age without realizing it. I remember being pulled out of my Kindergarten class at the parish catholic school that I attended. I was escorted to a 7th grade classroom where a fairly stern looking nun commanded me to sing. I sang, of course, and after some discussion in front of the class, the session was over, and I was taken back to my Kindergarten room. This happened a couple of more times in other classrooms. I didn't really understand why I was so popular for something that was so natural to me.

DISCOVERING THE BASS

After a while, as I got older. I was no longer in such demand. I no longer performed in the CYO variety show, and my musical life took on more normal dimensions. I briefly took accordion lessons and twice began lessons on the piano. Success was elusive, and I felt bad in the case of the piano, because after all, my mom was a piano player and I felt I had disappointed her. Then, when I was 10, there was an unexpected development. About a year prior, my dad indicated an interest in being able to play music with my mom. So my mom, with help from a family friend who was a bass player, went out and purchased a string bass from a member of the New Haven Symphony. My dad started learning to play the bass with my mom tutoring him in how to read the music, etc. This lasted only a few sessions and then my dad lost interest. And so the bass sat in a corner, untouched for an extended period of time. Fast forward a year, and then one day, I believe it was during a school vacation week, when I was generally bored and had no interest in watching soap operas, I picked up the bass and started fooling with it. I found the instruction book that my dad used and began to play from it. I could read bass clef from my piano instruction, so it was just a case of learning where all the notes on the bass fingerboard were located. As I was absorbed in this, my mom came into the room and watched what I was doing. She immediately sat down at the piano and showed me how to read the chords off a music lead sheet. As we played together, she on the piano, and I on the bass, a whole new music experience began to take shape with me. We found time to play together every day that week, and whenever we got a chance afterward. I took to the bass as I had never taken to anything before. My mom contacted our bass player family friend, who came to the house to watch me play. After watching me play with my mom, he made a couple of adjustments to my technique, and started giving me lessons. After a while I started taking lessons from another bass teacher, and then moved on to a third. I also listened to a lot of recordings from my mom's jazz collection. I would listen and zero in on how the bass players on each of the recordings would craft their bass lines.

In the summer between 8th grade and high school, I was given a chance to play with a band. I guess you could characterize it as a "wedding band". Four guys, all adults except for me, who would play dance music at weddings, dances, etc. A woman who was my mom's secretary for several years had a son who was looking to put together such a group and asked if I would be interested in playing bass with them. It wasn't really difficult. All I did was look over the shoulder of the accordion player and read the chord changes from the music, just like I did when I played with my mom. After a couple of rehearsals, they invited me to be their permanent bass player. More on that later.

HIGH SCHOOL

In the meantime, as any kid would, I was contemplating my entry into high school. I wasn't sure if high school would have anything of value for me musically. Family friends who were musicians would drop by our house as they always did on a regular basis, but now they would tease me about the prospect of me being in the high school band. They would say things like "Maybe they can find a float to put you on, so you could play the bass with the band on the football field." I took the kidding in stride, but the third day of my freshman year in high school, during the homeroom period, the announcement came on the school intercom- "Any student wishing to be in the band should report to the auditorium at this time". I was riveted to my seat, not really knowing what I should do. Would being in the high school band be valuable to me, or would it just be a distraction to my bass playing ambitions to be involved with such a group. After all, I had no experience playing in such a group because the catholic school that I attended through the 8th grade had no band program. As I sat in the classroom wondering what I should do, a girl in my homeroom, her name was Valerie, asked the teacher to go the auditorium, and proceeded out the door. Now you must understand, I had an intense crush on Valerie through the 7th and 8th grade. I never said anything to her. I was too shy. Here was this very pretty girl who was an absolute brainiac. She always knew the answer to every question the teacher asked and never received anything less than an "A" on every test. In comparison to myself, for who it would have been kind to say was at best a mediocre student. Perhaps it was the feeling that I could never be Valerie's intellectual equal, and therefore could never muster up the courage to speak to her. There was a lot to admire about her, and I guess you could say I admired her from afar. So, I was really surprised when I saw her leave the room to join the band. I didn't even know that she was a flute player. "That does it!" I thought, and I got up and asked to go to the auditorium having no idea the turn my life was about to take.

LAUNCH OF THE WEDDING BAND

In the meantime, or I should say a couple of days later my mom received a late-night phone call. I had already gone to sleep, so she wrote a note for me to find in the morning. The wedding band that I was now playing with had booked its first gig, and it payed $20. It was so cool! My mom took me out to get me a tuxedo, thus adding to the coolness. I didn't know of anyone who owned their own tux at the age of 14, except for perhaps Donny Osmond or Michael Jackson. Then at some point an interesting thought occurred to me, "Hey, I don't need to rent a tux for the prom". A couple of weeks later, we played the wedding. It was a new experience, of course, and I remember a couple of things. I remember that the time seemed to drag, and I was surprised at that. It was only a 3-hour gig, but I was really tired afterward. I also had a rather large blister on my finger because, of course, I was not used to playing this much.

During these same couple of weeks, I also started my participation in the high school band. The director, Mr. McWilliams was a knowledgeable guy, and he instantly understood that as a bass player we would both have to think a bit outside of the box. The most pressing issue at that point was that playing string bass with a marching band was not desirable for either of us. As with most band programs in those days, the band would concentrate on playing for football games in the fall, and the switch to more symphonic repertoire after football season. Thus, my first 3 months in the band would consist of mostly playing at football games. However, Mr. McWilliams explained to me that the bass drummer in the band wasn't always reliable to stay on the beat, and would I mind playing bass drum also, as a bit of extra insurance. I was agreeable to this, and so I took my place in the percussion section playing bass drum. Now, the band didn't have an actual standard bass drum for me to play, but it did have a type of bass drum that was referred to as a "flapjack". It was a very narrow drum, perhaps 3 or 4 inches thick, that had a swivel at the base of its metal harness, which allowed the drum to rotate while it was being played. However, it also had a lock that would prevent it from rotating, if necessary. To my mind, it was necessary. This type of bass drum was widely used by many college bands in the '60's, and it was most impressive to see a bass drum section with all the drums rotating.

When it was locked in position, it felt as if I was playing a huge pancake. One that was about 28 inches in diameter. I was not brave enough to try to play a rotating bass drum in front of hundreds, if not thousands, of people. And so, I kept the rotation lock on through most of the season. At the final football game of the year, I decided to try to play it rotating. It was exciting, difficult and stressful all at once. I hurt my hand a couple of times as it collided with the outside shell of the drum while it was rotating, and I had to momentarily stop playing a couple of times because the rotation of the drum had slowed, making it difficult, if not impossible, for me to play on the beat. So much for my bass drum career.

As the school year progressed, I started experimenting with various instruments. I spent some time learning the saxophone, and later the flute. When football season ended, I started learning the tuba. I wasn't sure that this was something I wanted to do. If Hamlet were a musician in today's world, he might ask- "Tuba? - or not Tuba?" that was the question. However, Mr. McWilliams was very encouraging through all this, saying that in college, a student who could play both the string bass and the tuba would be a valuable member of a music department. At the same time, he would occasionally set aside some time for us to play together, him at the piano and me on the bass much like I would do with my mom. Before I knew it, I was playing with him at school assemblies accompanying some of the really good singers performing before the entire school.

THE NEW YEAR'S EVE GIG

As football season ended, my wedding band became more active. We played a Christmas party at an upscale restaurant, and before I knew it, we were slated to play a New Year's gig. Now as many folks know, musicians have traditionally commanded higher prices on New Year's Eve than other times of the year. We were hired to play for a New Year's party at a local American Legion hall for $100 a man. Remember now, this was the 1960's and back then this was a pretty hefty paycheck for one night's work. Then to my amazement, we were not even halfway through the gig, and we were hired to return the following New Year's Eve. Not bad for a 14-year-old. After each gig, I gave the money I earned to my grandmother, who kept it in a strongbox for me. She kept meticulous records and never questioned me when I asked her if I could withdraw some money.

After Christmas, Mr. McWilliams encouraged me to try out for All-State, which was kind of an All-Star event for the best musicians in the state. In those days, the Connecticut Music Educators Association sponsored an All-State music festival in the fall. Students would have to audition the previous spring for a spot in the All-State Band, Chorus, or Symphony Orchestra.

Mr. McWilliams also nominated me for regional festivals,

that is to say similar honors festivals consisting of the best musicians of the participating high schools, but on a smaller scale. At one of these smaller festivals, known as the Southwest Connecticut Regional Festival, I had my first experience playing with a symphony orchestra. I had never even heard a live string section before, with violins, violas and cellos, and by the time the festival concluded with its grand concert, I walked away with a much greater understanding of the contrast between a band and an orchestra.

THE ALL-STATE AUDITION

As the weeks passed, I spent almost all of my practice time staring at the All-State audition piece. The Marcello Concerto in G may not have been the most difficult piece in the world, but you probably would not have been able to convince me of that. It looked really hard, and any attempt I made to play it failed miserably. To make matters worse, I was in between bass teachers at that point, and thus had no one to coach me with it. Finally, during the last week before auditions, I resolved myself to take one more stab at it. This time, I tried a different approach. I sat at my mom's piano and started playing the bass part on the piano. I would play a phrase on the piano, and then play the same phrase on the bass. I kept doing this back and forth until finally, the piece began to take shape. Feeling comfortable enough with the piece, my father took me to the All-State audition. Of course, I had never played before a judge before, and let me tell you, I sounded like it. I started playing the audition piece, and things started to go downhill very fast. I made errors in places that I had never made errors before. If I had to characterize the audition in one word, "disastrous" comes to mind. I left the audition really distraught and was considerably depressed. My parents tried to console me, but it was no use. It certainly looked like I could cross off being a symphony player.

A couple of weeks later, Mr. McWilliams told all of us students who auditioned that none of us had made All-State. "No surprise there" I told myself. However, the next day, another letter arrived at the school containing an All-State acceptance form with my name on it. "I don't understand," said Mr. McWilliams as he pulled out the original letter he received the day before. As it turns out, the original letter said that none of the students from my school had made the All-State BAND. But of course, I had auditioned for the All-State Symphony Orchestra, and was accepted as a bass player- 8th chair – meaning that I was the last bass player to be accepted.

I did not realize it at the time but bumbling as I had been in the All-State audition, my success at making the group would lead to other things. Toward the end of the school year, I received a phone call from some people who ran a one-week music camp for high school kids in the summer. It certainly looked like they had gotten my name from Connecticut All-State roster. The Laurel Music Camp took place every summer for a week at what would normally be a Boy Scout camp in the Connecticut hills. The camp needed bass players that year, and they asked if I would I be willing to accept a scholarship to attend. I said yes, and so began my first summer music camp experience.

THE HARTT SUMMER PROGRAM AND DR. PARANOV

I attended the Laurel Music Camp all of my four years in high school, but by attending that first year, I learned a great deal. I was able to improve my technique, increase my confidence and develop a vibrato. I also learned of another opportunity. All of us received fliers from, and were encouraged to attend,

5

the inaugural summer music program at the Hartt College of Music, at the University of Hartford. My father agreed to pay my tuition, and off I went for my second such experience of the summer. Hartt pulled out all the stops for their first attempt in hosting a summer program for high school students. Many of their best professors were involved in the program, including an orchestra conductor who would become a major influence in my life. His name was Dr. Moshe Paranov, and he was a legend at Hartt. Well into his 70's, he continued to teach at Hartt, working with students, conducting the orchestra, and holding musicianship clinics. In rehearsal, he was almost a volatile mix of grandfatherly support, excitement for the music, disarming humor when things became difficult, and general crankiness. "I hate kids!" he would often say, "but I love young musicians". Being under the baton of Dr. Paranov came with it an unspoken vow, to dedicate ourselves as a group to the mission of interpreting the music to the highest level we were capable of. Paranov was the personification of the Pablo Casals quote "Don't just play the notes, play the meaning behind the notes". Every nuance was examined, and nothing was out of bounds when it came to producing the desired musical effect. I can remember once when there was a particularly dramatic tympani entrance in a piece. "Lift your mallet higher!" he instructed the tympani player. Not satisfied, we tried it again. "Lift it even higher!" he said to the timpanist again. Still not satisfied, we did it one more time. "Higher!" he shouted. At this point, some of us could hear the tympani player mumbling under his breath, "We're not supposed to lift it that high". But finally, the effect he was looking for was achieved.

When it came to imparting a concept to the orchestra, Dr. Paranov was an endless fountain of stories and experiences, some of them coming from his association with Isaac Stern, and famous cellist Leonard Rose. I don't know if we ever met his expectations, but he was supportive and encouraging nonetheless. The end result for us in the orchestra was to take the music to a much higher level, higher than I ever would have thought possible.

Dr. Paranov's musicianship class was also an experience that I was unprepared for. Some of the best players in the summer program would play for him in the concert hall with all of the students present. These soloists were good, but not so good that Dr. Paranov would not be able to find ways to make the soloist play more musically. I think that was the difference. The issue was not to make the soloist play better but to make the soloist play with more musical sensitivity. At some point, I noticed the same thing happening with the orchestra. He did not seem so concerned about how well we would play a piece, as how musically we would play the piece.

Although this was only a 2-week program, I could feel a transformation taking place within me. Up to this point, I was just a kid with musical aspirations, just like other kids have aspirations to be president or to be a professional baseball player. But now, I was inspired like no one had ever been able to inspire me. I knew at that point that just being a musician would not be enough. I needed to be a music educator. Needed, in such a way like no other occupation could possibly be as satisfying. To be able to work with young musicians, to help them take their playing to the next level, to help them unlock the mysteries of what makes music speak to us all on a level that mere words could not possibly describe. I just knew, more than I knew anything else, that this had to be my calling. Nothing else could possibly compare with it.

As the old saying goes- "In for a penny, in for a pound".

Now that I had resolved to myself the direction I wished to go in life, it became my major focus. It dominated my day-to-day thinking and influenced practically every decision I made. As I started my sophomore year in high school, it was as if I were on a mission. I went to concerts at other high schools and read whatever I could find on musical instruments and ensembles. Boy, did my grades suffer as a result. If I received a "C" in a class, I considered it a success. If I were to receive a "B", it was cause for celebration. Getting an "A" was unheard of for me, so "D"s were more or less my default grade, with an "F" every now and then for good measure. Of course, this would come back to haunt me senior year, when I was looking at colleges, but it wasn't as if I wasn't learning anything. I could retain a lot of the classroom material; I was simply allergic to homework.

In October, it was finally time to go to the All-State Festival, where the All-State Band, Chorus, and Symphony Orchestra would rehearse for two days at the University of Connecticut, and then present a grand concert in the Jorgensen Auditorium on the UConn campus. I remember my first day there, as I left the dining hall having just had dinner, and hearing drums in the distance. I followed the sound until I came across the UConn Marching Band in the middle of their rehearsal. Of course, this was October, and it was dark out. The band was practicing on a lighted parking lot. There was a small rise on the "home" side of this asphalt football field, and from the rise, one had a great view of the band. It wasn't particularly warm out. It always seemed to me that the UConn campus had a lot of similar weather to its Canadian counterpart, the Yukon. However, the cold didn't seem to matter to any of the band members, and they just went through their paces as if it were shirtsleeve weather. I was mesmerized by what I saw. I watched as long as I could before I needed to head back to the

All-State rehearsal. I attended All-State for 3 years, and every festival day was the same. Rehearse in the morning, have lunch, rehearse in the afternoon, wolf down dinner as quickly as I could, and rush out to go watch the UConn band for as long as I was able. So now, I had a second component to my ambition, to study to be a music teacher at the University of Connecticut.

In the meantime, the wedding band I played with continued to play occasional gigs here and there. And although Mr. McWilliams no longer taught at my school, he did invite me to play some gigs with musicians that he put together. I can remember a wedding gig that I played with his group, and one of the wedding guests was a girl in my biology class at school. It almost seemed unreal for us to see each other at this event. In the high school band, I pretty much played tuba and string bass my sophomore year. Most days, when I would get home from school, my routine was essentially the same. Listen to some recordings; practice; listen to more recordings; more practice; etc. Homework? What a distraction! It usually didn't get done except when I was in study hall. As a result, my grades remained unimpressive, and I became a bit more withdrawn socially, except of course during band rehearsal. So, I continued to play in various festivals, and took up lessons with a new bass teacher.

DISCOVERING DRUM & BUGLE CORPS

Towards the end of my sophomore year, one of my fellow band members, Harry, invited me to come to a rehearsal of the drum and bugle corps that he was a member of. On the appointed evening, he picked me up, and we went to the rehearsal. I spent the rehearsal observing and at the end, I told Harry that I would consider joining. It made sense to belong to a group like this. I knew that as a music teacher, I would more than likely need to instruct marching band, and this seemed a good way to learn. But when word got out that I had gone to watch Harry's corps, which was called the Explorers, a couple of other fellow band members then insisted that I come to a rehearsal of their corps, the Royal Lancers. So I went to a Royal Lancers rehearsal, knowing that at some point, I would need to decide which group I wanted to march with. It's no mystery why I received such attention. The contrabass bugle is the drum corps counterpart to a tuba and playing that particular type of bugle is like playing a concert tuba that sits on your shoulder. In those days, it was very difficult for drum and bugle corps to find kids willing to play the contrabass bugle, or "Contra" for short. It was even rarer to find a tuba player who could also read music and was willing to play the contra. In those days, drum and bugle corps used written music to a minimum. Most of the learning of the music was done through rote methods. The instructor would play a passage, and the corps member would try to play it back. Having a corps member who could read music made the process go smoother. Such corps members were not unheard of, but they were not that common. And so, it appeared that I needed to make a decision. From an intellectual standpoint, the Royal Lancers would seem to be the better choice. The corps had a greater level of discipline and seemed destined to probably go on to attain a higher level of achievement. However, I took more of a liking to the kids in the Explorers, and the atmosphere was more relaxed. I surprised myself because I made the decision on my social needs rather than my intellectual needs, and so I became a member of the Explorers Drum and Bugle Corps.

I made friends fast in the Explorers, and a few weeks after joining, one of my new drum corps buddies, Wes, invited me to go with him to see a drum and bugle corps field competition for senior corps. The Explorers were classified as a junior corps, meaning that the age of all of the members were under 21. Senior corps had no age limit, and most of the members of a senior corps were adults. This particular competition was sponsored by a local senior corps, the Connecticut Hurricanes, who went on to win the senior drum and bugle corps world championship that year. I went with Wes expecting to see something similar to what most marching bands did, except with drums and bugles. Not so. The drum and bugle corps performances that I saw that night were more sophisticated than even many college marching band shows at the time. The marching patterns were much more complex and better executed. At that point, I became a fierce drum corps fan, and attended as many competitions as I could.

My junior year progressed pretty much the same as my sophomore year. I continued to attend festivals, and I continued to attend summer music programs, sometimes with scholarship help, sometimes without. I hooked up with a new bass teacher, who I got along with better than my previous teachers, and it showed in my progress and technique. Bill Duffney was a recent graduate of Hartt College of Music and had been an instructor in their high school summer music program. I worked harder for him than I had with any previous bass instructor. In the spring, he coached me intensely on the All-State audition piece. This would be the audition for my senior year in high school, and I really wanted to nail the audition. I still had nightmares of my first All-State audition, and the last thing I wanted to do was repeat it. As the audition neared, I was feeling more confident, and it seemed like I had a really good feel for the audition piece. At my final bass lesson before the audition, I did one final play through of the piece for Bill. He smiled, and said he had a surprise for me, if I would guard it with my life. I was curious and said I would. He left the room for a minute and returned with a case that obviously contained a bass bow. As he opened it, and I saw the black horsehair on the bow, I instantly suspected what it was. He confirmed it right away. "It's a Zimmerman bow." he said as he took it out of the case. Fred Zimmerman was an absolute icon of bass players. A long-time principal bass player of the New York Philharmonic, Zimmerman edited several instruction books and solos for the bass and was considered a guru of bass players. Unlike most string players who used bows with white horsehair, the horsehair on the bow Zimmerman used was black. It was kind of like a trademark with him. As I understand it, Zimmerman owned about a dozen such bows, and it seems that when he died, his bows were sold off. I don't know how Bill managed to get one, but the fact that he was willing to lend it to me for this audition was one of the coolest things I've ever experienced. It felt as if I had been given a bow made of gold. On the day of the audition, I confidently marched into the judging room with my bass, took out the Zimmerman bow, and played well enough that I received the second highest score in the auditions.

SENIOR YEAR

Before I knew it, I was a high school senior. Senior year is a really memorable year for most people, and I was no exception. I was drum major of the band, and we had a new band director who gave me a lot of freedom to pursue my ambitions. The new director allowed me to design the marching show for halftime. I used elements that I learned in drum corps and mixed it with some of the format that I had seen the UConn band use. The final product was not totally what I had envisioned, but it was close. I also started to write arrangements for the band. I started writing arrangements shortly after I became engrossed in drum corps. Wouldn't it be cool, I thought, to arrange drum corps music for band and vice versa? My first attempts were absolutely horrible. Some of the notes I wrote for some of the instrument parts were in their extreme ranges and not very playable. I wrote some arrangements for the bugle section of the Explorers, and again, there was a lot of room for improvement. In the meantime however, I had spent some time learning other instruments in the band. I learned trombone, bassoon, some trumpet, and even flirted briefly with the oboe. Now it was senior year, and I wrote an arrangement of "California Dreamin'" to close the halftime show. It worked really well, and for the first time I wrote something worthy of a public performance. As spring approached, I wrote an arrangement for the high school band of Chicago's "Make Me Smile" almost as a capstone project to reflect what I had learned through high school. I experienced a setback in preparation logistics though. In those days, all copying was done on a mimeograph machine. For those unfamiliar with the process, a master sheet is attached to a piece of carbon paper. When one writes on the master sheet, the pressure of the pencil or pen forces contact between the carbon paper and the back of the master sheet. The master is then affixed to a rotating cylinder, and as the cylinder rotates, the back of the master copy is then coated with mimeograph fluid and impressed upon a clean sheet of paper leaving an imprint of the master copy in blue ink. In my case, the issue occurred due to a protective tissue paper in between the master copy paper and the carbon paper when it is removed from the package, to prevent any unwelcome contact between the carbon and master. Before one starts to write on the master copy sheet, the protective tissue needs to be removed. Unfortunately, no one told me this, and I proceeded to write all of the parts of the band arrangement on special mimeograph music staff master sheets without removing the protective tissue paper. When I gave the finished parts to the band director to copy, he pointed out my error. All of the notes I had written ended up imprinted on the protective tissue paper rather than the master sheet. If he had he attempted to run the master sheets that I gave him, the result would only have been blank copies. In order to fix my error, I had to remove the protective tissue paper and redraw over each note that I had previously written, so the carbon would imprint on the back of the master sheet. Not only did it take twice the normal amount of time for me to write all of the band parts but having to write over the previously written notes made them harder to read once the copies were mimeographed and distributed. The first rehearsal of the music was a nightmare. It seemed as if the entire rehearsal was dominated by questions from the band kids because it was so difficult to read the music. Questions like "Is that an eighth note?" and "Is that note a "B" or a "C"?" were constant through the entire time. Eventually, all of the problems were worked out, and the piece was performed at the Spring Concert.

In the meantime, it was college application time and I faced a dilemma. My lousy grades had finally caught up with me and I noticed that there were a lot of colleges that I did not qualify for academically. My guidance counselor made several suggestions. She believed that I needed to be in a small school where hopefully I would be able to receive extra attention should I need it. Some of her suggestions were a community college with a music major in North Carolina, another similar college in Florida, and a small state college in

New Hampshire. I rejected all of these. I wanted to go to UConn. However, UConn didn't work out. It wasn't for lack of trying. My mom drove me through a snowstorm to Storrs on the day of my audition and accompanied me on the piano as I played my audition piece. I didn't play badly, but I wasn't great either. Also, I unfortunately had also never had any formal training in music theory, and I made some major errors on the music theory exam. So getting a rejection letter from UConn was hard to take, and I had to look elsewhere to pursue my dream. I started looking through just about every college guide I could find. More frustration, it seemed that every college or university I looked at either A) had no music major; B) was impossible for me to get into with my grades; or C) was incredibly expensive. I finally found one option that looked promising. The University of Houston had a music major. The cost of attending was not prohibitive, and it looked like I could qualify academically. Houston appeared to have a unique entrance qualification, which worked to my favor. In its admissions process, the university used a type of sliding scale correlation between SAT scores and class rank. Those who were in the top 25% of their graduating class only needed a combined SAT score of 700. In the next 25% one would need a combined SAT score of 800. In the third 25% group, one needed a combined score of 900. I only ranked in the 40th percentile of my graduating class, but I had a combined SAT score of 960, meaning that I would qualify for acceptance. When I inquired about an audition, I found out that they didn't require one. It seemed weird that virtually anyone could walk in off the street, and if they had a high enough SAT score they could be a music major at the university. But who was I to judge? So I started the application process for Houston, and once I was accepted, it became a choice between Houston and Western Connecticut

State College. I had also applied to Western Connecticut State, or "WestConn" as it is known, as another option. I had a good audition there and was accepted with no problem. As acceptance materials started coming in from Houston, the university looked more and more promising. From the photos, the campus looked very attractive, and it appeared there was a multitude of activities offered. As I looked over a brochure from the music department, one name caught my eye. Bill Moffitt was the marching band director at the University of Houston. For those unaware, Bill Moffitt was one of the most well-known and respected marching band directors in the country at that time. I remember when I was younger, seeing a feature on a TV sports program about marching band. The band in the feature was the Michigan State University marching band, and its director, Bill Moffitt. He had obviously made the move at some point to the University of Houston. In the meantime, he had an impressively large number of his arrangements for marching band published through Hal Leonard Publishing. I would be willing to bet that every marching band director in the country at that time was familiar with the Soundpower series of marching band arrangements by Bill Moffitt. Even as a high school student, I could see that his approach to arranging was very different from the arrangers that had come before him. Add to this, the fact that all of the University of Houston home football games were played in the Astrodome. Now at that time the Astrodome was the only domed stadium in the country. Folks called the stadium the "8th wonder of the world", and its high tech scoreboard was cutting edge at the time. There was no more doubt in my mind. I was going to Texas.

ON TO COLLEGE

After graduation, the summer seemed to fly by. I hated having to leave the Explorers before their season had concluded. But Marching Band Camp at the University of Houston started in mid-August and I had no choice but to leave early. When the day came, I was the picture of anticipation. We all went down to Kennedy Airport in New York City, where I would catch my flight to Houston, my mom, my brother, and a man my mom was seeing now that she and my dad had divorced. I was excited, no question about it. I was one of the first to board the plane and took a window seat, so I could see everything going on outside the plane. From my vantage point, I could see a public viewing deck that was adjacent to the boarding gates. My mom had walked out on to the viewing deck and was watching the plane. The world seemed to stop, as I was completely startled. She was crying. More than that, she was crying more intensely than I think I had ever seen her cry. And as I watched her, I instantly understood. I was her first-born child leaving home. This wasn't like going to a summer music program where I would return in a week or two. This time I would be away for a considerable amount of time. If anything were to go wrong in Houston, she would not be able to be there to help. She had never said anything to me, probably because she didn't want to say anything that might cause me to reconsider going to Houston. She had kept a brave face through packing, and the trip to the airport. Now that I was on the plane, she broke down. As I watched, I could feel tears welling up in my own eyes. It took every ounce of self-control not to go running off that plane, burst on to the viewing deck and say, "Let's go home". However, I felt committed to going and somehow managed to resist getting up and saying, "Hell with Houston!" and walking to the exit. I stayed where I was, but I continued to cry for at least the first hour after the plane took off.

Arriving at the airport in Houston, I called the director of the dormitories, and advised him I had just arrived. I had to make special arrangements to get into the dorm early, before the dorm was opened for students moving in. I found my way to the campus, and eventually checked in to my room. I'm guessing that one could have counted those living in the dorm at that time on one hand. As I was unpacking, I happened to look out the window of my dorm room. There, sitting on the lawn in the late afternoon sun were a couple of students, a girl and a guy. The girl was holding a leash. On the other end of the leash was a full-grown cougar. They all sat leisurely on the grass, the cougar lounging as if it were a house cat sunning itself. I found out later that the cougar's name was Shasta, and she was the mascot of the University of Houston. "Well, you don't see that every day" I thought as I turned away from the window. Later, as I walked the campus for the first time, I came across Shasta's enclosure. Some might call it a cage, but I wasn't willing to be that cynical. It was about a 12' by 12' building, with glass on three sides. There were plans on the drawing board to expand the enclosure, but it would take some time. There was a bench across the walk for people to sit and as I'll tell you later, I visited Shasta on multiple occasions.

The day before band camp was scheduled to start, I went to the band hall. I was one of the new students who needed to play for the director prior to camp starting. I had requested to play baritone horn in the band, but I didn't own my own instrument. Someone gave me a rather old instrument to play, with a moveable bell that was stuck in one position, pointing to the side instead of straight ahead. It was stupid on my part not to warm up prior to going into the band office, but no one was calling this an audition. As far as I knew, it was just supposed to be an informal session. In the room was Bill Moffitt, the marching band director, a guy I came to know as Charles, the graduate assistant of bands, and Mr. Matthews, Director of Bands for the University. Needless to say, I didn't play well. I sounded awful, not having played the baritone horn for two months, and in combination with an unfamiliar instrument, my playing was just dreadful. The Director of Bands said to me "I think the marching band may not be for you. Perhaps you should just stick with the bass and play in the orchestra". I was crushed. I left the band hall without saying a word to anyone. I went to my dorm room and for the second time in three days was reduced to tears. After thinking about it, I decided that I needed to at least make my feelings known to the staff, so I went back to the band hall. The staff were still listening to new students, and in between players, I asked if I could speak with them. I told them that I didn't blame them based on the way I played, and ordinarily I probably would make the same judgment they did based on what I sounded like. But I went on to say that the reason I came to Houston was to play with this band, not the orchestra, and that I wanted to be a part of this band if they could possibly accommodate me. They were silent for a few seconds, and then Mr. Matthews spoke up. He said that I would really need to bring my playing level up in order to play with the band. In the meantime, would I consider being a "substitute" band member, in case there was a hole to be filled? I agreed immediately. It was far better than not being involved at all. Next morning, at the first rehearsal, I watched as the band came together. A magnificent gathering of almost 200 musicians. As I stood and watched, Mr. Matthews came out of his office and said to me "Ed, we need to fix you up with a baritone horn". This time, they gave me a fairly nice instrument, a Besson, that had a great sound and responded well to my playing. So I took my place in the baritone horn section and noticed something interesting. In a band of this size, the baritone horn section should probably consist of 16 players. However, counting myself, there were only 14 players in the section. It began to dawn on me that perhaps there were some players that they were expecting, that for whatever reason did not show. That would suggest that they were giving me at least a shot at a spot in the band, and let me tell you, I wasn't about to waste it. The band camp was hard. They were demanding a lot of us physically as well as musically, and in the hot Texas sun, I was certain I was going to pass out at some point. However, I was able to hold it together, and on the next to last day of band camp, an activity took place that many in the band world would refer to as "shakedown" day.

The staff didn't call it that. They told us it was just an informal session, so they could evaluate us on what we learned at camp. But I wasn't convinced, and I decided to treat this as a life or death audition, which as far as I, as a player was concerned, it may well have been. We organized ourselves in squads of four. They had removed almost all the chairs from the rehearsal section of the band hall and marked the floor off as a football field with lines every 5 yards, for maybe a total of 35 yards. At the end was a table where the band staff sat, the same three people, Mr. Moffitt, the marching band director, Mr. Matthews, the Director of Bands, and Charles, the graduate assistant. One squad at a time marched down the 35-yard section playing the school fight song. Four flutes, followed by four trumpets, then four saxophones, etc. went through their paces through the 35-yard area. When it was time for the squad of four baritone horns that I was a part of to take the floor, I was extremely nervous, but I was able to keep my game face on. As my squad marched down toward the band staff, I made one error playing, and a marching error also, but generally, I think I did fairly well. The next day, the permanent squad assignments were handed out, and I had been assigned to a squad. Assuming the squad assignments reflected the "shakedown" results, my rank was most likely number 12 in a section of 14. I didn't care one bit. I had a spot in a band directed by Bill Moffitt, and for the time being, that was all that mattered

THE BARRIER EXAM

On the first day of classes, the first class I went to was my music theory class. It was then that we found out why the music department had such an open-door policy. As classes go, the University offered four sections of freshman music theory. One was an advanced class. One was a remedial class, and the other two sections were kind of in the middle. I was assigned to a middle class, and on that first day, we were informed that we had six weeks to master music theory basics. Key signatures, scales, intervals, triads, and 4-part choral writing were all included in that category, as well as ear training and music dictation. At the end of the six-week period, we would be given a barrier exam. If we passed the barrier exam, we would be allowed to continue. However, those of us who did not pass it would be required to drop music as a major. So, becoming a music major at UH wasn't the issue, but staying a music major was. I wasn't about to allow something like this to stop me, and I spent every free minute I had working to master all the material. After six weeks, I passed the barrier exam, no problem. I remember feeling very sorry for a really pretty violin player who flunked the exam. She was determined to try again the following year and I wished her well. While I cruised in music theory, some of my other classes didn't go as well. I struggled in piano class, and because of that, my keyboard harmony class also became difficult. It wasn't that I didn't know which chords to play, and how to play them. The issue was that I couldn't play them on the piano very well, and so that class became a challenge as well. It was interesting to be in a US History class of about 400 students. For the most part, we sat in an auditorium and listened to the professor lecture. There was a breakout section each week where we sat in groups in a class conducted by a graduate assistant. Now for the most part, I enjoyed history, especially US History. In fact, before I got to high school I considered that I might want to be a history teacher, although that was before my experiences in music. But this course was rather difficult. When I purchased my books for the semester, I was astounded that I needed to purchase 12 books for US History. That meant that in a 15-week semester, I would need to read almost a book a week. I tried, of course, but the books were really dry, and for the first few weeks I was only able to get through the first few chapters of the "book of the week". Finally, I stopped trying. I just couldn't keep up, and what I thought was important in the books that I read didn't seem to have any bearing on what the objectives of the class seemed to be. I also didn't care for being in the UH orchestra that much. The director didn't have much of a personality, and at times could be a bit dictatorial. I also was not fond of the rehearsal schedule.

The marching band met three afternoons a week, but that was not the case with the orchestra. One of the orchestra classes was scheduled for Wednesday nights, and I soon found out why. It appears that there were not enough string players at the university in order to make up a respectable college level orchestra. So the Wednesday night rehearsal was scheduled in order to bring in local high school string players into the group. It was a really lousy way to do things, but I suppose their options were limited. The repertoire that the director chose was quite good. But I guess I didn't appreciate it as much as I should have, because the night rehearsals really made Wednesdays very long and tiring. I also became a bit resentful during Homecoming week. I can remember pausing at the door of the orchestra rehearsal hall on a Wednesday evening. I looked across the campus and could see glimpses of the Homecoming parade, about 40 kids carrying torches, led by the marching band, headed for the bonfire site. I certainly would have loved being with the band that night, but I also couldn't miss orchestra rehearsal. Needless to say, I wasn't a very happy camper that night.

In the meantime, I was having a great experience in marching band. I was handling the music pretty well and starting to grasp what they called the "Patterns of Motion" system of field marching formations. Mr. Moffitt was fantastic. All of the music the UH marching band played were his arrangements, most of them already published. Here was a national superstar of marching band directors, and yet, if I, or any other student were to drop by his office, pick up a music score to one of his arrangements, and ask him questions about the arrangement, he would immediately drop what he was doing and address the question. Why did he write the melody in this particular way? Why did he use this particular chord voicing? What made him think of using this particular type of chord progression? There was no BS, just honest answers to what he was thinking, and how it could make us better arrangers ourselves. Then there were the football games. The first game of the year was at Rice University stadium across town. It was a very nice stadium, but after that came the home games in the Astrodome. Perhaps not as expansive as some of the domed stadiums of today, but it was nonetheless an imposing structure. The band was a major part of those events. We would play a pre-game show, which would always include the school Alma Mater and National Anthem, and of course, we would perform at halftime. We would also play a post-game show, which really didn't consist of much. We would take our places on the field after the game and play through a set of songs at a standstill. Yet, hundreds of people stayed to watch.

The third home game of the season was "Band Day". Now, a lot of college and university bands hold band days across the country. It's an event where many high school bands, some of them local and some of them traveling some distance to participate, come together to form a large massed band to perform at halftime. The band days at UH were particularly large. My anticipation was fueled by some of the photographs of band days of previous years posted in the band hall. These huge bands, some 10,000 plus players, filled the entire surface of the football field and beyond. They needed to bring in a set of airline boarding stairs, similar to what they use on Air Force One, for the conductor to stand on in order to conduct the band. For Band Day that year, Mr. Moffitt wrote an arrangement of "Tea for Two" which he christened "Tea for Tubas" because it was a tuba feature. When it was time to perform the piece, all of the sousaphone (tuba) players were brought to the sideline. The entire sideline was solid tubas, more than 300 of them. Of course, the sound of such a large ensemble was incredible. When the final note of a song was cut off, the residual echo of the band continued to roll around the dome for several seconds. There was no question that marching band was my favorite class, and when I got my University of Houston band jacket, I just swelled with pride. I was a "band geek" long before they coined the phrase. I would spend time in the band hall, even when I didn't even need to be there. I never missed a practice, and in fact was usually one of the first ones to arrive. I was fully committed to the group, and the staff, but at one point, I ended up disappointing them. The UH football team was pretty good that year, and there was a lot of talk about them going to a bowl game. I had very mixed feelings about this. If the football team were to go to a bowl game, then the band would most likely be traveling with them as well. It would be a great experience, but the prospect of such a trip was diluted by the fact that I was encountering a major case of homesickness, and when it came to the upcoming holidays, I knew I needed to be home with my family. The bowl picks were finally announced. The University of Houston was invited to the Bluebonnet Bowl. I couldn't help but feel disappointed. The Bluebonnet Bowl was scheduled for New Year's Eve- where? - In the Astrodome. Now, you have to understand. As the semester wore on, I developed a very serious case of homesickness. For all the people wandering around the UH campus, it was still a very lonely place. The weekends were especially difficult when we didn't have a game. I would walk the campus, sometimes stopping to practice in the bass studio, an unused classroom where all of us bass players kept our instruments. It also had a small electric piano, so I could practice on that whenever I had a chance as well. Afterward, I would visit with Shasta. Now I know these days it's not very politically correct for a college or university to have a live mascot on campus, but I can tell you, having that cougar on campus meant a lot to me. I don't fully know why, but I would come to see Shasta on a regular basis and sit on the bench opposite her enclosure. I couldn't really talk to her through the glass, so some nights we just stared at each other from each side of the glass. Other times she would totally ignore me and pace around the circumference of her enclosure as if she were stalking some unseen prey.

I would also go to the towers. The Moody Towers was a new dormitory recently constructed. It was 17 stories, and on top was an observation deck. I would go to the observation deck and stand in the northeast corner, looking off toward home, as if it were possible for me to actually see it. It seemed as if the only thing that kept me going were phone calls from home, as well as phone calls from my girlfriend, who would later become my wife. So it looked like it was a choice between going home to be with my loved ones through the holidays, or staying on campus, having to go out for all my meals, and being by myself virtually all of the time, in order to attend what for all practical purposes was a glorified home football game. Even though it was a major event, and on national TV no less, I just felt that I couldn't go through with it. I went to see Mr. Moffitt and Mr. Matthews. I told them of my decision. I don't think they really understood, and they certainly weren't happy about it. But they also realized that my mind was made up. So on New Year's Eve, I watched the University of Houston band perform on TV with my family and friends, while my spot in the band was filled, ironically by a girl who was a substitute band member.

TIME FOR A TRADE-UP

At some point, I made the decision that I couldn't stay in Houston. It was a great experience, but I totally underestimated the toll it would take on me to be away from home. Adding to that was the fact that the University jacked up its tuition for out-of-state students by 300% and I realized that I really couldn't afford to stay there. So with that decision made, I felt a lot of pressure had been taken off me, and I made some choices that some might find illogical, but to me were just fine in the light of my not continuing at the University of Houston after my freshman year. To begin with, I moved out of my dorm in the campus quadrangle and took a vacancy in the Moody Towers. It was a more modern room, and I only had one roommate instead of two, as in my previous room. I also made a change in my performing groups. Of course, marching band season was over, and in the spring semester, the band was split into three groups. The first was an advanced Wind Ensemble which was a group largely set up for music majors who were focused primarily on being professional players. Then there was another Wind Ensemble, which was made up of primarily those students who were music education majors. The third group was a Concert Band, set up for everyone else. Now, the music department had a policy that each music major needed to be a member of a performing ensemble on their instrument. This was why I had no choice but to play in the Symphony Orchestra during the fall semester, because it was the only performing group option for string bass players. However, once I was accepted to the string bass position in the music education wind ensemble, I dropped orchestra from my schedule. I just didn't like playing with the group, and I felt I just could no longer put up with those Wednesday night rehearsals. This created what Bill Clinton would call a "dust-up". The Orchestra director apparently was not happy about my leaving and had some words with the band people. Charles, the band graduate assistant, who was also a bass player took me aside and encouraged me to remain with the orchestra. He said I really shouldn't drop orchestra because doing so would "leave a bad taste in his mouth" referring to the orchestra director. Had I planned to stay in Houston there's no doubt that I would have followed his advice. However, since I knew I wasn't returning after the current semester, what the orchestra director thought was of little consequence to me. I had traded Wednesday night rehearsals in a group with high school kids, for a performing group of music education majors led by Bill Moffitt. In my mind, it was a considerable trade-up.

The Wind Ensemble was not the only performing group that I played with that semester. I also performed with the Cougar Brass at basketball games. The Cougar Brass was a group of all brass players along with some percussion players led by Mr. Moffitt, and we played at all of the UH home basketball games. Now, I enjoyed playing at the football games, but I enjoyed playing at the basketball games just as much. The UH basketball team almost always made the national top 20 rankings, so the quality of play was very good. And I have to say, one of the things I also looked forward to at games was the appearance of Shasta. Shasta was always accompanied by a contingent of students called the Cougar Guard. The members of the Cougar Guard were from a campus fraternity. They cared for Shasta, fed her, took her on daily walks, and cleaned her enclosure. When she was taken to an athletic event, they usually did not walk her in. Instead, they used a child size red wagon. Shasta loved her little red wagon and would immediately jump into it as soon as she saw it in anticipation of getting a ride. At basketball games, the members of the Cougar Guard would bring her in her red wagon down the tunnel and onto the arena floor. They would then take her around the circumference of the arena floor around the basketball court. I really think this cougar had an idea of what was going on. I can remember more than once, as she rode in her wagon around the court, and when they approached the spot where the cheerleaders of the opposing team were setting up, she would growl at them, with her ears pinned back. As the Cougar Guard continued to walk her wagon around the court to where we in the band were setting up, she was back to normal, practically purring.

As the season went on, the ABC network had decided to televise a late season Houston home basketball game. So, even though I missed the football bowl game, I would still get a chance to perform on national TV. I made sure that everyone at home knew to watch, and when the day of the game came, all of us in the Cougar Brass made sure we were at our best. For halftime, we moved our set-up out on to the court during a commercial break for the benefit of the TV cameras. As we played, the cameras panned up and down the line of players, and then focused on Mr. Moffitt conducting. As a baritone player, I was in the background of that shot. My mom thought it was wonderful when I checked in with her after the game. My dad, not so much. When I asked him if he had seen me on TV during the half time performance he said he wasn't sure, then asked if I was the baritone player that badly needed a haircut.

The rest of the semester basically went on without incident. Well, without any music-based incidents anyway. As the semester classes ended, the campus went into "study days". These were 2 days just before final exams started in which classes were not held, and students were given the opportunity to just study in preparation for exams. The whole dorm was relatively silent, and we all sat studying with the doors to our rooms open. As my roommate and I studied, another student walked into our room. "Is there a heaven?" he asked. I groaned. A Jesus freak, just what we needed. The movement was at its peak in the early 70's and although I felt these kids were well meaning, they could also be very annoying. What I wanted to say was "I don't know if there's a heaven, but you're going to find out if you don't get out of this room". But my roommate signaled to me non-verbally that he was on top of the situation. Now, you must understand that my roommate was a straight A student who also read the Bible before he went to sleep each night. When our uninvited guest started spouting off quotes from the Bible, I grinned inwardly as my roommate reached for his Bible. The Jesus freak didn't stand a chance. Each time he quoted from the Bible, my roommate would cite a different bible quote that could be interpreted as meaning the exact opposite. When our would-be missionary recited another quote, my roommate was already thumbing through his Bible to a different section, again, to an opposing meaning quote. "Yes, you are correct" he said to our intruder, "but in Matthew..." You could almost say that this was a joy to watch, and after about 5 minutes of this, the Jesus freak left our room looking somewhat dazed.

MEETING WITH "THE CHIEF"

When classes and exams were done, I said farewell to everyone and went to the airport to catch a plane for home. My eyes started tearing as the plane taxied away from the terminal. The tears surprised me. I was leaving Houston and not coming back. Had this place grown on me that much? Of course, it was a moot point as I was committed to moving on. I would be attending Western Connecticut State in the fall, and even though the experiences I would have there could not compare to UH, it was nonetheless close to home.

So, I returned home from Houston on a Thursday. On Saturday, Frankie, one of my drum corps buddies stopped by the house. "The Chief wants to see you!" he said. The managing director of the Explorers Drum and Bugle Corps, John Andrechuk, went by two names. The kids referred to him either as "John", or "The Chief". John was a very even-tempered guy. He was a member of the local American Legion post that sponsored the corps, and besides managing the drum corps, he also acted as liaison between the corps and the Legion post. He ran the corps in a quiet, but firm manner. I rarely heard him raise his voice, and all the kids really liked him. Many of us would drop by his house, unannounced, and both he and his wife were always very welcoming. So, I went with Frankie to John's house, and found out that things were not going as well with the Explorers as we all would have liked to. The bugle instructor of the corps the previous year had decided not to continue and recommended one of his fellow corps members of the Connecticut Hurricanes to instruct the bugle section. It appears this new instructor was not all that successful and walked away leaving the corps in the lurch. Some of the kids left the Explorers and moved on to other corps, while other kids simply left. At this point, toward the end of May, the Explorers field show was only half completed, with the first competition only a few weeks away. The selection "Under the Double Eagle" was only half completed when the instructor quit, and there was no music score that could be used to finish teaching the selection. John told me there was a rehearsal of the bugle section scheduled for the following day, Sunday, and would I be able to find a way to help salvage the situation. We agreed that it might be best to segue into another march, and perhaps the trio section of "Stars and Stripes" might be just the thing. That night, I wrote out the arrangement on a sheet of music staff paper. I didn't even need to use a piano to figure out the parts. I was able to do it in my head. My ear training skills were so sharp after spending my freshman year at Houston with music theory and aural skills that in my mind, this was child's play. The following day, I met with the bugle section. Of course, I knew a lot of the kids because after all, I had marched with them the previous summer. I think that helped me because they were willing to trust me. I knew the drill, that is to say I understood that I would need to teach the music to them by rote. I was very patient with them as they struggled with the parts. At the end of the 3-hour rehearsal, they had learned the entire trio section. The corps now had three complete selections for their field show with two more selections to learn. John and I agreed to continue, and he hired me as the bugle instructor of the corps. I really didn't think much about the prospect of being the instructor. I only knew that my corps was in trouble, and I was in a unique position to help. I knew that John had a lot of confidence in me, and I would certainly give the corps my best. However, John's decision did not go over well with everyone. Some of the kids in the corps and some of the adults as well had concerns about turning over responsibility for the field show to an inexperienced 19-year-old. However, when word got out that I was teaching the bugle section, some of the players that had left the corps, returned. Truth be told, I did make some rookie errors that summer. Overall, once the show was completed, the corps did not do particularly well in competition. It was mostly due to the fact that they fallen so far behind over the winter, and had to rush through finishing their show, while other groups started the season fully prepared. The Explorers didn't win any competitions, although they did place ahead of some of the other groups in some of the shows.

TRANSITIONING TO WESTCONN

In all, it was a busy summer. Besides my work with the drum corps, I also had a summer job at a local factory. I also got together with some kids that I had grown up with and we formed a rock group. As usual, my mom was pleased and supportive, and went out and got me an electric bass and amplifier. After all, there aren't many rock groups that use an unamplified standup bass, not since Buddy Holly anyway. As the summer ended, I attended the new student orientation at Western Connecticut State. As I settled into classes at "WestConn", I noticed that a great deal of things were different at my new school. For one thing, WestConn had no male dormitories. All male students needed to rent rooms off campus. I rented a room with a family a couple of blocks from the campus. The first thing I noticed was I had somewhat less privacy than what I had in Houston. I did have the option of subscribing to a meal plan at the campus dining hall, but the word from other students was that the food wasn't all that great. My classes weren't all that much different from what I had at Houston, except of course, there was no marching band. There were other similar groups, however, but the performing group requirements at WestConn were more extensive. In Houston, the only requirement they had was that one had to be in an ensemble on whatever instrument they were majoring in. At WestConn, however, one had to acquire a certain amount of performing group credits in both instrumental and choral performing groups. The amount in each category depended on the student being an instrumental or choral major. I had my Houston type of courses, such as music theory, ear training, keyboard harmony and bass lessons, but I also played in the symphony orchestra, wind ensemble, and sang in the chorus. Also, piano lessons were tied to the keyboard harmony course as opposed to Houston where piano class was a separate course. I also had a class in string methods. Now, of course, being a string bass player would suggest that I wouldn't have much of a problem mastering other string instruments. Not so. I started off on a violin, and just didn't do very well. I found it cumbersome to hold and of course, the notes on the fingerboard were much closer together than on the bass. The result was a lot of out-of-tune notes and a tone that was just awful. Later on, I moved to the viola, but things were not much better. I had my best success on the cello, perhaps because it was easier to adapt to and the playing position was closer to what I was used to with the bass. Another thing I didn't care for was my sophomore music theory class. I really did try, but it was boring, a major comedown from what I had in Houston. I did slightly better in keyboard harmony class, but it was still hard to play the piano.

Even though most of my classes were a drudgery, I fared better in the performing groups. Mr. Don Wells was the professor who conducted both the symphony orchestra and the wind ensemble. Mr. Wells was also my adviser, and clearly understood that as a transfer student into WestConn some flexibility would be needed. As a conductor, he wasn't as dynamic as Paranov was, and he certainly wasn't as dictatorial as the orchestra conductor at UH. He was knowledgeable and pragmatic, and he guided his performing groups with a steady hand. Each group had a more extensive warm-up routine that any previous groups that I had been a part of. As time went on, I began to understand the strategy of incorporating those skills in the warm-up routine that would be necessary to master the repertoire. Mr. Wells wasn't able to use his expertise quite as much with the orchestra though. The string section was small, just a handful of violins. There were five of us in the bass section, but our section of five was larger than the viola or the cello section. The struggle to balance such a group was significant. As far as the orchestra music went, it was interesting to play, but a mere shadow of the pieces I played in Houston.

However, as the semester unfolded, it seemed that orchestra was the only class I had that was POC – a piece of cake. I was also doing well in musical dictation, but that was all. My string class was problematic. My music theory class was very problematic. I had to get up early for a psychology class that most times seemed to put me back to sleep, and then there was this boring philosophy class that I had a really hard time dealing with. Not only that, but as time went on, I found that a lot of my activities were starting to conflict with each other. The rock group that I was a part of had played its first gig and was now engaged in an eight-week Sunday night gig in a small local nightclub. The problem was that the Explorers also rehearsed on Sundays, and I was forced into a situation where I would have to leave Explorers rehearsal early in order to arrive early enough at the gig or leave Explorers not quite as early and be late setting up for the gig. More times than not, the Explorers got the short end of the stick. The bugle section was shrinking, and it was becoming difficult to write music for a smaller group and still be able to keep them sounding good.

HITTING BOTTOM

In the normal course of the week, my mom would drop me off

in Danbury, where WestConn is located, and pick me up on Friday after my last class got out. However, there was this one particular week when I had her car with me in Danbury for the week. I can remember one morning as I departed the house where I was staying. I was late for my string methods class. After that, I would be struggling in a music theory class, followed by a rather stupid, but required, philosophy class. I looked at the car sitting there, and then over to the campus, then looked at the car again. "That does it!" I thought, and I jumped into the car to go somewhere, anywhere but here. I just drove. Before I knew it, I had driven into New York State, had crossed the Tappan Zee Bridge, and was headed down the Garden State Parkway into New Jersey. I stopped at the rest area there and had breakfast. I sat there and tried to console myself. If ever I could name a low point in my college journey, I would say this was it. The Explorers corps was coming apart at the seams, and it was largely my doing. The rock group I was in seemed to be going nowhere, and that was also partially my fault. I was struggling in more classes than I was succeeding in, and I could only come to one conclusion, my dream, my all-encompassing dream of teaching music was in big trouble. What would happen if I were to fail? In those days, one could still get a decent job with just a high school diploma. It wouldn't be the end of the world. As I pondered this, I also wondered what it would be like to never be able to musically inspire kids. To never guide them or lead them to the treasures of music, or to never conduct them in a performance that would make them smile and beam with pride as they left the stage. I had recently seen an advertisement in a music teacher magazine saying- "You never get tired of seeing their eyes light up". My mom ran a dance studio, and I saw kids' eyes light up more times than I could count. Would I be willing to trade it all for some safer, more predictable existence? "NO!" I said to myself. "No compromises!" "No alternatives!" "I'm going all in and damn the consequences!". Of course, I knew my grades would be taking a beating at the upcoming end of the semester, but I knew this wasn't me, and I could do better. Deep down, I knew I would do better. I would either succeed and every day I would speak the words "OK class, take out your music!", or I would crash in flames ending up in a job where my most common saying would be "You want fries with that?"

When my fall semester grades arrived, they were awful. I simply had to admit that I just really screwed up. The news wasn't all bad, however. Music Dictation class is something a lot of students dread, but I didn't. My ability to process notes and write them down as I heard them was very strong. Even when the instructor played a line of music in four parts, and we had to write down all four parts knowing only the starting note, I was not tripped up. As a result, the college sent me a letter stating that I would be exempt from having to take the final semester of Music Dictation.

As the spring semester started, I was full of determination. I was certain that there would be fallout from the previous semester, but I wouldn't let it phase me. In an unexpectedly pleasant development, over the holidays my mom decided that I really needed my own car to keep all of my commitments. She ended up purchasing a new car for herself, and giving her car, which was only a couple of years old, to my grandfather. My grandfather's old car was given to me. It really was wonderful to have a car at my disposal, and I made the most of it. With the new semester, I sensed that some changes would need to be made, although the first change was not my doing.

I walked into Explorers rehearsal, the first one of the New

Year, only to find a new bugle instructor teaching the section. At first, I was upset, and John, the managing director, took me aside before anything happened. He told me that I wasn't being fired, but that I would now be the assistant to the new instructor, Ray. The corps was in a rebuilding mode, something that I had no experience with. Even though we had lost some kids, new ones were walking through the door, and they would need to be brought up to speed when the new marching season started, which seemed like a long time away, but really not that far off when you consider that you only got to teach the group once a week. When I thought about it, I chastised myself for feeling upset. Bringing in a new instructor was entirely logical, and perhaps I could learn some things from Ray. Moreover, the fact that John was keeping me on the staff once again underscored the confidence that he had in me. I wasn't about to let that go to waste, and I made sure that there would never be any more leaving rehearsal early or arriving late. Ray was a pretty nice guy, and after a bit of adjustment, we worked well together as a team.

In the meantime, the rock group that I was involved with hit the wall. We were booked for a steady gig at a prominent restaurant for four nights a week, but things went badly, and we were fired after the second night. I was really upset. I had sacrificed a lot of time to be in this group, and all our efforts seemed to have been for naught. Finally, I made the decision to leave the group. It wasn't an easy decision to make. I had been jamming with some of these kids since I was 11 years old, and I felt like I had really disappointed them. However, I knew I just had to be smarter about how I spent my time.

As I contemplated what courses to take during the spring semester, I decided I needed to make some changes there as well. I had wanted to play with the college jazz band, but they already had a bass player. However, there were some trombone vacancies in the jazz band, and since I had some experience playing trombone in high school, I saw that this might be a way that I can be involved in this group. My mom, as always, was supportive, and we went to the music store to buy a trombone. I also decided that I didn't need to play in two ensembles on my major instrument, so I did not sign up for wind ensemble, but signed up for concert band instead. The concert band was less high profile, and I was hopeful that I might be able to play with the group on some instrument other than string bass. As it turned out, the conductor asked me to play trombone with the concert band. In fact, I was the only trombone player in the group. In my mind, playing trombone in both the concert band and jazz ensemble was only logical. After all, how many string bass players would I end up teaching in my classes during my career compared with brass players?

Also, since I was no longer involved in the rock group, I had some extra free time. I decided to join the college student radio station. At the time, I just was looking for a new experience in an area that I had always had an interest in. When I was in sixth grade, I got involved in a radio activity known as DXing. It involved picking up radio stations from some distance away. This was done mostly on the AM radio band. In the evening, radio station signals are inclined to skip off the ionosphere, allowing their signals to be picked up far away. Stations on the FM band were not as likely to "skip" as AM stations could. If I was fortunate to locate a station some distance away from my Connecticut home, I would keep a log of what was being programmed on the station. I would then send a copy of that log to the station, and if my log matched up with theirs, they would send me a confirmation of the reception. I had confirmations from AM stations in Baltimore, Indiana, North Carolina, Chicago, St. Louis, Canada, Mexico, and others. More than once, I even was able to pick up a station in Cali, Columbia, although I was never able to get a confirmation.

So I became involved in broadcasting at what was a very exciting time for the college station. Up to this point, the station had been broadcasting on a low power AM frequency. The station could be picked up in the Student Union, and a few other places on campus, but not much beyond that. However, they had applied to the FCC for a broadcasting license on the FM band, and a few weeks after I became involved with them, the license came through. Now classified as an educational FM station, we had a new radio station, WXCI, broadcasting from Danbury, Connecticut, on the campus of Western Connecticut State College.

In the meantime, the trombone parts in concert band were generally playable, and because the instrumentation of the concert band was fairly incomplete, the Director did not attempt to put a performance program together, and simply used the opportunity for us to explore a wide variety of band literature. As a result, much of my time in concert band was spent sight-reading. This wasn't a bad thing, and besides the varied amount and variety of band pieces, there was no performance pressure. In jazz ensemble, however, things were a bit different. At that time, there was a student director of the group, and I don't think he listened to me when I said that I hadn't played trombone since high school, because I was put on the lead trombone part. This is a part that you put your most experienced player on, not your least experienced. I had multiple problems right from the start. I had no experience being a lead player, and it showed. Some of the notes in the pieces were beyond my range, and I can't really say I had the type of tone that one would expect from a lead player. I was afraid that I would hold the group back with my inability, although my problems were among a multitude of difficulties that the group was experiencing. To make matters worse, they had already booked several performances for the jazz ensemble in area high schools and those dates were closing in fast. Finally, the help we needed arrived in the person of Mr. Howard Williams. Mr. Williams was the trombone professor for the college. More than that, he had an extensive amount of experience playing with top groups during the big band era. He spent some time with the Glenn Miller band, the Claude Thornhill band, the US Air Force jazz band, among others. He would sometimes tell us stories about being on the road. Apparently, more than once he would walk into a gig with a top band held at one of those very large dance halls. The halls were so large many times they would employ two bands in a given evening, one to set up at one end of the hall, the other to set up on the opposite side of the hall. It seems that on more than one occasion, after hearing Mr. Williams play, the other band would offer him a job with them, usually for more money, and Mr. Williams would leave the gig as a member of the other band. At any rate, he was just what the WestConn jazz ensemble needed. He took over the lead trombone part for me, and I slid down to the 2nd trombone part, which I was fine with. There were generally some very good players in the group, and most of the difficulties we were experiencing were coordination problems. We tackled issues one at a time with Mr. Williams giving feedback along the way, until finally we were sounding pretty good.

In general, I was starting to see things turning around a bit. When I fell behind in a speech class, the professor allowed me to do some extra credit to bring up my grade. I was playing better in my keyboard harmony class, and I was also faring well in a vocal techniques class that I had picked up that semester. The only fly in the ointment was sophomore music theory, which I was still having a really hard time with. Socially I was doing better as well. I made friends with several kids at the radio station, and the jazz band as well. Some of those friendships in the jazz band have lasted to this day. When I made my first newscast at the radio station, I was confident, but nervous. Most of the officers of the station had gathered for the event. The station's general manager, programming director, assistant news director, and others listened in the main studio while I read the news from a smaller booth. I was actually more nervous about making a mistake in front of them as opposed to on the air. I made a couple of errors, but generally did all right, and gradually I was worked into the schedule of newscasts. I went to New York City to take the test for an FCC 3rd class license. I received the 3rd class license, but not the broadcast endorsement, meaning that I would not be allowed to be on the air at the radio station by myself. It would take two more tries before I was able to pass the test for the endorsement.

The semester ended, and I received my grades. There was noticeable improvement, but there were two problems. First, my music theory grade was poor, and they would not allow me to continue as a music major unless I took (and passed) a remedial music theory course during the summer. I also noticed a possible dilemma. I had been able to bring my GPA up to a 2.1, not good, but an improvement. While I was no longer on academic probation since I had been able to bring my GPA above 2.0, the flip side of the issue was that once I graduated, I would most likely need to pursue a master's degree at some point. One needed at least a 2.5 GPA in order to be accepted at most graduate schools. I had a lot of work ahead of me for my last 2 years, and once again, I would have to step it up. Then I noticed a third problem. There, listed with all my courses and grades was Wind Ensemble, and the grade was an F. The problem was that I wasn't in Wind Ensemble. I had received an F for a course that I didn't sign up for. I was not part of the group, did not play with the group, and yet here it was listed on my report card. I talked to Mr. Wells, and he had no idea how it happened. I then went to the registrar's office. It was a textbook case of college administrative blundering. After two visits to the registrar's office, I was convinced that they felt that after a while I would just go away. It was then that I decided that I would stay on their case until this issue was resolved. I then made weekly trips to the registrar's office to inquire about the status of removing this errant grade. The excuses were many. They were out of the type of form that needed to be filed. The administrator they needed to talk to was away on vacation. The secretary was out that day, etc. I ended up making weekly trips to the registrar's office for an entire calendar year before it was finally resolved. For a college, it was truly an administrative response at its worst.

That summer, I ended up taking two courses during the summer term. One was the remedial music theory course. The other was US History, which I needed to retake, because my grade in US History at Houston was too low to transfer. The music theory class consisted of only myself and one other student. The instructor, the conductor of the concert band, was able to give a lot of individual attention to both of us, and it was an immense help. All of a sudden, I started to see things a whole lot more clearly than the regular class. Taking summer classes also opened up a major opportunity with the college radio station. There was a shortage of people around in the summer to run the station. At the beginning of the summer, the management of the station faced a dilemma. Without enough people to run the station, they would need to shut it down during the summer, a prospect that no one was looking forward to. When I told them I was taking summer classes, they immediately asked me if I would take a daily on-air shift. So each day, I would take classes in the morning, and after lunch go to the radio station to host an afternoon show. Supervision while the station was operating wasn't a problem, since the station had recently become an FM station, there was a need to upgrade some of the station equipment. While I was on the air each day, the chief engineer of the station was busy upgrading the auxiliary studio. He was a very talented engineer and had gotten his 1st class FCC license in the military. If there was a problem, he was only a few steps away. By the time the summer had ended, I had developed a very good on-air persona. My mom even drove to Danbury one afternoon to listen to my show. She sat in a parking lot with a portable AM-FM radio since most cars at that time only had AM radios.

JUNIOR YEAR AND THE BUGGY WHIP

As I started my junior year, one thing was clear. I was no longer just a music major. I was now a music education major. Instead of music theory, I now had Counterpoint with Mr. Wells. This time, there was no mist-shrouded instruction to wade through, and I was able to stay on top of things the whole semester. I also had Mr. Wells for conducting, and after a somewhat embarrassing start, I ended up doing well in that class also. But the first couple of classes were a bit rocky. Mr. Wells had ordered us to get 14" conducting batons at the local music store. I wasn't able to get to the music store until the last minute, and they had run out of 14" batons. I ended up having to get a baton that was 17" long. "Maybe it's no big deal" I told myself as I walked into class. But just the same, I

44

chose a spot in the back of the room behind several people hoping I wouldn't be noticed. The first task was to develop a standard conducting 4/4 beat pattern. So we stood in rows, everyone moving their batons in this very basic pattern. There was no talking or any other noise. Just the 20 or so of us practicing in silence. All of a sudden, I heard Mr. Wells yell "Judd! What are you doing with that buggy whip?" I guess it was a big deal after all.

An unexpected opportunity also presented itself at the beginning of my junior year. I found out that there was a shortage of tenors in the WestConn Concert Choir. While the WestConn chorus was open to any student, the Concert Choir was a select group. I knew that if I were to sing with the Concert Choir, that it would be a very valuable experience. I applied the same logic as when I got involved in drum corps. Chances were good that at some point in time, I would need to conduct a chorus, and I wanted to be able to do as good a job as I was sure I would be able to do with band. The Concert Choir featured the best singers on campus, and the conductor, Mr. Don Craig, was a former professional singer. Among his credits were choral arrangements of his that were published, and a stint with Fred Waring's Pennsylvanians. Now younger folks may not recognize the name, but Fred Waring and his group were extremely popular in their day. I had been in Chorus as a sophomore the year before, so I was familiar with Mr. Craig's conducting style. I went to see him, and we agreed to give it a try. This was a big jump for me. Thinking back to high school, as much as Mr. McWilliams had been a great band director in high school, I'm not sure the same can be said for his choral management. As the high school Spring Concert approached my high school freshman year, Mr. McWilliams enlisted several of the guys in the band to sing the male parts in the chorus. For me, it wasn't a very good experience, and I spent the rest of my high school years avoiding choral music. When I sang with the WestConn chorus my sophomore year, it was the first time I had sung with a chorus since my high school freshman year. Now, a year after my time in Chorus as a sophomore, I was angling to sing tenor with the more advanced vocal ensemble, most of the members being vocal majors. Since my voice changed during puberty, I had always sung bass. However, in my voice methods class sophomore year, I learned about falsetto, and learned to develop my own falsetto quite well. Falsetto is what one might call a person's "squeaky" voice. When you talk in your falsetto voice, you kind of sound like Mickey Mouse. Singing this way came in handy in trying to sing tenor with the Concert Choir. Many of the notes in the tenor part were beyond my natural vocal range, what vocalists would call my "chest" voice. Using falsetto allowed me to hit all of the notes in the tenor part, and I was able to blend in with the section and avoid sticking out when we sang the part. I learned a lot from Don Craig, and the literature that we sang was wonderfully eye opening.

Several classes that I took were finally starting to play to my strengths. I had Brass Methods class, Percussion Methods class, Woodwind Methods class, all of which presented no major problems for me. In addition, there was a transcription component to conducting class. Transcription, that is to say the writing of a part for an instrument in a different key could be a tricky situation for some. It works like this, certain instruments such as flute, violin, trombone, etc. are known as concert pitch instruments. Simply put, their pitches match up exactly with the piano. However, other instruments such as the saxophone, trumpet, French horn, etc. need music written in such a way that their notes have to be adjusted to match up in pitch to the piano. If, for instance, I want the piano and the flute to play a C, I simply write a C in each of their parts, but if I want the French horn to play the same pitch, I have to write a G in the French horn music. I had been writing transposed parts for these types of instruments since I was in high school, so transposition was a particular strength of mine. I almost could have done it with my eyes closed.

Academically, I was on a mission my junior year. I had a goal, raising my overall GPA to 2.5 by graduation, and I was determined to attain it. I approached every class with the goal of getting an "A". Besides the music classes, I had another psychology course, and another boring philosophy course. Physical Education classes were a requirement also, and I took classes in archery, and bowling. I enjoyed both of them. Now that I had a car, I was a commuter student. I liked it much better, although it made for some really long days. Wednesdays in particular were quite long. I would have to leave home at 7am in the morning to get to an 8am class. I had several classes and rehearsals throughout the day, and a radio show at night. Jazz Ensemble rehearsal ended at 5pm, and a bunch of us in the jazz ensemble would head over to the local Bonanza steak house for supper. It was a weekly ritual for us, and it was a great way to unwind. After supper, I would head back to campus to the radio station, where they had given me a Wednesday night jazz show. The radio station signed off at 11pm, and I usually got home around midnight.

The big challenge of the junior year was Elementary Music Teaching Methods, more popularly known as Junior Methods. The challenge was that we had to try to forget all of our preconceptions about what music education is. Of course, when one gets to this stage of college, one needs to understand that in most every course you have to approach it in the sense that "You don't know what you think you know".

In an innovative move, the professor of the Junior methods class arranged for us to work with the music staff of the Danbury schools. We were assigned to work with various music teachers in the school district. For me, it was a valuable part of my training, even though my first attempts at conducting a class were less than successful. If they were to put me in front of a drum corps, I would have been stellar, but this was elementary general music class, an entirely different animal. I had to make adjustments in my timing, lesson pace, expectations, and "teacher" personality.

My first two attempts at conducting a music class did not fare well. In the first instance, a third-grade class, I didn't get along all that well with the music teacher of the class. I made a few errors in conducting the class, but I didn't go crashing in flames. However, the teacher was very unforgiving when it came to the evaluation form that she sent to the junior methods professor. My second attempt, with a kindergarten class, was a dismal failure. I tried to teach the kids a song while playing guitar with them, but I didn't know the chords very well, nor did I have the classroom control ability for kids of this age. In the end, the music teacher of this class, who I also didn't get along with very well, ended up taking over the class, and I felt like a scientist whose lab had just exploded, and with singed hair and lab coat, wondering what happened. The professor of the junior methods class sat me down and went over the evaluations of the two teachers with me. She was totally unimpressed with what I had accomplished and suggested I should think about dropping the class. Of course, there was no way that I was going to do that. "Let her think that I'm awful" I thought to myself, "I'm going to learn to do this right". In my third experience, I fared much better. This time I was assigned to the music teacher at the Stadley Rough elementary school. In those days, Stadley Rough was a fairly new building and was designed as a school with an "open space" concept. There were no classrooms in the school. In fact, there didn't seem to be any interior walls at all, although ironically, the one class that was taught in a contained room was the music class. This music teacher was so much better than the other two that I had worked with. To begin with, she went over my lesson plan from top to bottom, making supportive suggestions as we went through all the details. The other teachers hadn't done that with me. What a difference! I followed the lesson plan as we had discussed and was spectacularly successful. When the kids left the room after class was over, I could see in their eyes that I had reached them, and I knew I was on my way to being a music educator. I continued to conduct classes at Stadley Rough, with almost all of my lessons meeting with success. When the junior methods professor saw the glowing evaluation, I had from the Stadley Rough music teacher, she poo-pooed it, saying that there was something wrong with the teacher there. The semester flew by. Before I knew it, I was looking at my fall semester grades. They were pretty good too, all A's and B's except for Junior Methods, where I received a C. I wasn't very happy about it, but on the bright side, I had made progress in bringing my GPA closer to a 2.5.

As the spring semester got underway, the Junior Methods professor told all of us that we would now be assigned a weekly elementary music class to teach throughout the semester. She then talked to me and told me I was being reassigned to teach a kindergarten class for the semester. I was assigned to work with the same teacher under which I had that disastrous kindergarten class back in the fall. At first, I was upset. I suspected a set-up. At this point, after the success I had at Stadley Rough, I was very confident in my abilities, but now I couldn't help but wonder if it would matter. However, after I thought about it, set-up or not, this would make a good challenge for me, to face my demons so to speak. It was time to get creative, and that's what I did. This time, I was able to utilize my experiences at Stadley Rough to craft some very creative lesson plans, which led to some fairly successful classes. One of my favorite lessons was to bring in an instrument that I played, such as the bass or trombone. I would teach the kids a song about the instrument and play the instrument with them as they sang. When I brought in the bass, we had to extend the class time an extra ten minutes so that all of the kids would get a chance to play a few notes on it. The elementary music teacher that I was assigned to was cautiously complementary, although she still didn't always see eye to eye with my approach. There was one instance when I brought a floor mat to the game "Twister" to use for class. I wanted to use the painted circles on the mat to teach melody and pitch movement, a central concept for kids of kindergarten age. But she didn't understand my objectives and would not allow me to use the floor mat saying, "We don't play games like this in class."

Ironically, several years later a manufacturer of music education materials came out with a floor mat to teach young kids melody, which looked suspiciously like the "Twister" floor mat. I have often wondered that if I'd had the foresight to patent the idea if I would have made any money.

My relationship with the elementary music teacher remained uncomfortable, but manageable. Then there was a day when she was absent from school. The kindergarten classroom teachers asked me if I would be willing to teach two kindergarten classes simultaneously. I wasn't wild about the idea. That meant teaching a combined class of almost 50 kindergarten kids. But I thought "What the hell, I'll give it a shot." and actually taught a fairly decent class.   The kindergarten teachers were most grateful for my flexibility, and I couldn't help but feel really good about it.

In the meantime, the Junior Methods professor introduced another component to the class, peer coaching. If one of the class members had talent or expertise that the rest of the class would find useful, we were encouraged to give lessons or a presentation. One of the girls in the class was a guitar player and offered to give guitar lessons to anyone in the class. I was one of six students who signed up for lessons. The plan was to spend a few weeks taking lessons and then give a presentation to the class. Over the next few weeks however, most of the kids who signed up for lessons gave up. When it came time to do the presentation in front of the class, I was the only remaining student. The student guitar instructor and I went ahead and gave a presentation to the class, both playing and offering advice to anyone who might find themselves teaching a guitar class someday. As for my own expertise, I decided that I would do a presentation on marching band for anyone in the class who wished to attend. I developed an overview with general procedures and required knowledge such as etiquette for the American Flag. I showed a film on field drill and presented an introduction to the Patterns of Motion system that we used at Houston. We even marked off the floor in the rehearsal room and spent some time doing a rudimentary Patterns of Motion drill. These contributions to the class, in addition to an evaluation from the elementary teacher that I had been assigned to where she cited that I had made "tremendous progress" in teaching the kindergarten class led to me getting an "A" in Junior Methods for the spring semester. As I look back on it, that "A" was one of the most difficult grades I've ever worked for, and one of the most satisfying.

In the meantime, I continued to be involved instructing the

Explorers. I wrote an arrangement for the corps, the theme from the movie "El Cid". Ray, the instructor that I was assisting, was very impressed with the arrangement. "I would have never thought of this type of voicing!" he said as he studied the score. He then invited me to go to with him to a drum corps clinic in New Jersey. There were major changes in the drum corps score sheets that year, and the organization of drum corps judges in the New York City area had set up this clinic in order to bring everyone up to speed. Ray also told me that there was a guy riding with us that he wanted me to meet. The guy's name was Paul, and he was an experienced judge as well as instructor. So, we went to the clinic, and Paul was actually one of the judges giving a presentation. In listening to him as he spoke, it was obvious that Paul was knowledgeable, and very intelligent. On the way home, I found out that Paul was a band director at a local junior high school. That got me to wondering. This was about the time when my Junior Methods class was discussing our senior year, which would also include Student Teaching. The only real guideline we had in choosing where we would student teach, was that it be in a school with a successful music program. I asked Paul if he would be willing to have me as a student teacher and he agreed. When it came time to meet with the professors to discuss our student teaching sites, it took some convincing on my part for them to allow me to student teach at Paul's school. Their concern was that Paul's school was not on their list of places that they historically sent student teachers to. They suggested to me that I think about a high school that they preferred in New York State.

Since Danbury was on the New York state line, they assumed that I wouldn't have to travel very far to go to a school that while in New York State, would still be relatively close to Danbury. This would have been a correct assumption if I had actually lived in Danbury, but I was commuting from home, an hour away in the opposite direction. When I pointed this out, they reluctantly allowed me to student teach at Paul's school. My decision to student teach at Paul's school also ran contrary to WestConn's general practice of students doing their student teaching in a high school. It wasn't really a requirement, but something they strongly suggested. However, I felt that since I had spent almost two years teaching drum corps and working with kids that were mostly high school students, I felt that I didn't really need to focus my student teaching on that age level. To be a well-rounded music educator, I would need to experience teaching at all levels. I already had a lot of experience working with kids in the elementary grades. Add that to my work teaching drum corps, and that left one glaring hole in my overall teaching experiences, junior high.

INSTRUCTING A NEW DRUM CORPS

At about the same time that these discussions were taking place, about the beginning of May, I was approached by one of my drum corps buddies, Vic. Vic lived in the city of Torrington, and there were some folks there looking to start a drum corps. Several years before, there was a drum corps in Torrington called the Connecticut Vagabonds. It was a respectable senior corps in those days, but for one reason or another, they ended up ceasing operations. Now, some former members of the Vagabonds were looking to revive the group. Vic was the drum instructor of this new edition of the corps and asked me if I would consider being the bugle instructor. I agreed, and went with him to meet the management of the corps. Now, I was under no illusions that this would be a beginner group in every sense of the word.

The managers of the corps had been able to acquire some of the equipment that the old corps used. For drums, that didn't make much of a difference, but the bugles were the old-fashioned G-D bugles. For those that may remember, bugles of those days were pitched in G, as opposed to most brass instruments and the bugles of today that are pitched in Bb. But in those days, bugles had only a single valve located under the lead pipe, as opposed to trumpets where the three valves are located on top. The standard Boy Scout bugle can only play open notes, that is, notes that do not require valves. But when pressed, the valve on a G-D bugle would lower the open pitch by four notes. This allowed the player to play a somewhat crude sounding scale, although there were also some notes that the G-D bugle was simply incapable of playing. This made writing and arranging for such a bugle section a tricky task indeed. When I started in the Explorers, all of our horns were G-D bugles, so I was at least familiar with the instrument. So when I went to my first rehearsal with the new Vagabonds corps, I had eight players of various degrees of playing ability. Most were kids and although there were a few adults that were part of the group, classifying it as a junior corps might have been more accurate than as a senior corp.

Some of the players were barely large enough to hold the baritone bugles that they were playing. This group was really starting from scratch. The rehearsals were held in the garage of one of the corps managers. Most of the eight players were beginners, but I had assumed that was the case in my preparations. I started them out with the very basics of playing the bugle, and at the end of the rehearsal, taught them the first few measures of an arrangement that I had prepared for them, the theme from "2001, a Space Odyssey". There were only a couple of weeks left in the semester but teaching two drum corps made it a very busy two weeks.

Classes ended, and so I began my summer with a focus on drum corps and the two groups I was teaching. The Explorers had made an admirable comeback and now had a fairly good corp. They were not ready for field competitions, but they had made great strides. The Vagabonds were a work in progress. They would eventually get to the point where they would be performance ready, but it would take some time. As it turned out, time was not a luxury. The corps management had made arrangements to set up a drum corps field competition for the beginning of July. While the Vagabonds would not compete in the competition, as the "host" corps, they were expected to give an exhibition presentation at the end of the show. It was traditional, but it meant that I only had about six weeks to get the bugle section ready. In the drum corps world at that time, where nearly all teaching was done by rote, six weeks was the blink of an eye. I prepared a second arrangement for them, the main theme from Mussorgsky's "Great Gate of Kiev". Because I was writing for G-D bugles, the melody was barely recognizable, but it would suffice given the circumstances. Putting tunes together in this "old school" style of rote learning, the process was slowed by the fact that the drum section learned a song after the bugle section had completed learning it. It took three weeks, rehearsing in the garage, to teach the first tune, "2001" to the bugle section. Then, we had to make a recording, so Vic could write the drum parts. I then started teaching "Great Gate of Kiev" to the bugle section, while Vic was teaching the drum parts for "2001".

A week before the Vagabond's drum corps competition, I went to Vic's house to see him before rehearsal and work out some details that would allow him to put together a basic drum part for "Great Gate of Kiev". Vic met me at the door and hesitated. I instantly sensed that something was wrong. "I've been fired." Vic told me. It seems that the drum section wasn't making what the corps managers considered sufficient progress. At this point I had to wonder about the managers of the corps. Even if they didn't care for the job that Vic was doing, firing your drum instructor a week before your premier performance isn't very bright. Before rehearsal started, I met with the managers and let them know that I wasn't very happy. I really wanted to tell them that if Vic goes, then so do I, but that would mean leaving the corps membership in a bind, and I just couldn't do that. Not performing at their own show would be an embarrassment, one that a new, fledgling corps might not be able to survive. So at this point, the issue was how to salvage this situation and somehow allow the corps to give a respectable performance at the competition. On the day of the competition, which was a Saturday, I met with the drum section on the field at the stadium at 8:30 in the morning. We worked until noon, on a drum part for "Great Gate of Kiev". I had never written music for a drum section before, and in creating the parts, I had to walk a tightrope between a basic beat, and a part that sounded somewhat respectable. In the end, I was able to fashion a part that worked, although it was very crude sounding. After lunch, the full corps got together to prepare for that evening's performance. It was then that I found out that there was no field drill preparation, and it fell to me to make something up on the spot. All I could do was fashion an opening drill move for the first minute or so of the performance. After that, the rest of the performance would have to be done in a standstill position.

After rehearsal, I noticed that they had set up a microphone at a field level table for the competition. Out of curiosity, I asked one of the managers who the announcer was going to be. "Probably me." he answered, "We don't have anyone". Again, I was concerned. Trying to run a competition, and deal with a myriad of details, oversee the admissions gate, see to any needs that any of the competing corps might have, be able to address any needs the judges might have, as well as line up and prepare your corps for a performance would be near impossible. I was almost tempted to let him find that out the hard way, but again, that might have an impact on how the corps would look in front of their hometown. "I'd be willing to do the announcing, if you like." I offered. It would be a great opportunity to put my radio station training to use. He agreed, and I began to go over the announcement scripts of the competing corps and other details I would need to prepare to do the announcements during the show.

Once the competition started, things ran pretty smoothly. After the last competing corps left the field, the Vagabonds came out and took their starting positions. I got the sense from the crowd that their appearance was a bit of a surprise, I'm certain many of the Vagabond veterans from the old corps were aware that the group had started up again, but it was clear that a significant percentage of the crowd was not. I read through the script that the managers had given me. At the end, I thought to myself "the most important component of this introduction is missing". So I improvised. I said, "Ladies and gentlemen, the performance you will see tonight is a result of six weeks of rehearsal and preparations". There were some audible gasps from the crowd. Drum corps veterans would understand what a small amount of time that was and giving out that information would put the performance a little more in perspective. There was also some polite applause after my announcement. "I'll take that." I thought as the

Vagabond performance started. As I watched the performance, my misgivings turned into pride. Their performance was near flawless, and I could sense that this was making an impression. When the corps finished their performance, the polite applause that I was expecting didn't materialize. Instead, a huge cheer rose from the crowd. Moreover, the cheering continued even after the corps had left the field. I imagine the pride could be seen on my face. Even more so when one of the judges said to me "Wow! That's impressive for only six weeks!". So the Connecticut Vagabonds, the hometown drum and bugle corps was back.

As the summer continued, the Vagabonds marched in several parades. In one parade, they were awarded the 2nd place trophy for best musical unit. At another parade, they were awarded 3rd place. This was working out better than I anticipated. At the end of the summer, I asked one of the corps managers for a professional recommendation that I could put in my file for when I started looking for a school teaching position. He wrote a very glowing recommendation and at the end, he wrote "In a year when the Vagabonds should not even have appeared in public, they were able to make a respectable showing, and attain the status of an award-winning unit. All of it due mostly to Mr. Judd's efforts."

THE STUDENT TEACHING EXPERIENCE

The rest of the summer went by quickly, and soon it was time to start my student teaching. Fairfield, Connecticut is an interesting community. It contains aspects of being an adjoining community to Bridgeport, but a very large segment of the residents' commute to New York City. The Metro-North rail line goes right through the town. In addition, it can also be considered part college town. Fairfield is the home of Fairfield University, and Sacred Heart University. At the time I taught there, the town had a population of about 50,000 and the school district had two high schools, two junior high schools, and a multitude of elementary schools. Tomlinson Junior High School was located toward the center of the town, with the rail lines running right next to the school. The school itself contained about 900 students that fed directly into one of the high schools.

One of the aspects of a successful music program is that the school administration gives the music program the support it needs to succeed. That certainly was the case with Tomlinson. In fact, during that time period, Tomlinson would have made a good case study of the type of scheduling and music program infrastructure that it takes to be successful on the junior high level. Each student in the school had one of the seven periods of the school day designated as a study hall. In reality, it was not a study hall, but a utilization period for subjects like Industrial Arts, Home Economics, PE, Art and Music. The beauty of this schedule was that music had the priority in scheduling for the utilization period. The process started during the summer when class schedules were put together. The students, who were band members in their 6th grade band in elementary school, were identified and placed homogeneously, by instrument, in their study halls. All of the clarinet players were given Period 1 as a study hall. Trumpet players were placed in the 2nd period study hall, etc. On the first day of school, I followed Paul to the auditorium 1st period, to meet with the clarinet players. All students that had a period 1 study hall were called to the auditorium, and sat in different areas with the music teachers, chorus on one side, and band members, that is to say clarinet players on the other. Using information furnished to him from the elementary band directors, Paul proceeded to divide the clarinet players into five classes, one for each day of the week. Advanced players would meet on one day, weak players on another, and the rest of the players placed accordingly. Once the band classes were set, the students were dispersed to other areas of the auditorium where the other utilization subject area teachers awaited them to place them in classes other days of the week. When 2nd period came, it was the same procedure, except with trumpet players. This played out for all of the class periods, each period a different section, flutes, saxophones, etc. By the end of the day, the music schedule was set for 260 band students. Actually, there were two bands, the 8th grade band, which had 125 students, and the 7th grade band, which had 135. The only drawback to this schedule was that the time for full band rehearsal was limited. The daily schedule called for an activity period of about 25 minutes each day. So, on Mondays and Wednesdays, the 7th grade band met during the activity period, while on Tuesdays and Thursdays it was the 8th grade band. During the first couple of weeks, all I did was observe the classes.

Paul knew of my drum corps background, and I think he had a lot of confidence in me, but this was junior high, and it is considered universally the most difficult of levels to teach. That was the issue, and as time unfolded, Paul tutored me in the techniques that would be most effective as well as the classroom control protocols that would work best. I had to rethink things like classroom pace, amount of playing time vs. talking time, and level of expectations. Paul also sent me to observe at the high school, and elementary school. He felt it was important that I understand how the band programs of the different levels mesh together. At the time, I was not aware of how important the infrastructure of the entire program is. I would not learn that lesson for many years. When it was time for me to start actually teaching, Paul assigned to me a mix of classes across the board. I took on a low-level clarinet class, an advanced trumpet class, a mixed level flute class, etc. In the beginning, I did moderately well, and started to improve from that point. I only had difficulty with one class in the beginning. I had a class of two tuba players. They were both just starting out having switched over from trumpet. The first couple of classes were difficult. They were both using very weird valve fingerings, completely wrong for many of the notes. Add to that the fact that they were both trying to adjust to the larger horns from trumpet, and the result was just a mess. By the third class, I was completely frustrated. "Who taught you guys these fingerings?" I asked. After some discussion, it occurred to me exactly what the problem was. The tubas that the kids were playing were Eb tubas. They looked as large as the standard BBb tuba, and any Eb tubas that I had previously seen were noticeably smaller than the BBb type, but not these. Add to that the fact that if one were to read the bass clef as treble clef, the Eb tuba fingerings line up almost exactly. So what the kids were doing was treating the tuba music as if they were playing trumpet. The thing is, that if they had been able to make the adjustment to the larger horn, and if I wasn't watching their fingers, they might have been able to play the tuba part fairly accurately, and I might not have noticed the difference. Although, giving these kids such a short cut struck me as kind of short sighted. After a few weeks, one of the assistant principals of the school came in to observe one of my classes. The comments that he provided me were generally positive, and when the student teaching supervisor from WestConn came to observe me, I did well on that evaluation also.

DRUM CORPS IN A TIME MACHINE

In the meantime, about the beginning of October, Paul asked me if I would like to instruct another drum corps. A very traditional senior drum corps had approached Paul to be their instructor, but Paul was busy with some other folks who were trying to start a new junior drum corps in the Bridgeport area, and Paul felt he did not have the time to take on the senior group as well. Now, although it is not a requirement, it is strongly recommended that student teachers do not work at another job while they are student teaching. The thinking is that for the duration of student teaching, one is already involved in a full-time job. At that point in time, the Explorers had advanced over the last year to become a very formidable junior corps. Ray, the bugle instructor I had worked with at Explorers decided to leave and take on some new bugle instructor positions closer to his home. That left me as the Explorers' primary bugle instructor. The Vagabonds were progressing, and as their first season drew to a close, we were looking to build upon what was accomplished. Taking on a third drum corps would mean having a second job for three nights a week. However, I wasn't taking on any playing gigs, and my radio show was moved to Saturday afternoon, freeing up another night. I was willing to take a chance that taking on a third night of drum corps would not seriously impact my student teaching. As it turned out, it wasn't long before my three nights of drum corps a week was reduced to two again. Although the managers of the Vagabonds realized that we could not practice in a garage throughout the winter, they had difficulty locating a place that would suffice for rehearsals during the cold weather. We started rehearsing at one of the local firehouses on the outskirts of town, but this only lasted a few weeks. When the group lost the firehouse as a rehearsal site, there was no place to go. The managers told everyone that they needed to suspend operations until the issue could be worked out. They told the instructors that they would call once they could get things up and running again. Unfortunately, the call never came, so I was left instructing the Explorers and this new corps that Paul had referred me to, the Yankee-Peddlers. The corps itself was not new, and I had seen them in various parades over the years. Walking into a Yankee-Peddlers rehearsal seemed like walking into a time machine. It was as if some of the older adults who were in the corps had been able to re-create their drum corps experience as kids, and while drum and bugle corps as a whole continued to make advancements, the Yankee-Peddlers seemed immune. Their uniforms seemed to come from a time many years in the past. Their equipment appeared to be decades old. Drums that seemed to have come from the 1950's, and, of course, G-D bugles. The only advancement, a rotary valve to play half-steps, flats and sharps. In the old-style G-D bugles, the only way to play flats and sharps was to manipulate the tuning slide. There was no contrabass bugle player and no baritone bugles. The bugle parts were primarily for soprano and French horn bugles. Their military bearing was also very traditional with an old school style protocol. The drum major sometimes used a mace. This was partially due to the fact that the corps, while not participating in the regular drum and bugle corps field competitions, instead took part in standstill competitions put on by the Connecticut Fifers and Drummers Association. Nearly all of the units that were members of the CFDA were fife and drum corps. The format of their standstill competitions required the drum major to use a mace. The guys in the bugle section of the corps were great to work with, although I did encounter an unanticipated difficulty that I never had to deal with while teaching school age kids. Once in a while, during the course of rehearsal, a couple of the players would have a few too many beers, and it became problematic to work with them.

On the student teaching front, Paul was starting to allow me to conduct parts of the band rehearsals. I was really nervous. The last thing you want to do is appear nervous in front of students, especially junior high students. It's not that I couldn't conduct. I had been conducting drum corps ever since that first day that I started working with Explorers. But even when conducting the entire corps, I was never conducting more than 45 or so people. Now, I was conducting a 125-piece band, and although the conducting mechanics are pretty much the same, there just seems to be a lot more room for error. Fortunately, I was able to navigate the rehearsal setting without any serious breakdowns. After a few times conducting the band, Paul assigned me to conduct one of the three selections the 8th grade band was going to play at the Christmas performance. Note that I didn't say "Christmas Concert". The only performance the band gave while I was student teaching was held during the school day. An assembly, just before Christmas vacation. There was no evening concert for parents. I never knew why.

A few weeks before the Christmas performance, I asked Paul to evaluate how I was doing. Nothing formal, just an opportunity for me to hear his thoughts. What was going well, what could be better, things I needed to work on. As it turned out, he said none of these things. What he told me was "You need to lose about 40 pounds. Kids, parents, and administrators will always make judgments based on how much you weigh". Paul's warning had been well timed. In another six months, I would be looking for a teaching job, and the last thing I needed was for administrators interviewing me to make judgments based on my weight. I had always been overweight, even as a kid, and yes, even to this day. I took Paul's warning to heart, went on a diet, and lost a few pounds. But as always, the weight came back.

If I do say so myself, I did a really good job conducting at the Christmas performance. It was the last day before Christmas vacation, and the students filed in to the auditorium. The Chorus performed first, followed by the 7th grade band, and then the 8th grade band. My mom had even come down to the school to view the performance. For some reason, I wasn't nervous at all. The piece that I conducted was an original arrangement by Paul called "Variations on 'We Three Kings'". Not only did the kids play it accurately, they played it very musically. I was fairly satisfied with how it went, and it made for a great punctuation mark on my student teaching.

THE LAST SEMESTER & SENIOR RECITAL

And so, I entered spring semester of senior year. The finishing stretch, the last hurdle, the final act. I calculated the last of the courses I would need and was taken back by how much coursework I had to finish. I had taken massive course overloads my junior year. I carried more than twenty semester hours both semesters. And now it looked like I was going to have to do a similar size of overload in order to graduate on time. I needed to take two philosophy courses, a Spanish course, which I thought I was exempt, but it turns out I wasn't. I also needed an English literature course, and a science course. Those courses alone made for a full class load, but I also had additional music courses that I had to take, including performing groups, and my applied bass study. While I was student teaching, the college brought in a new bass instructor, and from the start, I just didn't get along with the guy. He hated every aspect of my playing technique. He didn't like my hand position, or the way I stood with the bass, or the way I held the bow, or my bowing technique, my fingering technique, or vibrato. You name it, and he hated it. He then made me change just about everything about my playing. I couldn't believe it. It was astounding. Here I was, in my last semester in college, and this guy wants to change my entire playing technique. Not only that, but I only had about 10 weeks to accomplish all of this because that would be about the time of my senior recital. It's not that I didn't learn anything from him. Some of his corrections worked well for me. But it was a struggle for most of the semester.

In a more positive development, the music department announced to us that there was a new course that was being offered by the physics department. One of the professors there was also a musician, and he wanted to offer a course in the physics of music. Several of us jumped at the chance to take this course. How wonderful to have such a useful way to meet a degree requirement. It sure beat the heck out of having to take a biology or chemistry course. The two problem courses I had to deal with that semester were Spanish and English Literature. In each case, I needed to talk to the professor for extra help. In Spanish, I hadn't taken Spanish since high school, and I had forgotten much. After a couple of tutoring sessions, I was caught up, and was able to hold my own in the class. The English composition class was a different animal. I just couldn't understand where the professor was coming from. Every time I would try to analyze a literary passage, my ideas were in total opposition to what she expected. It was maddeningly confusing, and it took a lot of conversations with her to at least partially understand her approach. The philosophy classes were boring, as expected, but I was fairly confident I could navigate them without too much of a problem. Among my music classes, I had to take Orchestration. Of all the classes I took in college, this was the class where I was at my strongest. With my previous arranging experience going back to high school, I wasn't just good, I was great, if I do say so myself. In Jazz Ensemble, there was a freshman girl who came in to play trombone while I was student teaching. Ironically, she was from Fairfield, where I student taught. She was playing the 2nd trombone part, so I dropped to 3rd. I didn't mind. I just wanted to continue to play with the group. Over at the radio station, I still had my Saturday afternoon jazz show, but they had a problem finding someone to take the suppertime top-40 slot. So I simply continued into the shift. I would run my jazz show from 2-5 in the afternoon, and then switch to top-40 from 5-7.

So the semester wore on, and the progress I was making was slow. The "A" I received in student teaching went a long way to bring up my GPA. I knew I had a shot at bringing it up to 2.5, but I also knew a couple of bad grades would sink it. And through this time, I was still struggling through my bass lessons, and I had to start planning for my senior recital. The bass instructor gave me a choice of a couple of pieces. Neither one was easy, and I ended up choosing the Eccles Sonata for Bass, which any experienced bass player will tell you is a challenging piece. I was starting to get really concerned. I was caught up in making all these changes to my playing technique, was trying to learn a very challenging piece for my recital and realizing that if I allow the bass teacher to select a second piece, it would probably be just as difficult. I could feel this whole thing closing in on me, and I knew I had to come up with a creative solution in order to have a successful senior recital. One of the guys that I played with in the bass section of the orchestra was a music composition major. I asked him if he was interested in composing a bass piece for me to be premiered at my senior recital. Having played next to me, he was aware of my playing level, and if he could write a piece at that level, I wouldn't have to worry about having to deal with another difficult piece that might throw me for a loop. He very quickly agreed, and I knew if I could get this idea approved, my recital repertoire would be set. Permission was granted, and a few weeks later, the piece was completed. I looked at the piece and tried not to show any disappointment. I had expected that the piece would be contemporary, but this was downright Avant Garde. It called for an amplified string bass, which was a problem in that I didn't own an electric pick-up for my bass. It also called for a vast array of percussion instruments, another problem in that I had not lined up a percussionist to play with me. The piano part was just plain weird with the player needing to pluck piano strings and perform other strange sounds on the instrument. And that wasn't all. Only a limited portion of the piece used standard music notation. The remaining music was written in a type of shorthand, in which the composer obviously knew what all the symbols meant, but I certainly didn't. We managed to locate a percussionist who was willing to play with us, and we went into rehearsals, myself on bass, the percussionist, and my piano accompanist. At first, the rehearsals didn't go very well. All of the shorthand symbols had to be explained, and that was very time consuming. In addition, our budding composer did not have a lot of experience conducting, and just getting the three of us to play together was a struggle. Things were sinking fast, and I started to doubt that the piece would ever be performance ready. During the third rehearsal, another music composition major walked in. This kid was a senior and seemed a bit cynical about the whole project. I think he might have been a bit perturbed since it was a composition by a sophomore that was being presented, not a senior such as himself. He saw what was going on and offered to conduct. The pianist and I exchanged smiles. We knew that this senior was just dying to get a look at the music. He tried to conduct us as well, but he had limited conducting experience also, and was no more successful than the composer was. Finally, at the next rehearsal, the composition professor walked in and spent some time observing the situation. He offered to conduct the piece himself and we all readily agreed. Once he took over, things started to fall into place quickly. We asked if he would be willing to conduct it at the recital, and he agreed. The program for my senior recital was now set.

Finally, the day of my senior recital arrived. That morning, when I walked in to the music department, there were fliers posted all over the building announcing the "world premier" of this new piece, and there seemed to be a "buzz" about it among the music majors. I wanted the day to be as normal as possible. As far as I was concerned, this was just a requirement that I had to do. As a candidate for graduation, I needed to show competency on my instrument. This was just another hurdle on the way to my degree. My mom saw it differently. She invited all of the family to attend, went out and rented a top of the line tuxedo for me, arranged to record the concert on what was then a high-tech reel-to-reel tape recorder, and set up a reception for everyone at her dance studio. I really didn't want the extra attention, but considering all the support she gave me throughout the years, I couldn't say no. I wasn't totally sure why she wanted to do it up this big. I mean yes, I was aware that she felt this was a milestone. Her son, the music major, was going to graduate, and there was only going to be one senior recital. However, in the back of my mind, it also occurred to me that this might well represent an event that she could identify with since she was never able to experience it for herself. When she graduated high school, my mom was a top-notch piano player. Of course, I wasn't around to witness it, but as a young kid, I remember her playing what seemed like some very difficult piano pieces, including one that years later I identified as the piano part to Gershwin's "Rhapsody in Blue". When I came to appreciate the difficulty of that piece, I realized how good my mom really was. When she graduated high school, she wanted to attend music college, but my grandfather had recently opened his own business, and was in no financial shape to send her. In those days, there was no such thing as a student loan program. So she instead went to nursing school, became a nurse for several years, and finally opened her own dance studio. But I can remember several times over the years when she would ask herself "What if?". In the evening, as concert time approached, I started to get my stuff ready. I skipped supper that night. I always do when I have an important performance in the evening. I find supper to be a distraction, and I find that I can concentrate better without it. Everything was in place. I checked my watch, it was 7:30, and the concert would start at 8. "Excellent!" I thought. That gives me about 30 minutes to change into my tux, with time left over. Plus, the concert partner I was paired with would be opening the concert. Almost always,

WestConn would pair two seniors together for senior recitals. Each student was to perform a minimum of 25 minutes of music. Factor in applause, and a short intermission, and the entire affair was over in an hour. I was paired with a girl who was a piano major, and since she was performing first, some quick calculation told me that I would have more time to change than I would need. I grabbed my tux and went to the men's room adjacent to the recital hall to change. I took my time, there was no need to rush. All of a sudden, I could hear applause in the recital hall. And then I could hear a piano. I was horrified as I looked at my watch. It was ten of eight. They started the concert early, and the piano player that I was paired with had already started performing. I only had on socks and tux pants. I immediately went into panic mode. "It will be alright." I told myself as I threw my tux shirt on. Having to perform for 25 minutes would suggest that this first piece she was playing ought to last at least 10 minutes. Wrong! The piece lasted only about 3 minutes. I hadn't even been able to finish putting the studs on my shirt. "Maybe she has other pieces to perform." I thought hopefully. But nothing, just stone silence through the walls in the adjacent recital hall. I hurried to put my tux on as quickly as I could, but this dead time was weighing on me more and more, and the silence was deafening. Finally, I finished putting on the tux. How long had it been since the end of the piano piece? Seven or eight minutes? Maybe ten? I had no idea, but I went to get my bass and brought it backstage. My accompanist was nowhere to be found. I quickly looked across to the other side of the stage. There he was, obviously looking for me. When he spotted me, he motioned that he was going to come over to my side of the stage. In order to do that, he had to run through the hallways around the circumference of the recital hall. He finally arrived, out of breath, and after a few seconds of assuring each other that we were alright, we went on to the stage. The first piece I was to play was the Eccles sonata. I made a couple of minor errors but got through the piece without any major problems.

After a short intermission, the recital continued with the girl I was paired with performing on piano. This time, the piece she played only lasted about 4 minutes. I was completely puzzled. Either this girl did not know what the time requirement was, or she was somehow unable to pull together enough music to perform in order to meet it. If that was the case, then I couldn't understand why she would perform in a recital that she knew she was going to flunk.

But I put those thoughts aside as we started setting up for our "premier". The irony struck me. The piece itself was about 15 minutes long, but it took us about 20 minutes to set up. The major reason for the long set-up time was the huge array of percussion instruments. The percussionist was hurrying as fast as he could, but there was just a lot of stuff to set up. It was time to perform, but first, the composer went on to the stage. He talked for several minutes about composing the piece, and how he wanted to dedicate it to his grandfather, who had passed away recently. I think everyone thought it was a nice gesture. We then proceeded out on to the stage. Because I was so rushed in the beginning when I performed the Eccles, I did not take the opportunity to scan the audience. It wasn't until now that I had the chance. Most of the people in the audience were music majors, and I guessed that probably all of the music composition majors were present. There were also several members of the faculty in the audience. Many of my family were present, of course, including my Godmother and some of my cousins, none of which I'm sure were fans of contemporary ensemble music such as this. We started performing, and the piece went a lot better than I thought it was going to be. Towards the end, the piece included a pretty melody for me to play from a later Bruckner symphony. I played the theme about as good as I could possibly expect to perform it. Afterward, many of us gathered at my mom's dance studio for a reception. It was an enjoyable time, except for a couple of folks who commented on my "late" entrance. As it turned out, the girl that I was paired with, who did not meet the performance time requirement, was not allowed to graduate with us, and I felt bad for her.

After the recital, it was just a case of mopping up and getting ready for finals. I did a couple of really cool projects in my Physics of Sound class. I did a study of dynamic properties of several instruments. I borrowed a decibel meter from the physics department and produced of graph of different instruments playing at their loudest and softest volumes. For class project, we mapped out the acoustic properties of the recital hall. I also designed the interior of an auditorium, making choices of what materials would be used for the walls, floor, seats, etc. while keeping the reverb of the facility within certain parameters. In one of my philosophy classes, I wrote a really great final paper, and received an excellent grade for it. As I reviewed it, I could see the higher-level thinking coming through, and I kept asking myself "Did I really write this?"

Another notable event of the semester was the music department sponsoring an Aaron Copland Festival. The festival was comprised of several concerts featuring the music of Copland, but the big bonus was that Copland himself attended. Well, not that big a bonus. I was absolutely thrilled when he came in to conduct the college orchestra in one of his pieces for a concert that evening. Here was a chance to learn from one of the giants of music. What kind of insights would he share with us? What kind of advice or philosophies would he share with us? The short answer was – not much. Copland spent the rehearsal in the role of what we refer to in conductor slang as a "fireman". That is to say that he spent nearly the entire rehearsal putting out fires. The trumpet player was too loud in a particular section, or the English horn player needed to crescendo more intensely. But there was no mention by him about the piece itself. No insight, no real guidance. It was great playing under his baton, but it was also a disappointment.

GRADUATION AND THE BIRTH OF A DRUM CORPS

Finally, graduation arrived. Not only did I get my diploma, but I achieved my GPA goal of 2.5, and had a final GPA of 2.598. I'm certain it would have been over 2.6 if I hadn't gotten a lousy grade from the bass teacher. Those who have graduated from college are most likely aware that there is a difference between the cap and gown for a bachelor's degree candidate, and that of a master's degree candidate. Well, they gave me a master's degree cap and gown by mistake. It was irritating, but I figured I'd just roll with it. Nearly all of my family was present, and I could sense the pride in my mom and my grandfather.

There was a graduation party at the house afterward, and a lot of my drum corps buddies stopped by. As we talked throughout the afternoon, the conversation, most predictably, turned to drum corps. Many of us lamented the we missed marching with a drum corp. We were all over the age of 21, meaning that we were ineligible to march with a junior corp. The only local senior corps. the Connecticut Hurricanes, required a major time commitment, two weeknights and every weekend in the summertime. So, that left us with no real options. Then someone said "Well, what are the chances that we could just start a corps ourselves?" We all looked at each other. If a lot of our friends were feeling the same way we were, maybe we could do it. At that point, the idea went into overdrive. We spoke to the director of a defunct drum and bugle corps who had kept the set of bugles from his old unit. He also agreed to be the manager of the corps. We managed to get a set of drums, and we all reached out to our drum corps friends to see if they might be interested in joining up. When we started rehearsals at a local firehouse, we had about 30 people attend. We adopted the name of "F Troop" for the new corps and arranged for everyone to get uniforms that resembled the cavalry uniforms of the old west, which we fashioned from clothes at a local Army-Navy surplus store. I arranged a couple of western style songs for the group, and five weeks later, we marched in our first parade. I was back to teaching three drum corps, although I taught the bugle section of F Troop gratis. In the meantime, the Explorers had developed into one of the most impressive junior corps in the area but were now experiencing membership difficulties due to a change in management. The Yankee Peddlers were doing well, and on the day of the Connecticut Fifers and Drummers Association Stand-Still Championships, I went to watch them perform. The first event was a parade, and the weather was quite hot. I watched as the corps passed the reviewing stand and thought they had done fairly well. I walked toward the end of the parade to meet them. As I walked, I came across a tavern called "The Yankee Peddler Inn". I took it as a sign of good things to come, and went inside and ordered a beer, then went outside to greet the corps as they walked by. When they passed by me holding the beer, the corps halted. The Drum Major ordered them to fall out, and the entire Yankee Peddler corps went inside the Yankee Peddler Inn, equipment and all, to take a break from the heat and have a drink. When they were finished, they struck up a tune for the patrons before heading out to the local stadium for the competition.

DISCOVERING FRYEBURG

And so, diploma in hand, I went about seeking my first music teaching position. Actually, I did do one interview before I graduated. The Fairfield school system, the same school system where I did my student teaching came to the WestConn campus to do interviews, and I took advantage of that. However, the problem with Fairfield was that they had no music teacher openings. In fact, it seemed as if the entire state of Connecticut had no music teacher openings. I realized that if I were to find a teaching position, I would have to open up my options. The music faculty at WestConn discouraged the use of a teacher agency to find a teaching position. It's not as if there was anything wrong with the teacher agencies themselves. It's just that the professors felt it was unnecessary. But after watching the postings for the last couple of months prior to graduation, and finding only a few music teacher openings, nearly all of them out of state, I realized that I was probably going to need some help. I contacted a teacher agency and brought my resume to their office for a consultation. They pretty much confirmed what I had observed. There were very few music teacher openings in the state of Connecticut, and if I wanted to find a teaching position, I would probably have to expand my search to northern New England. I signed a contract with the agency, and within a couple of weeks, I started receiving responses from school districts. The first interview I went to was for an elementary school music vacancy in Marion, Massachusetts. Marion is a very pretty town on the coast, just a few miles before Cape Cod. The school was very nice, and the people were friendly. However, I didn't get hired. I didn't let it get me down. The next interview I went to was in southern New Hampshire. It was one of those days when nothing went right. I totally underestimated the travel time to the school, got caught in construction traffic, and ended up having to call the principal to reschedule my interview time. When I arrived at the school, it was totally unimpressive. The principal seemed as if he would rather be just about any place else rather than conducting music teacher interviews, and he was rather vague about several details of the music program. I couldn't help but feel that this trip was a complete waste of time, and to make matters worse, I was so far behind schedule, that I was late for an Explorers rehearsal in the evening. After a couple of more unproductive interviews, I received a call from the Headmaster at Fryeburg Academy, in Fryeburg, Maine. I had not considered the possibility of teaching at a boarding school, but I was willing to go in with an open mind. On the day of the interview, my girlfriend (future wife) went with me, and I allowed a lot of extra time to reach my destination this time. As it turned out, I needed it because we got lost and it took us a while to find our way again. I wanted to arrive in Fryeburg an hour early, but actually got there less than 20 minutes before the interview. The town of Fryeburg sits on the edge of the White Mountains, right along the state border with New Hampshire. The scenic area is among the finest that can be found anywhere. One can see Mt. Washington from most places in town, including the Academy campus, and even if you can't see it, at times you can certainly feel the wind whipping down from the mountain in the winter time.

The interview began with the headmaster, who explained to me that Fryeburg Academy was part boarding school, but it was also under contract to the local school district, and therefore provided a high school education for the students of Fryeburg, and the surrounding towns. He went on to explain the recent history of the music program. For more than two decades, the music program at the academy consisted only of vocal music. An Italian gentleman who emigrated to the area taught chorus for about 25 years until he retired a couple of years previous. Another gentleman was hired to continue teaching chorus and start a band program. He was a part time teacher and only stayed a year. The headmaster felt that if the music program was going to grow, there needed to be a full-time music teacher in place. He told me that there was a 20-piece band, but that the instrumentation was unbalanced. As I listened to him, I began to believe that this was a situation where I could make a difference. I then found out another reason why he was interested in me. He had just arranged for a student radio station to be installed on the campus, and he was looking for someone with radio station experience to lead the project. This was right up my alley, and I assured him that I was indeed the right person for this position. I then went to follow-up interviews the Guidance Counselor and Dean of Students. The salary was a little bit lower than the average public-school starting salary but considering that they were providing me with housing and meals, I thought it was a pretty good deal. I left the interview fully expecting that I would be their guy. And why not? Besides having the radio station experience that they were looking for, I also had superior ability to arrange and orchestrate music compared to the average music education graduate, which was exactly what the band needed. I could play all of the standard band instruments to a reasonable degree of mastery, and it didn't matter what the band instrumentation was, I could write music for them that would put their best foot forward. Also, with my experience in the Concert Choir at WestConn under Don Craig, I knew I would be comfortable teaching the chorus.

When I arrived home, there was a message waiting for me. A local high school near my home had a part-time band teaching position, and they wanted to interview me. This complicated things, because I really wanted to teach near my home, and even though this was a part-time position, I felt I had a good chance to grow the program so that it would eventually become a full-time position. I went to the interview, and things went well, but I didn't get the positive feeling I did at Fryeburg. I finally decided at the end of the interview to ask them point blank if I was a leading candidate, because if so, I would be willing to turn down the offer from Fryeburg that I was expecting in the next day or two. I guess they felt that since I was being honest with them that they should be honest with me. So they told me that I was not their first choice for the position, but probably their second. I thanked them for their honesty, and a couple of days later I accepted the offer of the teaching position at Fryeburg Academy.

Moving to Fryeburg was a big undertaking. Myself, my mom, brother, girlfriend, cousin, all went in two vehicles containing all the stuff that I wanted to bring. My room was in a former dormitory on the second floor, and there was a bathroom that I was to share with another teacher who would be in the adjoining room. On the first floor, there were two classrooms that were used during the daytime, and across the hall from our rooms there were a couple of rooms used during the daytime for working with students who needed remedial reading instruction. However, at night, we had the entire building to ourselves. The music classroom was not connected to the main building but was an old one-room schoolhouse in back. It was fine for my needs. There were about a dozen instruments in the closet, and a spinet piano on a platform at the head of the room. The radio station had mostly old but functional equipment and was connected to a small AM transmitter in each of the dorms. Another responsibility I had was to oversee the Student Union. Unlike major college campuses where the Student Union is a large, multi-functional building, the Student Union at Fryeburg Academy consisted of a large room in the basement of the unoccupied dorm that I lived in. It had a few lounge chairs, a bumper pool table, and a couple of soda machines. The headmaster told me that since my teaching position had been part-time up to this point, that I would need to take on some additional responsibilities to compensate for not having a full-time teaching load.

On to the start of the school year. The Labor Day holiday was move-in day for the students in the dorms, and classes started the following day. I had put fliers all over the school announcing the first band and chorus rehearsals. In the back of my mind was a class discussion in my junior methods class back in college. The topic of the class that day was small ensemble music. The focus was on how to be flexible when choosing music for small instrumental ensembles. One of the students asked why this was a topic that required so much class time. The instructor replied, "Well, what if you were to find yourself in the first day of school as a new teacher, and only five kids show up for your band rehearsal?" I was in the back of the room with a bunch of my jazz band buddies, and we all started laughing. "C'mon!" some of us said. "This is the 70's! Where are you going to find a band program where only five kids show up?" Well, at Fryeburg Academy, at my first band rehearsal as a new teacher, the size of my band was-- five kids. Soooo, this presented a dilemma. I had assured the headmaster that I would be able to have the band ready to perform at football games, but that was going by what he had originally told me, that there were 20 kids in the band. Dealing with the lack of instrumentation in a band of five kids would be difficult. I outlined what the goal was to the students, but also told them that we needed to grow the organization. Word got out, and after a couple of weeks, the band had grown to 12, although many of the students were beginners and near-beginners. Eventually, we were able to get the band out to play at a football game, although it was in more of a rudimentary fashion. The music schedule worked more like what one might find in a high school in the 1950's or early 60's. An activity period was scheduled once a week for band, and once a week for chorus. I then formulated a band and chorus lesson schedule that pulled students from study halls. So, this meant that my lesson schedule was subject to the whim of the study hall schedule. It was workable, but not to the extent that most of today's music programs work. I instantly knew that a full program for the Christmas Concert was not an option. There simply was not enough rehearsal time for that. I knew that given such a schedule, that the best I could hope for was perhaps three band selections, and three or four chorus selections for the concert. My chorus and band lesson schedule had an interesting mix of really good and talented classes, and beginners or struggling students. While I didn't really care to rehearse Christmas music in early October, it was entirely necessary when the group rehearsals were limited to once a week.

My days were really busy. I had my class schedule during the school day. After school, it was the radio station that occupied most of my time. At first, it was developing an on-air schedule and training the kids to use the equipment. It wasn't necessary for the kids to have FCC licenses like we had to have in college, because the academy radio station was such low power that the FCC considered it not much more than a wireless PA system. Once everything was rolling, all I really needed to do was just be around to monitor things. Once in a while, I would have to step in if one of the kids played a record with questionable language, but usually there wasn't a problem. I also had to keep an eye on the Student Union, stock the soda machines, and perform any of the other duties I was scheduled for. Private boarding schools have a much more demanding supervision schedule. Of course, I received meals free in return for dining hall supervision. For lunch, this worked fine. Dinner was fine too, after some adjusting to the format. During the day, Fryeburg Academy was a combination boarding and local high school, but in the evening when only the dormitory students were present, the prep school side of the academy took over. Dinner was a formal event. The boys all dressed up in ties and jackets, while the girls were also dressed accordingly. This also applied to the adults. Students acted as waiters and waitresses by rotation, and once everyone was seated, they brought the food to the tables. One staff member was assigned to each table and was expected to monitor the manners of the students at their table. Once dinner was finished, the students had a few minutes of free time before the evening study hall began. If school was to be in session the following day, then there was an evening study hall that ran from 7-9pm the night before. There was a rotating schedule for the faculty to circulate through the dorms during study hall to supervise and assist students with their studies (if they could). Evening study hall was not the only duty to run on a rotating schedule. There was also after school detention, and weekend duties. Each weekend, faculty members were assigned to weekend activity duty, which consisted of planning activities for the dorm students on the weekends such as shopping trips, canoe trips (the academy owned its own set of canoes), Student Union supervision, etc. There was also a duty called the "Week End Master" or WEM. This person was responsible for supervision of the entire campus from Friday evening to Sunday evening. The WEM was part supervisor and part security detail. When I had the duty, I had to check in with each dorm at curfew to make sure that all of the students were accounted for. If there was a problem, I had to deal with it. I would also then make rounds among the campus buildings to make sure that everything was secure. On duty weekends, I usually didn't get to bed until well after midnight. It's not that things were difficult, there was simply a need to try to anticipate problems. One evening, when I checked in with one of the dorm supervisors, we found that one of the students, Pat, was missing. Since this was in the middle of ski season, and Pat was a dedicated skier, the first place I went to look for him was the ski shed. Sure enough, there was Pat, polishing skis. I took Pat back to his dorm and placed him on dormitory restriction. I wasn't a big disciplinarian, but sometimes it just needed to be done.

The thing that I remember the most about Fryeburg was that it was a lot of work. I was really tired most of the time, and there wasn't much time for resting and recharging. Even on a weekend when I didn't have a duty and could look forward to a couple of days of rest, it didn't always work out that way. After the first couple of weeks of school, I was approached by the pastor of the local congregational church. I had two of his sons in the music program, but he also asked me if I would conduct their church choir. In a small town such as Fryeburg, there wasn't always a person available who could conduct a church choir, and it didn't seem as if the pastor had a lot of options. The interesting part of this is that he offered to give me technical assistance with the radio station, since before he became a minister and once worked in radio. Therefore, it was only logical that we helped each other out.   The only problem was the fact that I had never conducted a church choir and was not familiar with the service in a congregational church.   No matter, every Wednesday night I conducted a church choir rehearsal, and they sang at the following Sunday service. They paid me a few dollars for directing. Nothing much, but that was okay. Even though I didn't have the experience, nor did I understand how to be a church musical director, I still felt that

I was helping and making a situation better than it would otherwise be without me.

THE FIRST "QUITTERS" AND MY FIRST CONCERT

So everything was up and running, and my lesson groups were mostly functioning well. Students were for the most part progressing on schedule, and I was generally satisfied with the way things were moving along. Then, at the beginning of November, I had two freshmen girls come up to me and informed me that they were quitting chorus. Of all the things they teach you in as a music major in college, the one thing that I don't ever remember being covered is what to do when kids quit. I was devastated. I couldn't eat for two days. Even though the two girls were generally weak singers, all I could think about was what I might have done wrong. I can tell you, after 40 years, the sting doesn't go away. After many years, I have learned to trust myself in that when a kid quits, there are probably a wide variety of reasons, and it usually isn't my fault, but it still hurts.

I did my best to put it out of my mind, and I started working in earnest in preparing the band and chorus for the Christmas concert. I had a lot of beginners in the band. There was a tuba player, and although he made great progress, he was a beginner nonetheless. There was a beginning drummer, who also made great progress, and a Bermudian rhythm section. Three students, Kenny on drums, Darren on bass, and Brandon on piano. All were from Bermuda, and were beginners starting from scratch. In Brandon's case, he was a PG, or post high school student, and would likely only be attending the academy for one year. So instead of starting him out on a primer piano lesson book, or similar manual, I started teaching him using a keyboard harmony approach learning chords and accompaniment techniques so that he would be able to back up a soloist. I thought that maybe by the end of the school year he might be able to be functional in that capacity, but Brandon worked diligently, and spent a lot of time after school and weekends practicing in the music room. He ended up being able to accompany students in the Christmas concert. The strongest student I had was a sophomore, Brent, who played trumpet and baritone horn, and could also hold down the tenor part in chorus by himself. Brent was the son of the elementary music teacher in town. Brent's mom was also an excellent pianist, and since I couldn't play piano well enough to accompany the chorus, I was gratified when she volunteered to play. I really needed to depend on her to fulfill that role. The problem was her schedule did not allow for her to be present for choral rehearsals, so for the most part, I conducted choral rehearsals "a cappella". The only way I could facilitate a rehearsal with her and the chorus was to schedule a special chorus rehearsal after school on the day before the Christmas concert. This special rehearsal was scheduled to be held in the gym, since that was where the Christmas concert was slated to be. When I walked into the gym on that afternoon, I was surprised to find an array of Christmas trees lining the section of the bleachers where the chorus was to perform. The maintenance folks told me that they would take care of setting up for the concert, but I certainly wasn't expecting this. They had gone into the woods that morning and cut down nearly two dozen small pine trees to use as a background behind where the chorus would perform, and they weren't done yet. The day of the concert, they installed a white curtain behind the Christmas trees, adorned with a wooden cross. The cross threw me at first. After all, one would not find this in a public school, but of course, Fryeburg Academy is a private school, and this was obviously a long-standing tradition for this concert. They also set up the chairs for the audience and lined the center aisle with battery operated electric candles. It was a wonderful setting for the concert.

Evening arrived, and the students and audience began to file in. Students in the dorms were excused from evening study hours if they wished to attend the concert. I did not set up the program as most teachers would, with a chorus performance followed by a band performance of all their pieces. Instead, I mixed the program up between choral pieces, band pieces, and soloists. I started off with the chorus singing "Carol of the Bells", also known as the Ukrainian Bell Carol. The chorus sang it flawlessly, and I was very pleased at how it went. When it ended, I thought the audience would receive it well, but --- stone silence. I didn't know what to think. Was it also a tradition here not to applaud for selections, or was the piece so short that they didn't realize it had ended? I kept my game face on and moved to the band. Their first selection was the "March of the Toys". It started out a little shaky, but the rest of the piece went fairly well. This time, a lot of applause. The rest of the concert went rather well, and then came the finale, the "Hallelujah Chorus". I guess this was where I made a rookie mistake. It probably would have been helpful to inform the students prior to the concert that it was a tradition for the audience to stand during this piece. But with all the other last-minute details, I forgot to mention it to them. When the audience stood for the piece it was a surprise to most of them. They sang the piece quite well, but after it was done, and everyone started getting ready to leave, some girls in the chorus came up to me with puzzled looks on their faces. "They stood up!' said one girl in disbelief. "Why did they do that?" another said as if they might have done something wrong. All was well once I explained it to them.

And so, the first concert of my career was in the books, so to speak. If I had to rate it, I would say it was reasonably successful, although for the first of many times I experienced what I call "future concertitis". No sooner did we start packing stuff away when the concert was over, and I was already thinking about what I would do for the Spring concert. Not that I felt that I needed to "top" the Christmas concert with something more impressive. I was satisfied to simply program music that would stretch the boundaries of the students just a little bit. The issue was that I wanted to choose good quality music, and until I had a set program. I heard from the students several times that they considered the music that the previous teacher had chosen to be both boring and stupid. When I saw what the teacher had programmed, it appeared that he had chosen material that he thought the students would find fun to sing. But it seems he wasn't able to get that across to the students. It isn't the approach that I would have taken. To me, a song shouldn't just be "fun", but should also allow the student to grow musically and speak to their self-expression. The stuff that he had chosen for them to sing just didn't do that.

The second half of the year started, and I was looking forward to the debut of a music festival that we would be involved with. I was contacted in the fall by a music teacher from another prep school who was looking to put together a festival of massed choirs from several prep schools in the state. Many of the prep schools in the state had very small choirs. My chorus at Fryeburg was one of the bigger ones with 38 kids. Still, I jumped at the chance for my students to be involved with a massed choir event. So, all of the prep school choral directors were contacted to see if there was enough interest to put such an event together. I mostly observed the process, since as a new teacher I had no idea how to organize a festival and all of the details involved. Many prep schools declined to participate. For some, it was a case of scheduling. With some schools on a semester schedule and others on trimesters, there were certainly coordination problems. In other cases, some schools simply were not willing to be involved. There was a religious school that told us that they would be willing to participate only if the entire concert program consisted of sacred and religious music. Another school told us that if there was sacred or religious music on the program, they would not participate. In the end, neither school participated. The directors of the participating schools met a couple of times to agree on which pieces would be on the program, and who the conductor would be. We ended up asking a choral teacher at Bates College to be the conductor of the massed choir, and he agreed. He also arranged for the festival and concert to be held at the Bates College Chapel.

On the day of the festival, I arranged for a bus to take us to Lewiston. We rehearsed throughout the afternoon with a combined chorus of about 70 kids. The pieces were not difficult, although the Randall Thompson "Alleluia" challenged my students. After rehearsal, everyone dressed up for a formal dinner at a local establishment. The concert was in the evening, and besides the massed choir selections, most of the individual school choirs also performed. I had the Fryeburg chorus do "Bridge Over Troubled Water" with a pianist that I had never rehearsed with before. I did not realize until we started performing that the pianist might have difficulty maintaining tempo. Although we started out at an acceptable tempo, the song started to get faster. Eventually, it began to sound like a rhumba. I guess it was the kind of experience that makes music teachers wiser.

I was making plans for the Spring Concert. One of the things I wanted to do was find a way to incorporate something visual into the concert. When I mentioned it to some faculty members, I received various suggestions, but it led to some larger discussions as well. The discussion eventually focused on dates how to schedule the various other arts areas as well as music. There was an art show that needed to take place, and every class performed a one-act play towards the end of the year. We finally ended up planning an arts festival weekend. It was only logical to try to combine all of these activities into one weekend. Rather than having a concert one night, followed by four one-act plays the next night, we set it up so that there would be two one-act plays presented one night along with half of the spring concert program. The following evening, the remaining half of the spring concert would be performed along with the remaining two one-act plays. In the end, it worked really well, and I managed to work in the visual effect in the concert that I was looking for.

I wrote an arrangement of music from the tornado sequence from "The Wiz" that had recently opened on Broadway. I managed to utilize two overhead projectors and station them backstage on each side of the stage. Using clear glass dishes with a small amount of water, I had students add small amounts of food coloring to the dishes. When the liquid was swirled around in the dishes, the overhead projectors would capture the colors blending together. It made for a bit of psychedelic effect, but it worked well.

One of the students involved in the lighting was a fairly shy kid by the name of Barry. I don't remember how I came to involve Barry in the concert, but he was very reliable behind the scenes. After the concert, I was contacted by Barry's parents. They were so thankful to me for involving Barry in the concert. It seems that the parents were very concerned that Barry was not involved in anything. He didn't do any sports, nor was he a member of any of the student organizations. He pretty much stayed in the dorm most of the time and didn't socialize, nor did he seem to have any friends. This apparently was the first time they had seen him involved in any kind of activity, and they were thrilled.

The school year ended, and I had some choices in terms of what to do with my summer. I decided to start taking some graduate courses, and perhaps begin my journey to a master's degree. I took two summer courses at the Hartt College of Music. One was a course in teaching jazz band, the other was a course in Musical Theater. I figured it would be something valuable to take, since perhaps at some point I might be involved in a musical.

FRYEBURG, THE 2ND YEAR

When I returned to Fryeburg for the start of the new school year, I found out that several different duties were going to be assigned to me. First, I was being placed in a dorm. The previous year, each dorm had a teaching couple living in the adult apartment on the first floor. Then on the second floor was a small two-room apartment for a single adult. The single adults had been older women who served as "house mothers" to the students. However, the academy had deemed that to be too expensive, and now single teachers would be assigned to the small apartments rather than housemothers. Being in a dorm would mean some additional duty time although I would no longer have to do the Weekend Master Supervisory duty. I would nonetheless need to be in charge of the dorm one weekend a month and one night a week. I still had weekend activities duty at regular intervals, but those weekends would have to be scheduled around my dormitory duty weekends. Also, I no longer had to supervise the Student Union, but I would instead supervise a new work-scholarship program. I had no idea how difficult overseeing this new program was going to be. The real problem was that in previous years, scholarships were given to students with no expectations placed on them. Now, students would have to work for their scholarships, and for most of them, it wasn't a welcome development. However, everything was final, and the kitchen employees that were responsible for cleaning dishes, trays, pots & pans, etc. were laid off. In my case, the first thing I had to do was develop a work schedule for the students. There was a lot of resistance from the students, and I had to do a lot of consulting with the headmaster. Add to this, part of the scholarship program consisted of giving a tuition break to families that sent more than one child to the academy. It was basically a discount, but it was officially a scholarship. Initially, I was told to include such students in the work schedule, but after parent complaints, that aspect was dropped.

I finally set a schedule that appeared to work best with everyone, but problems still persisted. Students did work that was a) incomplete, b) unsatisfactory, c) accompanied by a poor attitude, d) all of the above. In addition, students were squabbling with each other over who was doing more work than the other, or didn't get along with the remaining kitchen staff, etc. After a while, I learned which students to put together, and which ones should work by themselves. It was a help, but I still couldn't sit down for a meal without being interrupted by a problem in the kitchen. Add to this, one of the cooks left the academy to start his own business. However, he had been covering for some of the incomplete work of the students, and never told me. Once he left, it was a complete mess, and the only way that I could make sure that everything would run smoothly was to be in the kitchen myself. When lunchtime came, I ended up cutting the line and wolfing everything down as quickly as I could, then going to the kitchen to supervise the students. I would sometimes help out if necessary, and I needed to restructure the work schedule to have some students go to the kitchen after school to finish what the lunch crew may not have been able to complete. In the evening, I would arrive at the kitchen with the students who would be waiting on tables for that meal and eat supper early. Then, once the rest of the students and faculty would enter for the sit-down dinner, I would be in the kitchen supervising and helping out as necessary. At least I no longer had to dress up for dinner.

The good part was that my band was bigger than the previous year and so was my chorus. The lesson plans that I had designed for chorus were having an effect, and I could see an improvement in their skills. In the fall, I decided to send kids to the Maine All-State auditions. They had the ability, I was certain. I was also sure that some of them would be accepted, no problem. In those days, in order to audition for the Maine All-State Chorus, one had to learn their part in a piece that had four-part harmony. I started teaching the piece to the students, but in order to do so, I had to schedule the practice times during the evening study hours. I couldn't do it on Monday evening because that was my dorm duty night. Wednesday evening was still rehearsal time for the choir at the Congregational Church, and the students were pressing me to start jazz band rehearsals on Thursdays. That left Tuesday nights for working with kids on the All-State auditions. Eventually, there were seven students that learned the piece. The breakdown of parts were fortunate since the kids had to audition in groups of four. Two of the kids were sopranos, two were altos, and two were basses. That left Brent as the one tenor. When we went to auditions, he would have to sing the piece twice so that all of the kids would get a chance to audition in a quartet. When we went to auditions, I was concerned. As I did with all of the choral pieces I taught, since I couldn't play piano I needed to teach the piece a cappella. All of the other schools appeared to have piano accompaniment for their students, but of course I did not. I walked into the judging room with the students and tried to explain that I was unable to teach the piece with the piano part. One of the judges stood up and his face brightened. Addressing the students, he said, "You mean that you can all sing the piece a cappella?" The students nodded, and the judge smiled and said, "Well, I really want to hear this! Please, let's start." It seemed that many students from other schools appeared to be using the piano part as a crutch for staying on pitch. Having students sing the piece without the help of the piano required a higher skill level, and that was something the judges could appreciate. The first quartet performed the piece followed by the second. They did very well, and I was pleased. In the end, five of the seven students were accepted to the All-State Chorus, and the two who were not accepted had scores that were just under the cut-off. Brent, the tenor, received the second highest tenor score in the state. I found the results to be quite satisfying.

In the meantime, I was dealing with my new set of teacher duties. There was one fall weekend where I was on activity duty. This meant setting up weekend activities for the dorm students. Faculty members were assigned to this duty two at a time, and I was paired with an English teacher who was new to the academy. We decided to do a canoe trip with whatever students were interested in going. The school owned a set of canoes, so there was no other arrangements that needed to be made. All we had to do was hitch up the trailer of canoes and go. On the day of the canoe trip, I went to check out the launch area, a place called Swan's Falls, which was on the Saco river only a couple of miles from the academy. As I entered the area, I was greeted by a hand-written sign, which apparently had been placed by the warden service. The sign said that there were flooding conditions on the river that day, and that they did not advise navigating the river by canoe. I looked over at the river, and the water was not only high, but very rough as it flowed over the falls. I went back to the campus and told the other teacher what I had found. She did not seem impressed by what I had to say and said we would go over to Swan's Falls and make a decision. I found it annoying that she wouldn't take my word, but we hitched up the trailer with the canoes and headed for the launch. One look at the sign and the water, and she immediately changed her mind. It just looked too dangerous. The students, who were in the van fully expecting that the trip was on, were upset. They protested vigorously, pointing to a couple of canoes that were some distance upriver, and either didn't know of the warning, or they ignored it. However, the other teacher and I weren't budging, and we told them that if the flooding subsided, we would do the trip the following day. Grumbling, the students got back into the van, and we all went back to the campus. I would find out afterward that later, after we left the launch, a canoe overturned at Swan's Falls, drowning a young boy. The postponed trip took place the next day, and while the other teacher went with the students instead of me, everyone appeared to have an enjoyable time.

I also rearranged my duty schedule in order to go to Connecticut to attend my mother's wedding. She had divorced my dad several years before, and now was apparently ready to get married again. Her new husband, Bill, was a great guy. He spent many years going to sea with Woods Hole Oceanographic Institute, and like any seaman, was never at a loss for stories.

During the fall, the band played at all of the football games, and did a fairly good job. It was still too small a group to make a good impact in outdoor acoustics, but it was an improvement. We did the Christmas concert the same as the previous year, and it worked fine, although I was missing two low brass players because they had a wrestling meet on the day of the concert and didn't get back in time. In a large band program, that may not make all that big a difference, but in this case, where I had written arrangements customized for the group of students I had, it was like a sonic jig-saw puzzle with two important pieces missing.

After Christmas, a set-back. One of my five students who made the All-State Chorus was kicked out of school for possessing marijuana. Fryeburg Academy had a zero-tolerance policy when it came to drugs, and any student caught having or using drugs was immediately expelled. It was frustrating to have to deal with this kind of situation.

And then, one night just before jazz band practice, my phone rang. It was Bill, my mom's new husband. My grandfather had a heart attack that afternoon and had passed away. As soon as I hung up the phone, I talked to several people to trade duty days so that I could go home, and then I went to jazz band rehearsal. Getting through the rehearsal was tough. I think it was the first time I had to teach with a complete poker face the entire time.

So I went to Connecticut to be with my family and went to the funeral. When I got back to Fryeburg, I faced a dilemma. I had been neglecting my project that I had been planning for the Spring concert. The musical "A Chorus Line" had recently opened, and I really liked the music soundtrack. I wanted to write some of the tunes for the spring concert, but I had been delaying it because of all the other supervision duties I had to deal with. It some point, I was wondering if I was a music teacher or a student work supervisor. The latter seemed to take up more of my time. Then, on a Saturday when I didn't have a duty, I figured I had better start on this project or else I needed to make alternative plans. I locked myself in the music room, with a stack of blank music staff paper. I started at 8:30 in the morning, stopped for lunch and then continued working. I almost missed dinner because I was so involved in what I was doing. After dinner, I continued to work. At some point, I realized that curfew had occurred in the dorms, and I was still working on the music. Finally, I looked at my watch. It was 2:30am. I had been working on these arrangements for 18 hours straight, stopping only for meals, and I didn't even feel all that tired. The kids loved the arrangements, and now I only needed to put one more component in place. As you might know, the show "A Chorus Line" starts in the middle of a dance audition. I wanted to stage the dance audition while the band and chorus performed the music on the floor in front of the stage. So I gave my mom a call and explained what I wanted to do. She agreed to help me and set up a time when she could come to Fryeburg to work with the students initially.

In the meantime, I was preparing for the prep school festival for its second year. This time, the festival was being held at a school about two and a half hours travel from Fryeburg. In addition, we were going with a more challenging program. We decided to have the massed choir do a choral master work, the Vivaldi "Gloria". Also, we were going to form a massed band, and do a couple of band pieces. I was selected as the conductor of the band. I chose two pieces for them to perform, the Frank Erickson "Air for Band" and the Bach Prelude and Fugue in F. The day of the festival came, and because my chorus was now more than 50 kids and I was also bringing band kids, there were too many students for one bus. I ended up driving a school van with the overflow kids behind the bus. We traveled to the festival and began rehearsing. I was very confident in my chorus kids. The first time we rehearsed the opening movement of the Gloria, they sang it with almost no errors. The only misgiving I had was how good the instrumental players were from the other schools. As the day went on, I felt better about the band and how they were playing the music. Like the previous year, we had a formal dinner in the school dining hall. We then started preparing for the concert. The audience started filing in, and I got to see my mom, grandmother, and girlfriend, who made the 7-hour trip from Connecticut. Also, the academy headmaster made the trip up from Fryeburg. The concert started, and the chorus sounded great. When it was time for the band, they performed well also, but then I made a rookie error. While the "Air for Band" went great, and so did the Bach prelude. When I went to start the fugue, I gave a bad cue, and the students did not come in together. It was disappointing, but still, it was a good concert. When it was over, I wanted to get the kids on the bus and van and leave. We had a long way to travel. But the other teachers wanted us to pose for a photo, and then punch and cookies, etc. by the time we got on the road, it was after 9pm. For the first hour of the trip home, I was fine. Then, the long day started to catch up with me. I had to fight to stay awake. The kids were all asleep. If one of them had not been, I could have had that student try to keep me awake. But I tried to carry on, eyelids growing heavy. Finally, we got to the Lewiston rest stop on the Maine Turnpike. Shortly after we pulled in, the headmaster parked beside us. I probably should have told him that I was tired, but I thought that it would make me look weak, so I didn't say anything. At any rate, I took a break, and got myself a drink before getting back on the road. Again, I was fine for a while, but then, once more, I started getting tired again. At one point, I caught myself nodding off, and it was so shockingly alarming that all of a sudden, I was wide-awake, at least for a little while. I knew I just couldn't let that happen again, not with a van full of kids. The battle with fatigue continued until finally we arrived at the campus. The time was a few minutes before midnight, and the thought that I would have to be up, fresh faced, in the classroom in 8 hours was daunting. The following evening, I had reserved the gym for the first practice with dancers for the "Chorus Line" sequence that I wanted to do for spring concert. My mom, grandmother, and girlfriend arrived at the campus in the afternoon, having stayed at a hotel the previous night. Eleven girls showed up, and first we had a discussion. My mom would be outlining the choreography to them that evening, but after that, they had to be willing to take direction from me in the following practices as we would work to refine what they had learned. All were in agreement, and so we started with the dance segment. After explaining the setting for the scene, and what they needed to portray, the girls responded and learned a large part of the dance segment that night. We then scheduled regular rehearsals where I taught them the remainder of the choreography, and we worked on their technique to perform the entire routine.

This was working just fine, and then about a week or two before the concert we had an incident with the baseball team. For some reason, I couldn't get the gym that evening, and had to use the wrestling room, which was located behind the stage. The only door to the wrestling room was through the boys' locker room. This wasn't a problem except for this one night when the baseball team was overdue from a game. I guided the girls through the locker room as quickly as I could, expecting the team to arrive any minute. After I closed the door, I realized that a couple of girls were missing. I was about to open the door to go look for them, but- too late. The team was coming in to the locker room. It wasn't long before we heard a couple of girls screaming in the locker room. Our latecomers had arrived in the locker room just as the team was preparing for the showers. It would have been amusing if it hadn't been somewhat serious.

As if I didn't have enough free time, I also became assistant track coach. I didn't have a whole lot of qualifications. I was on the track team my senior year in high school. I hadn't done anything else with it since. I basically worked with the kids who did the throwing events- shot put, javelin, and discus. The time commitment cut into my preparations for the spring concert, but I managed to get everything in place in time for the concert itself. Again, we did the arts festival format with half the concert on Friday night, followed by the other half of the concert on Saturday night. Both the band and chorus were set up in front of the stage, so that the stage could be used for the "Chorus Line" segment. The Friday night performance went well except for a glitch in the sound system. After the performance, I examined the sound system and ended up kicking myself. The settings on the sound system were off, and the microphones sounded awful. If I had half a brain, I would have checked the sound system beforehand. Another rookie mistake. Saturday brought difficulties of another kind. During the day, we attended the state prep school track meet in the City of Bath. Instead of giving us a bus, it was decided that both the head coach and myself would drive the students in vans. It was a two-hour trip, and I was a little concerned about returning on time for the evening performance. As it turned out, we arrived back on campus in plenty of time for the evening performance. However, once we pulled into the driveway, the weekend supervisor, or WEM, was waiting for us. Two of our students were still in Bath. It appears that once the track meet ended, we loaded our vans and took off. Apparently, these two students had wandered off just before the vans left. I thought they were on the coach's van, and he thought they were on mine. One of the students was a band member. Once we received the news from the WEM, the coach saw my concern, and told me to stay and get ready for the performance while he went back to Bath to retrieve the students. As it turned out, he must have broken a few speed records, because he managed to get the students back well in time for the performance.

The kids performed well. However, I realized that I had a decision to make. The music program was moving forward. My second year at Fryeburg was more successful than the first, and I had every reason to believe that the third year would be more successful than the second. In addition, the headmaster asked me to be a part of a committee to look at the way classes were scheduled at the academy. There were multiple objectives in designing a new schedule, but among them was to increase the number of rehearsals for band and chorus in the course of the week. I enjoyed teaching at Fryeburg, but the other aspects of the job were getting to me. The supervision duties were extensive, and with supervising the scholarship students, I rarely had a meal to myself where I could just relax. There were times when I had to drop what I was doing musically, to deal with a supervision issue. At some point, I had to wonder if I was just a supervisor who happened to teach music on the side. Besides the supervision, I also struggled with quarterly reports to parents. I was assigned about a dozen students for which had to write an official progress report four times a year. Sometimes the students that I needed to write a report on were not doing well. Some of them were slackers, had lousy attitudes, and were irresponsible. When I would try to communicate those things in my report, I would be called to the guidance office. The guidance counselor, who had been at the academy for many years, was very sensitive about what went into the reports. If I wrote something negative about a student, he would make me re-write the report. He would say something like "The academy has a good relationship with this family, and we can't say negative things about this student". In one case, I had to re-write a report several times. By the time the parent received the report, it was too late to address the problems with the student. The father of the student was very upset, and I can't say I blamed him. I believe that if my report had gone out on time without the editing, the situation might have been salvaged.

I also missed working with drum and bugle corps, but having to spend so many weekends on duty did not allow me the time I would need to work with a drum corps. This wasn't like Connecticut, where at that time, there were corps in almost every town and weeknight rehearsals were commonplace. There were far fewer corps in northern New England, and most of them rehearsed on weekends. Some weekends, when I wasn't on weekend duty, I would drive down to Portland and watch the drum corps there rehearse. I enjoyed my time observing them, but in the back of my mind was the knowledge that my schedule would never allow me to work with such a group. In addition to all of this, it also appeared that my family was having difficulty dealing with the death of my grandfather. I felt it was time to return home, not because anyone ever asked me to, but I just felt it was something that I needed to do.

Finally, I decided that I needed to leave Fryeburg. I didn't have a job prospect, and I had no idea what the future would hold, but I needed to find out. I might have reconsidered if I had known how prominent Fryeburg Academy was in the history of music education.

MUSIC EDUCATION HISTORY AND FRYEBURG ACADEMY

Because Fryeburg Academy was founded in 1792, it most certainly qualifies as one of the early American Academies, that is to say, schools that were founded before the establishment of public schools. The school has many distinguished alumni, including Robert Peary, who was the first person to lead an expedition to the North Pole. After attaining that achievement, he returned to Fryeburg, and set a small monument to true north, in a park across the street from the campus. I think I would have been more appreciative of teaching at Fryeburg if I had been aware of the musical history of the academy. I only taught there for two years, but the following year after I left the academy, I became interested in the musical history of the school, strictly by accident. The summer after I left the academy, I started work on my master's degree at the University of Bridgeport. One of my classes, a research in education course, was set up primarily to orient master's degree students to the realm of research, since many of us would be doing a master's thesis, which would probably require some sort of research. The final project of the course was to fashion a mock thesis proposal, which was to include a plan for researching the thesis topic. I decided I wanted my mock thesis proposal to be in education history. I wanted to explore the origins of music education in American schools. To help put this proposal together, I went to the University library and looked up every book I could find on the subject. One book, on the old New England academies, contained just the information I was looking for, but it was a big surprise for me. It turns out that the earliest record of any of the early academies including music in its curriculum was-- - wait for it ---Fryeburg Academy. It appears that the trustees of the school added music to the curriculum in 1803, some 30 years before music was taught in any public school. The 1803 date jumped out at me for another reason. The headmaster of Fryeburg Academy around that time was none other than Daniel Webster. Now I need to digress here just a bit. There are many institutions across New England, both prep schools and colleges, that have a building on their campus named for Daniel Webster. Fryeburg Academy also has a Webster Hall. The difference is that Daniel Webster actually taught at Fryeburg. Before he became a master statesman and historic legislator, Daniel Webster was the headmaster at Fryeburg Academy, having just graduated from Dartmouth. As I did my research, I got the impression that Webster was not entirely happy at Fryeburg. For one thing, socializing for a young man just out of college was difficult in those days. The nearest location where one might find opportunities to socialize was North Conway, just across the state line in New Hampshire. Although it is only about 12 miles away from Fryeburg, a horse and buggy ride to North Conway, depending on weather conditions, could take up to 4 hours. Webster also undertook a second job while he was headmaster at the academy. Fryeburg was located in the newly designated Oxford County in Maine. This meant that all of the property deeds of the town needed to be duplicated. In those days it needed to be done by hand. Webster would spend evenings in the town office copying deeds by hand in the candlelight. I understand that some of them can still be seen. It allowed him to earn enough money to put his younger brother through school.

Was it possible that the first school music program in the nation was established under Daniel Webster's leadership? I wanted to research it at that time, but the situation did not allow for that. Then, in the following semester, I took a graduate course in American Music. The focus of the class was primarily the music world in the United States in the early days of the country. As part of the class, we were assigned a research paper of our choosing focusing on some aspect of American music. Here was my chance, and I scheduled a road trip that would take me to Fryeburg, the public library in Portland, and the Antiquarian Society in Worcester, MA. Other members of the class also did their research papers on interesting topics. One member of the class had a grandfather that was a member of John Phillip Sousa's band, and her paper provided very interesting information about the Sousa band during its heyday. Another member of the class did his research paper on American Musical Theater, and actually managed to get an interview with Stephen Sondheim. Some of the other members of the class reported on early American composers.

I couldn't wait to take my road trip, and the headmaster at Fryeburg Academy was very accommodating, and even allowed me to stay in guest quarters on campus. The evening that I arrived, he led me into the inner office and opened up the school safe and took out a very old looking ledger. It was a record of the trustees meetings of the school going back to its founding. The edges of the ledger were singed in black as it survived a fire in 1853 that destroyed the original academy building. When I opened up the book, it was like opening a door to history itself, just astounding. All of the entries were written in ink quill pen. The handwriting done as it would have been in those days, with penmanship in which script S's looked like script lower case F's. I located the entries from 1803 and, disappointment! It turns out that the music program at Fryeburg Academy was not founded under the leadership of Daniel Webster but was instituted a few months after Webster left. Webster's replacement was a gentleman by the name of Rev. Amos Cook. Rev. Cook is described as a man of many talents, including a talent for music. It was Cook who convinced the trustees to establish a music program at the academy, and he himself was the instructor. In part, the entry read:

"That as the cultivation of Music has a direct tendency to soften the ferocious passion, ameliorate the manners, etc., instrumental and vocal music be attended to by those students who have talents and indication to improve therein."

The above words are historic, and I'm surprised that they have been ignored by most, if not all, researchers in the history of music education. The above quote is the earliest known record of an educational institution adopting music into its curriculum in this country. Many books and articles cite the "singing schools" of Boston and other places in the early 1700's as the first examples of music education in the colonies. However, it should be pointed out that the early "singing schools" existed as an end unto themselves and did not represent actual institutions of education. When the pilgrims and others settled into New England in the 1600's, the Puritan churches of the time did not allow music of any kind in their services, except for singing. The normal practice of the time, since few people could actually read, was for the deacon to stand in front of the congregation, sing the chosen hymn line by line, with the congregation repeating each line. This worked fine, if the deacon could actually sing. But through the years, people would become deacons with little or no ability to sing. Over time, these monotone deacons would have the congregation also responding in monotone, and after a while, no one understood the difference. In the early 1700's, when some folks who were knowledgeable about music came to settle in Boston, they were alarmed at the turn that music had taken in the churches and worked to establish "singing schools" at each church. But that was the only task of the "singing school", to teach congregations how to actually sing. Anyone wishing instruction in math, science, literature, etc. needed to attend an actual learning institution.

Students at Fryeburg Academy in 1803 could study vocal music, or instrumental music. The academy purchased two flutes and two violins. Students received lessons once a week for 12 ½ cents a lesson, and any student that studied instrumental music could receive vocal lessons gratis. This was in contrast to many other academies where music was expressly forbidden, or at least not allowed without written permission of the parents. As I continued my research, I found out that the little one room schoolhouse behind the main school building that I taught in actually had a name. At that time, it was called Thompson Hall. As I went through the various academy documents, there were several students that were identified as composers, and I went to the Portland Public Library to research them. Most of the names turned up nothing, but one name stood out.

Stephen Emery was a Fryeburg Academy graduate who went on to become a major force in the Boston music scene in the late romantic period. But Emery's mark in music education is more prominent than his career as a composer. Emery was a professor at the New England Conservatory in Boston, and besides teaching classes and working with the most promising composers of the day, he authored a textbook on music theory that went on to become the standard music theory textbook used in colleges across the country for decades.

My last stop was the American Antiquarian Society in Worcester. At first, they wouldn't allow me access to the building because I didn't have a letter of introduction from my professor. However, since I only needed to view one item, and wouldn't need to leave the research room with it, I managed to convince them to allow me in. The Antiquarian Society had a file of several copies of "Russell's Echo", an early newspaper in Fryeburg at about the time of the music department's founding. I knew that at many of the early American academies, there were frequent student exhibitions presented at various times in the school year. Most of the student presentations in these exhibitions consisted of performing poems or other recitations. At various times, after several student readings or recitations, there would be something known as "musical bits" to help break up the program. I wanted to see if there was any mention of these events in "Russell's Echo". Disappointment again! Although student exhibitions at Fryeburg Academy were mentioned a couple of times in the newspaper, there was no mention of any specific music presentation. I outlined everything I had discovered in my research paper. I received a grade of "B". I could not help but wonder if my grade suffered because my research didn't turn up what I had hoped it would.

HOLY CROSS

Towards the end of the summer, I began to wonder if I had made a mistake by not returning to Fryeburg. I went to a couple of interviews, but the music programs were far from impressive. I didn't want to take a position where I would simply be minding the store for a struggling music program. I started to wonder if I would be unemployed at the start of the school year, when a job opening caught my eye. Holy Cross College was looking for a Band Director. I didn't think I had the qualifications to conduct a band at the college level. Most folks in that type of position held a Doctorate degree or at least a master's degree. I had barely started work on my Masters, and I figured I would probably be a weak candidate compared to people who would more than likely have more experience and have superior academic credentials. However, I decided to apply for the position anyway, and Lo and Behold! I was invited to an interview. My girlfriend once again accompanied me as I went to the interview, and as soon as I arrived, I realized that this wasn't a typical college band director situation. The first indication was that I wasn't interviewed by anyone in the music department of the college, but by the Director of Student Activities. As the interview progressed, I was told that the band at Holy Cross was an extra-curricular activity and that the band's performances were limited to football and basketball games. The band director position was part-time, and with only 13 members, the band was not really considered a part of the music department. There was a budget for the band, although there were no uniforms. The students wore rugby shirts for performances.

The band had been an entirely student run organization for the last several years, and although they were now hiring a director, that director had a limited role in the band leadership. In other words, the band director need only be concerned with music issues of the band, while the administrative role fell to the students. It was far from a perfect situation, and I immediately realized that any college instructor of any stature would be inclined to stay away from this situation. But in my case, with no job prospects, it would make sense to pursue this position, and I had no doubt that being a college band director at the age of 24 would brighten up my resume considerably. I left the interview realizing that I had a good shot at being hired, and a few days later, I received the call.

The school year had already started, and I had to begin immediately. The band had already held a couple of rehearsals, and their first performance was in a week. Rehearsals were limited to two evenings a week and Saturday mornings during football season. I went to the first rehearsal, and the Student Director introduced me to the group. There were 22 students present, and the band rehearsed in what at one time was the college chapel. I asked them to show me what they were working on, and as they played for me, I realized that I could help them right off the bat. I made some adjustments to the percussion parts, and some stylistic changes that I think made more sense to the music they were playing. When the rehearsal was over, everyone was upbeat and looking forward to the next rehearsal. The following rehearsal consisted of mostly bringing me up to speed on selections such the school fight song, and other songs the band traditionally played. A couple of days later was the band's first performance, an away football game at Dartmouth. When I boarded the bus, I had no idea what kind of culture shock I was in for. On the bus were two garbage cans full of ice – and beer. The drinking age in Massachusetts in those days was 18, and apparently, it was commonplace for the band to stock up on beer for away games. It seems this practice had been ongoing for several years, and I had to restrain myself from speaking up. After all, my boss, the director of student activities, had made it quite clear that my role was strictly to deal with music. We pulled into Dartmouth, and I have to admit that it was a bit daunting to go from a football field at Fryeburg Academy where the bleachers could only hold a few hundred people, to a college football stadium with an audience capacity in the thousands. The band took their places in the stands, and at halftime, their performance began. For what up to that time was a student led group, I thought they did as well as could be expected, given the circumstances. The show itself was not complicated, only three or four marching formations. They would change formations for each song they would play, and the song itself was played at a standstill. It was a typical Ivy League style show, although the theme was fairly thin.

The Ivy League style show is supposed to be a result of utilizing a format designed for students that requires a minimum of rehearsal time. I'm not sure I buy that. When I was a kid, I remember watching the bands from Yale, Brown, and Princeton, all of which used a conventional marching band format in those days. At that time, there did not seem to be any indication that their performances suffered, or that there was a need to cut corners. The more modern Ivy League style show is actually centered upon the PA announcer, who lays out the theme of the show, supported by the music that the band plays. The announcer, who is usually a student, reads off a script that generally contains jokes, puns, and sarcastic digs at the opponent that their team is playing that day. I'm not a big fan of the format, and in fact, I think it cheapens the concept of a marching band. I will concede that in the case of Holy Cross, it makes sense to minimize the amount of rehearsal time that a student must commit to a marching band. I could not help but notice the large number of pre-med and pre-law majors in the band, and of course, students in those majors face considerable competition to be accepted to a medical or law school after graduation. When I was in the marching band at the University of Houston, we practiced six hours a week, while at Holy Cross, the band functioned with only a two or three-hour rehearsal week.

However, it was clear that I was stuck with this format. When I set up the pre-game show for the first home football game, I set the band up on the sideline in front of the opposing team bench and had them march across the field to the home sideline while playing the Holy Cross fight song.

The following Monday, I was called in to the Student Activities office. The Director of Student Activities wanted to impress upon me that "This band does not march". It seemed that this new position of Band Director was not without controversy. It appeared that the Director of Student Activities needed to assure the students that they would still be able to run their band, even with a Band Director. She was obviously concerned about student complaints, and fears that I might attempt to turn everything upside down. I assured her that I wasn't planning to do that. However, I felt that the concept that the band should march to its own fight song was a valid one and I continued to do it for each pre-game show.

It didn't take long, however, for folks to notice the improvement in the band. The membership of the group was growing, and I received positive comments from several people, but one event in particular stands out. The Holy Cross football stadium, Fitton Field, holds about 25,000 people, but it is very cramped. The home grandstand is built into a hillside, like most of the rest of the campus, while the other side of the field is bordered by the local interstate highway. The sidelines are very narrow, only a few feet, with the team benches lined against a fence that separates the field from the public walkway and bleachers. In order to be seen by everyone in the band while I conducted, I needed to stand on the team bench during the show. During halftime of the second or third home game, as I was standing on the team bench, conducting the band, I felt a tap on my shoulder from someone on the other side of the fence, on the walkway. I turned around to see an older gentleman, obviously a Holy Cross alumnus, decked out in a Holy Cross jacket adorned with several award and booster pins. He seemed somewhat oblivious that I was in the middle of a performance before about 10,000 people. "I want you to know," he said "that this is the best I've heard this band sound in at least 10 years!" I said, "Thank You, but I'm a little busy right now".

Not everyone was impressed with the improvement however. A couple of weeks before the Holy Cross-Army game, I received a phone call from West Point. It was a sergeant connected to the athletic department there. Earlier in the year I was made aware that it was a tradition of the Holy Cross band to travel to West Point whenever the Army-Holy Cross football game was held there. Band members had already spoken to me about playing at a reception for Holy Cross Alumni from the New York City area after the football game. But I was a bit troubled by this phone call. The sergeant was very somber as he explained to me that the Holy Cross band would not be able to perform during half time at the game because West Point had a ceremony planned honoring past Army football players. I told him I understood, and I did. But I couldn't help but get an underlying negative vibe from this sergeant. Although he didn't say it, I got the feeling that he would rather the Holy Cross band not attend this game at all. However, the band went anyway, and sat in the stands the entire game. After the game, I thought, "well, maybe it was worth the trip to play at the Alumni reception". But I had to question that thought as well as we arrived at the reception. No one came to welcome the band when we arrived, and some of the looks we got from some of the alumni were quizzical, as if to say, "What are they doing here?".

In the meantime, I was meeting other people on campus. As I was exploring the campus, I found the chorus room, and walked in. I met the Director of Choral Activities, Bruce, and we talked a bit. I didn't get along well with Bruce at first, but I came to appreciate his sense of the political landscape of the campus as it related to music. He confirmed what I had suspected, that the faculty of the college music department would go out of their way to devalue the band at Holy Cross. It seemed as a way for them to protect their territory. I could understand that. After all, it had to be disquieting to them for the band to perform in front of more people at one event, than their entire music department would in course of an entire year. Bruce also confirmed what I had also suspected about my own position, that I was the band director at Holy Cross because of the complaints from fans about the quality of the music when the band had been an entirely student run organization. I wasn't really sure what Bruce thought about the progress I was making with the band. I don't know why, but his opinion of how I was doing seemed important. Although, one day I was walking by the choral room while he was in the middle of a chorus rehearsal. He was working with the tenors, and I thought that I knew what piece they were working on, but I wasn't sure. I poked my head in the doorway to listen a bit more, but instead, Bruce stopped what he was doing, and it was clear that I had accidentally disrupted his rehearsal. "Is that the 'Cantique de Jean Racine?'" I asked. It turns out that it was, and I think Bruce was impressed that I could identify a piece just by listening to a couple of phrases of the tenor part.

I had also been asked to report to the publications office for an interview. The gentleman there, who I think considered himself a photographer more than a publisher, had various questions for me for an article he was planning for an upcoming edition of the alumni magazine. As we talked about the band, he told me about a band photo that he was planning to put in a future issue. The photo was from a baseball exhibition game, which I believe took place sometime in the 1920's. The Holy Cross baseball team was playing an exhibition game against a pro baseball team, the Boston Red

Sox. The photo from the exhibition game shows the Holy Cross Band seated in the bleachers and seated in the middle of the band playing trombone is none other than baseball immortal Babe Ruth, who was a player with the Red Sox at that time. I'm not really sure that the Babe was a trombone player. For one thing, he's holding the trombone backwards in the photo, nor does he seem to be really playing. I got the impression that Ruth was probably clowning around with the band for the benefit of photographers.

As football season was winding down, I faced another dilemma. The athletic department informed me that for home basketball games, the size of the band had to be limited to no more than 24 students. I was upset. After all, the size of the Holy Cross Band the previous year was 13 members. Now, it numbered nearly 40. The basketball team was expected to be a top 20 contender in the national polls. No doubt, a number of students would be upset at being left out of performing at basketball games. I could not understand why the college would on one hand encourage a larger size band, but then on the other hand systematically limit its growth. I spoke with the students. It seemed the only option open to us was to rotate students among the home games. So that's what we ended up doing, although I couldn't help but feel there were some students resentful over it.

In the spring, it was time to unveil the project that I was working on with students. When I started in the beginning of the year, a number of the students asked me if I would work with them in reviving the Holy Cross Jazz Band. It seems there was a jazz band many years prior but had been inactive for some time. The jazz band charts in the music files appeared to have been current about 15 years prior. I ordered more current music for the group and began holding rehearsals with the group twice a week. Each of those evenings, there would be the general band rehearsal for football or basketball games, and afterward I would meet with students interested in the Jazz Band. Now, it was time for the group to perform. A concert was set up in the campus ballroom, and invitations went out to the college administration. The college president declined to attend, but the Vice President of the college not only came, but also gave an introduction to the audience at the beginning of the concert. The concert went rather well. It was the first time that many of these musicians played for an audience outside of a sports event at Holy Cross, and they rose to the occasion. The Jazz Band received a standing ovation at the end of the concert, and the following day I received a letter from the college Vice President commending the band, and the work that I did with them.

At about the same time, Bruce, the choral director approached me about a project that he had been pondering. There are several songs written for and about Holy Cross by its students over the years. Most of them were written in the 1890's or the early 1900's in the march style, or anthem style of the times, and some of them are really good. Bruce wanted to create a medley of these songs and asked if I would be willing to write the band accompaniment to them. I thought it was a worthwhile project and said yes. Over the summer, I met with him and he showed me his first sketches. I thought he had made some good judgments in the choice of songs and the order in which they were set up. However, I felt the transitions from one song to another needed some work, and I told him I would try to rectify some of this in the band accompaniment. He had settled on a title for the piece, "Songs of Holy Cross", and wanted to debut it at a concert planned for parents' weekend in the fall.

ANSONIA

I started work on the "Songs of Holy Cross" band parts toward the end of the summer. In the meantime, I wanted to find a position that would be compatible with my position at Holy Cross. I watched for music teacher openings in the Worcester area, but the only response I received was for an unimpressive middle school band program, and it seemed to me that they we not interested in sharing me with Holy Cross. Then, I received a call from a music teacher friend of mine. "Ansonia is open! Apply!" she said. Now, in the interest of disclosure, Ansonia is the high school that I graduated from. It seems that the music program had been somewhat in decline, and the administration decided to cut back on the program. They did this by eliminating the position of the high school music teacher. Because the teacher in that position had the most seniority of any of the music teachers in the district, he ended up "bumping" an inexperienced elementary music teacher and taking over her job. So in the high school, music appreciation courses were eliminated, along with high school chorus. However, they decided to keep the band and look for a part-time director. The chances of anyone taking the job were very slim, but I saw this as an opportunity to expand my teaching beyond Holy Cross, and at the same time help out my alma mater in a very difficult situation. My meeting with the superintendent was almost a formality. No one had applied to the position, and I had no problem being hired.

Meanwhile, back at Holy Cross, they had started the school year and the band members went all out to recruit freshmen musicians. Band rehearsals started with 70 members on the roster, so seeing that the situation there was going well, I turned my attention to the situation at Ansonia. I met with the band on the second day of school. There were 10 students on the auditorium stage, and the first football game was in 10 days. An actual field marching show was out of the question. The best I could do was prepare them to play at a standstill for the games. Because of the time factor, I decided to go with music they had played the previous year and would try to introduce new music to them as time went on. My buddy, John, also offered to play. John and I were in the band when we were in high school. He was now teaching history at Ansonia, and with my taking the band directors position, it was kind of like a reunion. John was a trumpet player, so his playing with the band would stabilize the brass section. In the week and a half before the first football game, I was able to give the band a basic set of songs to get through the game. The band sounded fine, but some of the fans were dismayed at the low number of band members and wanted to know what had happened. I really didn't have an answer for that at the time, but I came to find out later some issues that may have contributed to the decline. For one thing, I had set up a "lesson day" for band members, and scheduled lessons with them during their study halls on "lesson day". I was a bit dismayed when the freshmen and some of the sophomores came for lessons. They were really struggling to read music. I started to suspect what was going on when some of them would ask questions like "Is that a 3 or a 2?" meaning the number of holes they had to cover with their fingers in order to play the note. On the other hand, if I were to ask them to play a particular note such as a "D", they would ask what fingers they had to use. After asking a lot of questions of these students, my suspicions were confirmed. The elementary band teacher was using what he called the "number system" to teach instrumentalists. He would take the music of each band member, and under each note would write in the number of fingers needed to play the note. He only referred to the notes by their "number". Some may believe that this system would be a help to young students, but to me, there didn't seem to be much difference between this "number system" and the rote method that was used to teach drum and bugle corps. Students didn't really know how to read music, and when they advanced to the high school band, where reading the music was pretty much a necessity, they had a hard time functioning. However, this was one situation where I refused to compromise. I insisted that all band students be able to read music, and I was willing to spend whatever extra time that might be necessary with students to help them make that transition, but there was no way I was going to write all of the fingerings into everyone's band music. A local newspaper reporter called me asking me about the small size of the band, and what could be done about it. I tried to be as positive as I could, saying that we could see light at the end of the tunnel. What I didn't say was that sometimes, though, the light at the end of the tunnel is an oncoming train. The sad truth that I didn't mention to the reporter was this band program was broken, and it would take years to fix it, if indeed it could be fixed.

Shortly after, a parent wrote a Letter to the Editor to the local newspaper wanting to know why the band wasn't playing at more football games. I was astounded. Here I was, trying to save the band from oblivion, and parents complain in public that they want the band at more football games. It was annoying, but it was also representative of the lack of respect that was part of the culture at Ansonia. More on that later.

Meanwhile, at Holy Cross, the first football game with the larger Holy Cross band was a great success. The only thing that bothered me was that one of the priests had criticized the show script that the students had written. I should have realized what was happening. There was a new Director of Student Activities, and either he was unaware of the policy that show scripts needed to be cleared by the Student Activities office, or he didn't bother following up on the issue. At any rate, the band came under a lot of fire for their show at the second game, where they "saluted" the City of Worcester by forming a zero on the field. A huge cry of protest erupted among city officials, media, and Holy Cross alumni who now lived in Worcester. On two occasions, I was called into the Student Activities office for a meeting with Administration regarding the show script and student behavior. I was upset. For all the pains that they took to impress on me that my role was simply a musical director, and that I wasn't to get involved in the running of the band, now I was being blamed for these problems. I told them in no uncertain terms that they needed to have a consistent policy regarding my role, but it didn't seem to do any good. A few weeks later, the ABC television network contacted the college that they were going to televise the Holy Cross-Brown football game in Providence. As is apparently the normal procedure, ABC hosted an orientation luncheon a few days before the game that involved the athletic and football team officials, as well as the heads of the band and cheerleaders. The only problem was that no one had contacted me about the luncheon. The college decided to send the band's student leaders instead.

Finally, Parents Weekend arrived. The Jazz Band played for a parent reception, put on by the college president, and that performance went well. But the really memorable performance took place the following evening at the Parents Weekend concert, which took place in the college chapel. The chapel was full of students and their parents, many of which were Holy Cross graduates. The first half of the concert went fairly well, with the college choir performing a varied repertoire. In the second half of the concert, a composition by one of the students was featured. It was a really wonderful piece, and the student received a standing ovation from the audience. I stood backstage awaiting the final selection of the concert "Songs of Holy Cross", the piece that Bruce, the choral director, and I had collaborated on. Bruce conducted the piece, with the band seated in front of the choir, which stood on risers. Both Bruce and I knew we had created a great piece of music. He did a marvelous job of writing the choral parts, and I was able to write a great accompaniment for the band while at the same time solving the transition issues from the earlier sketches. When the piece ended, the audience was immediately on their feet and cheering. The response was overwhelming. Bruce took his bows, acknowledged the band and the choir, and then motioned for me to come on stage. As I joined him on stage, the audience cheered even louder. Not only that, but we didn't get a chance to leave the stage. The audience insisted that the piece be performed again. And so, "Songs of Holy Cross" was repeated, and once more, the audience stood and cheered when the piece was over. It was probably my most treasured memory of my time at Holy Cross, and ironically, it occurred with the band in the role as a symphonic group, as opposed to all its other performances where they were simply playing for athletic events. It is my understanding that "Songs of Holy Cross" is still performed each year, although the instrumental parts that I wrote have needed to be modified and updated over the years.

In the meantime, in Ansonia, folks were noticing that although the band was small, it was still very good. Having my buddy, John play lead trumpet with the group made it a formidable ensemble for its size. Respect for the group was still a problem, and the two issues came together when the band traveled to a football game in a nearby town. When we arrived, the band students took their instruments off the bus, and walked over to the visitor bleachers. Now, in this town, as might be found in many places, the visitor bleachers section was small, way too small to accommodate the Ansonia fans. When the band arrived at the visitor bleachers, they were full of people and the section of the bleachers that were marked off for the band was ignored. For a while, it looked as if the band would have to play the entire game standing next to the bleachers. Fortunately, a policeman on duty nearby noticed the situation, and walked over to the visitor bleachers. He addressed the crowd in the bleachers, basically shaming them for not allowing room for their band, and he managed to clear out the area of the bleachers that was supposed to be set aside for the band. Once the band set up and started playing, the impact was noticeable. Fans from the other side of the field were commenting on how the Ansonia band sounded better than their own school's band.

For the last football game of the year, there had been a tradition from the previous few years of inviting alumni to play with the band at the game. I consented to continue with this practice again, but when I held a rehearsal for the alumni on the night before the game, I ran into some unanticipated difficulties. I should have anticipated that nearly all of the alumni had not done much playing on their instruments since they graduated. The only tunes that really worked with them were tunes that they themselves had played in high school. Anything that I put in front of them that was totally new didn't fly. Although I was no longer a rookie teacher, this was still a rookie error.

In the meantime, I was working on my master's degree at the University of Bridgeport. Since I started after leaving Fryeburg, the first couple of years of my graduate work were filled with core courses, only some of which I found to be actually helpful. However, now I was at the point where I could choose courses that really interested me. In those days, the University of Bridgeport had a very strong jazz program. Since Bridgeport is fairly close to New York City, this allowed the university to hire some of the best professional musicians from the New York City area to work with their students. This was a benefit that I was able to take advantage of. When I was an undergraduate at Houston, and later WestConn, my primary instrument was the string bass. Now, as I was starting graduate work, I realized that the string bass might not serve me well in terms of being a band director. It would make more sense to switch my primary instrument as a graduate student to an instrument more commonly associated with band. Since I had played trombone in the jazz band during my years at WestConn, and since the University of Bridgeport had such a strong jazz program at the time, it made sense to switch to trombone as my primary instrument as a graduate. As a result, I ended up taking trombone lessons from Moe Snyder, who was not only a professional trombone player who primarily worked in the city but was also a national clinician for Getzen band instruments. When I started with Moe, my trombone playing was not in good shape. I hadn't really played that much since my days at WestConn, and since I never took trombone lessons as an undergrad, I had a lot of catching up to do. Moe was very patient with me, and we took things one step at a time, working on my technique, clearing up my sound, etc. and I was making good progress. Then one day, during my trombone lesson, Moe took out a piece of music and asked me to play it. The piece was not particularly hard, and when I finished Moe was smiling at me. "You managed to catch the error!" he said, and when it was clear that I didn't understand what he was referring to, he went on to explain. It seems the music had a misprint, and in the middle of the piece, there was a modulation that required the note D to become D-flat. However, there was no flat in front of the note, as there should have been. If someone had played it as written, it would sound wrong. When I played the piece, and got to that section, I played the note as a D-flat without even consciously realizing it. To me, I was just playing what my ear was telling me the melody should sound like. It was so second nature to me that I didn't even realize there was a misprint. Moe was very pleased and explained to me that many times when a musician goes into a recording session, it usually is not an epic event where you're backing up a superstar musician. Most times, it is something mundane like a detergent commercial, or some other type of jingle. A lot of times, the composer is rushed and doesn't always proofread the parts for the musicians. As a result, sometimes errors get through undetected. When high-end recording sessions can cost hundreds of dollars an hour, a musician who can pick up errors on the fly is very valuable. Of course, I had no intention of being a sideman and doing recording sessions in the city, but if I ever did, it was nice to know that I would be valuable.

As football season ended, at Holy Cross, I had a meeting with the athletic department. Unfortunately, I didn't make any progress with them in terms of being able to get more students to play in the band at basketball games. Here we now had a 70-piece band, and although some of them would not continue to play during basketball season, that still left me with a lot of kids to rotate in and out in covering the basketball games. However, the athletic department wouldn't budge, so again I had to draw up a rotating schedule of students for the basketball games. I just did not understand. What was the point of building up a band if only a fraction of them would be allowed to perform? Perhaps I should have capped the band membership at 24. The basketball season was still a success. For 24 players, the band sounded pretty good at the games. A couple of the games were regionally televised, and the band performed well.

In March, I put another plan of mine into action. After football season, I had started kids in Ansonia working on a jazz band, although we called it a "Jazz-Rock" ensemble. Things started off rough. To begin with, my bass amplifier was stolen after the first rehearsal. Also, the concept of improvisation was new to the students, and although a couple of them picked up on the idea, and could do some basic improvisation, the group itself, rehearsing once a week, would not be performance ready for months. I wanted to find a way to expose them to a proper jazz band. So, I put together a jazz event for the school. I called it "An Evening of Jazz", and it featured a local community jazz band, as well as the Holy Cross Jazz Band. The Holy Cross kids were more than willing to make the trip. I gave some tickets to the local radio station to give away for free and had the Ansonia students run the event.

On the night of "An Evening of Jazz", there was a pretty good size audience of about 400 people. The community jazz band started off and played really well for the first half of the program, then the Holy Cross kids took the stage. Unfortunately, there was one glitch. It seems that the drummer of the Holy Cross band had run into some problems with grades. I should have anticipated a problem when he missed the last couple of rehearsals prior to the event. What I had a big problem with, is that he didn't say anything to me. It seems he arranged for another drummer to take his place, and when the band showed up, there was a drummer that I had never seen before. I was fairly upset, and I wasn't even sure that I wanted the group to perform. However, it was too late for that to be an option. So I kicked the band into its first tune, a standard swing tune. They sounded fantastic, exactly the kind of sound that I wanted the high school kids to see and hear. The next couple of tunes were rock tunes, and they went incredibly well also. I began to think that this could turn out well after all. The substitute drummer was following the charts well and catching all the cues properly. So far, it was impressive. Then, we hit Waterloo. A Chuck Mangione tune, an easy, laid-back rock style, and she totally mis-read the drum part. She ended up playing the tune at double speed, and the whole thing almost broke apart. The following tune she also messed up on, and again it was all I could do to keep the band together and prevent it from splitting apart and playing at two different speeds. Finally, things settled down and we performed a few more jazz standards. The final tune, "In the Mood" was the favorite of the evening, and the audience immediately gave the group a standing ovation. After the difficulties we had, I wasn't sure the standing ovation was merited, but it was nice to have anyway. I didn't realize it at the time, but that was my last performance with Holy Cross. A spring jazz concert that we were planning fell through, partially due to my drummer's problems, as well as some other difficulties that a couple of students were experiencing.

Now that I was finished with Holy Cross, I turned my attention to Ansonia. The band had a Spring Concert scheduled for May, and they were scheduled to march in the Memorial Day Parade, as well as perform at Graduation. The Spring Concert was magnificent, or at least as close to magnificent as one could get with a 16-piece band. The auditorium at Ansonia was, for the most part, a cave. The reverberation time very high. If one were to clap one's hands as loudly as possible, the hand clap would continue to ring and echo for almost seven seconds. In truth, I really didn't like the idea of performing there, but when the concert started, I was astounded. I had forgotten a lesson from the Physics of Sound class that I took in college. The most sound-absorbent factor in an auditorium is – people! With a couple of hundred people in attendance at the concert, the sound absorption the audience provided worked to lower the reverberation time to just the right level. The band sounded crisp, and balanced, and played better than they had all year. The newly re-formed Jazz-Rock ensemble premiered, and they did very well. I was totally pleased with the performance, and looked forward to the parade, where I felt they would also do well.

I just had this feeling that if the group was playing well, then the students would get the respect they deserved. In some cases that worked. In others, not so much. When we marched in the Memorial Day Parade, the band sounded great. Their marching was excellent, and I thought the performance would go far in dispelling some of the attitudes that I was seeing in the community. However, it didn't work out that way. The primary reaction of the spectators was once again the small size of the group rather than how they sounded.

I tried to put my feelings aside. Obviously, it was going to take more time to change attitudes. It was time to get the band ready for graduation. Now, this was the first time I had ever done graduation as a band director. Fryeburg and Holy Cross did not utilize their bands for graduation. I did the best I could in preparing the band for the event, and on graduation day, I felt comfortable going into the ceremony. Nearly all of the band members arrived on time, and I set them up, tuned them, and awaited the start of the ceremony. Then two of the trumpet players asked if they could go to the bathroom before graduation started. Graduation was set up on the school football field, and the field house, which contained the bathrooms, was located across the field. I checked my watch. It was 15 minutes before the start of the ceremony. I told them they could go, but they had to be quick about it. They assured me they would, and off they went. After a few minutes, I caught sight of the graduates making their way on to the field. I checked my watch. It was still 10 minutes before the ceremony was supposed to start. I couldn't understand why they were starting early, but I quickly got the attention of the band members and started them playing "Pomp and Circumstance". As the first of the procession of graduates reached their chairs, I could see out of the corner of my eye two students running across the field in band uniforms. It was fairly embarrassing, but what was there to do?

As the school year was finishing, I had a meeting with the administration. The elementary band instructor, who had been teaching students the "number" system, decided to retire. While that solved one problem, it presented another. The school district, facing falling enrollment, initiated a policy that in the event a teacher left the district, that the teacher's position would not be filled. For band, to have the elementary band teacher leave, and not have the position filled would be devastating. I tried to impress on them that there was a need to have instruction in the lower grades. We wouldn't start teaching algebra to high school students if they were never taught math in elementary school. The idea of having a high school band when the students had never had any previous music instruction was equally ludicrous. They asked me if I would be willing to cover some of the responsibilities of the elementary band instructor. I told them I would be willing, but I expected a greater compensation for the added responsibilities. The agreement we reached was that they would put me on a half-time contracted position. It was better than being paid by the hour, and I was hopeful that eventually the position could become full-time. They also agreed to allow 7th and 8th grade instrumentalists to play with the high school band. It would still be a small group, but it would allow me to get an early start in teaching those kids how to play properly and undo the damage from having them play by the "number" system. I outlined to them the means in which this could be accomplished. My vision was for 7th and 8th grade band members to ride to the high school by taking the normal high school buses. After band rehearsal, a special bus would pick the students up at the high school, and take them to their elementary schools, where they would be slightly late for class. The school superintendent was not willing to allow this on a daily basis, and so students ended up coming to the high school two days a week. It was far from ideal, but I would also have extra time to give them lessons to compensate for not seeing them every day.

When the school year started in September, I met with the 7th and 8th grade band members from the three elementary schools. I had no idea how many band students there were in those schools. The now departed elementary band director didn't leave any records. Of the students I met with, eight of them were willing to commit to the high school band. I was hoping for better, but it was a start. Add to the incoming freshmen band members, and the fact that the band had only lost two seniors from the previous year, and the size of the band had grown to a bit more than 20 students. Of course, I still had no budget. When I wanted to purchase a few new selections for the band, the superintendent agreed to cover the cost through some funds that he had.

My second year at Ansonia fared better than the first. To begin with, having the summer to plan was a big advantage, and when football season started, the band was ready. I was even able to teach them a half-time field show, although it was somewhat basic. Football season went fairly well, although during the final game, the lead trumpet player was bored in the latter stages of the game. He decided to practice "taps" facing away from the field. The only problem was that he didn't realize that there was an injured player lying on the field at the time. The rest of the band yelled at him almost in unison, and he stopped. But the incident wasn't finished yet. He then started yelling "I'm sorry" at the top of his lungs at the injured player, which I don't really think helped the situation much.

At about the same time, I received a flier for the National Music Festival Regionals. I thought about the idea. Certainly, the band was not in any kind of shape to perform at any of the really prominent music festivals of the time, but the National Music Festival was in its beginning stages, and I thought that maybe participating in such a festival might work for a group such as Ansonia. I registered the Band for the Regional festival at Wildwood, NJ and started the group on fund raising for the trip. When I began trying to arrange for a candy sale, I found that most of the dates had already been reserved by other groups. The only open time that I could arrange for a candy sale fundraiser was the first two weeks after Christmas vacation. I was upset. Certainly, when kids come back to school after the holidays, they most likely have been able to accumulate a major stash of candy. How much candy would they be willing to buy once they returned to school? Well, as it turned out, the answer was- quite a bit. One week into the fundraiser, I ended up having to contact the fund-raising company for an additional candy order. The band members selling the candy couldn't keep up with the demand.

Now that it was fairly certain that we would be able to afford the trip, it was time to start preparing the students for the festival. I entered the band in the Concert Band and Parade Band categories. I also entered the Jazz-Rock ensemble in the Jazz Band category, although I entered them for "comments only" meaning that they would not actually be competing against the other schools. Since the Jazz-Rock ensemble didn't have the instrumentation of the standard high school jazz band, it made sense to enter them only for comments. That way, the festival performance could still be a positive experience for those students, and they wouldn't face the pressure of competition with incomplete instrumentation. I also entered a quartet of rifles in the color guard competition.

When I started rehearsals for the Jazz-Rock ensemble, one of the newer kids stood out. His name was Scott, and he was one of the new 8th grade members of the band. During the football season, he played in the drum section, but now, he was playing keyboard with the Jazz-Rock ensemble, and his skills were nothing less than impressive. While the rest of the kids in the group were struggling with the blues scale and basic improvisation, Scott's improvisational skills were way ahead of the rest of the group, and he sounded like an improviser of many years' experience. In addition, Scott was into composing, and had the skills to invent chord progressions on the spot. I tried to help him put together some melodic ideas with his chord progressions, and the result was some pretty good original tunes. The last few weeks before the festival, I began holding rehearsals in the evening. In the first part of the rehearsal, I would work with the rifle quartet in setting up their performance. The second part of the rehearsal involved preparing the band for the parade competition. I didn't know what kind of groups they would be up against, but I certainly wanted them to be prepared and to do well. Having only 22 kids competing against most bands that were three times, four times their size, or even larger, it would be difficult to go toe to toe with such large groups, but I wanted to impress on the students that I wanted their performance to be respectable, and without any basic flaws. My buddy, John, helped out considerably. We would start the band marching down the driveway of the school to an area that was similar size to the judging area that they would encounter at the festival, and we would critique them each time. John and I marched in drum corps together, so he knew exactly the types of errors to watch out for, and what my expectations for them were as they marched. Finally, the day of the festival arrived, and everyone boarded the bus with great anticipation. The trip to Wildwood was uneventful, and when we arrived, I reported to registration, and we checked into our hotel afterward. John assisted me as a chaperone, although there were also a couple of other adults. The first evening featured the Jazz Band competition at one site, and marching auxiliary units such as color guard judging at the other site. Our evening started at the first site, where the Jazz-Rock ensemble performed. As I said before, the group was not in competition, but was performing only for comments from the judges. As the group performed, the judges used cassette tape recorders to comment on the performance. The comments the judges gave were generally very positive, but when they heard Scott's improvisation solo on the synthesizer, it was obvious that they were highly impressed. One judge continued to comment on the solo for a considerable amount of time after the solo was finished. The judges at the other site, where the rifle quartet performed were not as kind. I was not surprised. My only training in rifles was a one-week summer course at VanderCook College of Music in Chicago. I developed a few skills, and I was able to teach them to my rifle quartet, but I really wasn't knowledgeable about structuring a competition performance for them. Bands that do field competitions on a regular basis usually have an assistant instructing their color guard, and such an assistant is usually experienced and reasonably knowledgeable. So the judges were fairly hard on the girls in the rifle quartet. However, since they were one of only two entries in the rifle competition, they automatically received the second-place trophy.

The next day, the band participated in the Concert Band competition. I wasn't expecting a lot. The required piece for the competition was a bit of a stretch for the students. I had considered having them perform for judges' comments only, like I did for the Jazz-Rock Ensemble, but I thought "What the heck! Let's see where they stack up." As it turned out, Ansonia was one of three bands in class C (small school) division of the Concert Band competition. So again, they received a trophy just for showing up. In the evening, the parade competition was held on the Wildwood Boardwalk. Most of the bands were quite large, and I knew it would be difficult to compete against groups that size. "Please", I thought, "Don't let them come in last place". If that were to be the case, then I would have to question my reasoning in bringing them to an event like this. However, all the previous preparation paid off, and Ansonia placed 10th out of 12 bands. They received a participation trophy for the parade, but the important part was that they had accomplished at least a small degree of success, and that was something I could build on. On the trip home, the kids continually played the judges tapes, and I realized they were thinking the same thing.

At the Spring Concert, I wrote an arrangement of Maynard Ferguson's "Conquistador" and brought my buddy, John, in as a guest soloist. He did a magnificent job of playing it, and the band responded well in the accompaniment parts. I think it was a good thing for students to see John as a performer, outside his realm as a teacher. My second year at Ansonia ended on a fairly positive note, and I was looking to see if I could improve on that. As the school year ended, I received a surprise in the mail. It was an invitation for the band to participate at the Peach Bowl. Of course, I realized that most likely we had received the invitation because we had attended the festival in Wildwood. There was no evidence that the band needed to attain a particular level of excellence in order to receive such an invitation, but it seemed like a great opportunity anyway. However, if we were to take the idea seriously, the playing level of the band would need to improve. At rehearsal, I talked to the kids and told them about the invitation. I told them that if they wanted to attend an event such as this, we would need to rehearse throughout the summer. And so, I held a band rehearsal once a week through July and August. The rehearsals were not all that successful, and less than half the band attended. Finally, in mid-August, I abandoned plans to take them to the Peach Bowl.

In another development, there was an opening for the director of the Pom-pom squad, and I convinced my mom to take the position. The school Color Guard and Pom-pom squad performed on the field with the band during football season. I was excited at the prospect of working with my mom on a coordinated field show. One of the influences of the drum corps movement on marching bands was called "Total Show Concept". It called for a coordination of all of the elements on the field, drill patterns, instrument placement, choreography, etc. to be designed in conjunction with the music being performed. In previous years, the typical Ansonia half-time show consisted of the band playing at a standstill, with the Color Guard and Pom-pom squad staked out in different sections of the field performing on their own using whatever routines they wish to fashion. Basically, everyone doing their own thing. Now, the opportunity presented itself to coordinate the movements and performances of all the groups on the field together. I designed a field show over the summer that would address these goals although it would be a big departure from what had previously taken place.

Since the concept was so different from what the groups were used to, the process was a lot more difficult than I had anticipated. We ran into some snags. To begin with, the girls in the Pom-pom squad were not happy over the changes that my mom and I made. We made adjustments to their uniforms and changed the type of Pom-poms they used. The girls previously used Pom-poms that were dual-colored, that is to say blue and white strands mixed together. We changed the pom-poms to solid color. The girls would have a pom-pom solid white in one hand, the other hand would hold a solid blue one. This would allow for an enhanced visual presentation by alternately using the different colors. However, the girls were unimpressed with the change. As time went on, they were more receptive, but it was slow going at first. The other issue concerned the band. I made the mistake of putting all my eggs in one basket, so to speak, by giving them music that was a bit more difficult than what they had played the previous year. Due to the increased difficulty of the music, in conjunction with the substandard attendance at the summer rehearsals, and the more challenging marching formations, the band was not yet ready to perform for the first football game. It was embarrassing to have the Pom-pom squad perform to a recording that day because the band music was not performance ready.

Fortunately, once school started, I could work on the music with the band nearly every day. After a week or so, I was able to start teaching a field drill to the music. By the second football game, the band was ready, and we were finally able to perform the show as I envisioned it. After football season, I continued to schedule practices for the Pom-pom squad and the Color Guard. I decided it was best for the program to return to the National Music Festival Regionals at Wildwood, NJ again. However, the lack of respect issue reared its head once more through a series of events. I once again scheduled a candy sale fundraiser for the same two weeks after Christmas vacation. Unfortunately, this time a problem arose when several students who were selling candy had their candy boxes stolen from their lockers. It created some financial difficulties because the music department was still financially responsible for the stolen candy. The next issue occurred one morning during band rehearsal. The school did not have a music room. Therefore, the band rehearsed in the auditorium, on the stage. There were two dressing rooms located in the wings from backstage, and another two dressing rooms located above the ground floor dressing rooms. All four of the rooms also functioned as storage for instruments, and a band office. This one particular morning, as I was rehearsing the band, I noticed a trashcan, upside down, on the floor of the stage. It was a typical metal trashcan, the same type found in all the classrooms. As I was conducting, I absently kicked at the trashcan, not knowing what was underneath. The students saw it before I did. Someone had defecated on the stage and covered it with the trashcan. I can tell you, that particular rehearsal ended fairly quickly.

It wasn't just lack of respect from the students and community. There was also lack of respect from the administration. In the orchestra pit of the auditorium was a

Steinway baby grand piano, which as far as I know, had always been kept in the auditorium. When I was a student at Ansonia, the piano was used all the time, but at some point, an upright piano was placed on the stage, and it appears that the Steinway fell into disuse. The school district received an offer from someone from New York City who wished to purchase the piano. Not that this person was a pianist. As I understand it, the piano would be set up in this person's apartment as a showpiece. It might have been that the administration was afraid that I would protest the selling of the Steinway, or perhaps they just didn't care, but they sold the Steinway without telling me. Certainly, I would have wanted to keep the Steinway in hopes of bringing it back into use. After all, this was the instrument that Mr. McWilliams used when he used to practice with me. Not only that but using an instrument such as this as nothing more than a showpiece seemed like the waste of a good instrument.

To make matters worse, a couple of weeks after, someone went into the auditorium, and ripped out most of hammers on the inside of the upright piano. It cost hundreds of dollars to fix, and I didn't have a piano to teach with for weeks. Now, lack of respect was affecting my ability to teach. I was beginning to wonder if this lack of respect issue was going to undo the good things that I was accomplishing with the students. Then one day, a man who apparently lived near the school came into one of the backstage storage areas in the auditorium. He seemed like a pleasant gentleman, and we talked a bit about the band and about music in general. He then made a strange request. He wanted me to give him an oboe. Now, I only had one oboe in the instrument inventory, and even though I didn't have a student playing the instrument at the time, there was no way I was going to give it away. He seemed quite unhappy about my decision, left the auditorium. I just thought the whole thing was weird, and I didn't give it much thought.

As we entered the spring, the preparations for the Spring Concert and the return trip to the festival at Wildwood began to intensify. When the day of the trip came, we put everyone on two motor coaches, and headed for Wildwood. The festival had the same general flow of events, and on the first evening we first went to the performance of the Jazz-Rock Ensemble. Like the previous year, the performance went well, and Scott's keyboard solo again impressed the judges. We then went to the second venue where the color guard and pom-pom squad would be in competition. I applied what I had learned the previous year in designing their performances, and I was much more confident this time. However, the color guard did not perform well, and as a result, their score was not as high as I had hoped. Still, they were awarded the 4th place trophy. The pom-pom squad was another story. I had worked closely with my mom to design a performance that would stand up to the best of groups, and there were several top of the line groups in this competition. I think we did quite well, both in the show design and the performance quality. The group had a great performance, and my buddy John, who had not seen the group perform since football season was highly impressed. The pom-pom squad was awarded 2nd place.

Things were working out really well, and then the lack of respect issue reared its head. We returned to the hotel, got the students settled down in their rooms, when a van pulled into the hotel with four boys from Ansonia. We knew that there was a chance this would happen. John and I had both expressed concerns about it to the administration in the days before the trip. What should have happened was the administration should have stepped in as soon as we heard about these plans. They should have set the boys down and told them in no uncertain terms that they had no business interfering with an out of state school trip. However, the administration did nothing, and now I had the problem of additional supervision and having to anticipate possible problems that the appearance of these boys represented. Things were tense during the rest of the trip, and that's unfortunate because it shouldn't have been.

The following day we had two performances scheduled, the concert band in the afternoon and the parade in the evening. The concert band performance was a disaster. In the middle of the required piece, a flute player came in on an entrance one beat early. The rest of the flutes followed her, and now the flute section was playing a beat ahead of the rest of the band. This led to a string of errors that followed in all of the sections. In all of the years I have taught, this was probably the worst performance I have ever conducted. I listened to the judges' tapes hoping for some advice to help if a situation like this occurred in the future, but nothing they said was of any help. They simply pointed out the errors that occurred, which of course made me upset because I was already aware of what happened. John helped put things in perspective for me when he said, "I don't understand. You raise all this money to bring them here. You know what the problems are going into the performance, and then you get upset when the judges find the problems that you already know about". What could I say? He was right. The parade went much better. I set up the band in the line of march with the color guard in front of the band and used the pom-pom squad around the outside of the band on each side and the rear. The choreography with the two different color pom-poms in sync with the music made for a very effective presentation as they marched down the Boardwalk. I was pleased with the performance and pleased with the results. Again, being a small 24-piece band, it is difficult to compete against larger groups that are three of four times that size. However, we scored higher than two 80-piece bands in the competition, which I was happy about. We used the same setup for the Memorial Day Parade, which also had good reviews, and I was looking forward to the end of the year.

However, about the same time, there was a renovation under way to create new science classrooms and update their facilities at the high school. Of course, that would mean that the entire building would have to be brought up to code, and I noticed various places in the building where construction was under way to do just that. What I didn't know was that the doors to the stage and dressing rooms to the auditorium had been declared as not up to code, and I walked into the auditorium one day to find all of the doors had been removed. I was alarmed. If only someone had mentioned to me that this was going to happen, I could have secured all, or at least most, of the equipment and instruments. As it turned out, the workmen took off the doors and simply walked away leaving it all in the open.

It didn't take long for a major theft to occur. When I discovered the open doorways, I immediate did an inventory of the equipment. The only instrument missing was the oboe, but the entire sound system had also been taken, speakers, amplifier, microphones, even the connecting wires. We filed a police report, but I didn't think anything would happen. We had no idea who had taken the sound system, although I had an idea who may have taken the oboe. I just didn't know the identity of the thief, or where to find him. Then, we caught a break. A few days later, Scott went to his weekly keyboard lesson at a local music studio and spied the school sound system sitting in the studio. As soon as he told me this, I got in touch with the police. The proprietor of the music studio told police some high school kids had sold him the sound system, and that he had no idea that it had been stolen. I was amazed though when he had the audacity to ask that the school to reimburse him for what he paid for the sound system. The principal laughed at the request, and I certainly could understand why. This guy was lucky he didn't get arrested for receiving stolen property. This whole incident happened because of a lack of respect in not informing me what was going on. I complained about this to the administration, and shortly after the conversation, I was informed the following academic year, in September, the high school band class would be moved from the 1st period of the day, to the 3rd period. I was alarmed. The repercussions of this decision was that the high school kids would be on their own. It would be impossible to schedule the 7th and 8th graders to rehearse with the band during the school day. I lost 9 seniors in the band to graduation, which left only five students registered for band the following year. This was bad. I certainly couldn't do much with a five-piece band. I argued this point as strongly as I could, but to no avail. It was clear the my fourth year at Ansonia would be very different from the other three. I don't know of any folks who would call in a plumber to fix a leak, and then refuse to allow him to use his tools. And yet, the tools that I needed to build success in the program were being stripped away from me.

But that wasn't the end of it. About a week after school was let out for the summer, I received an urgent call from John. "You better get down here" he said. "They're using jack hammers to take out the door frames in all of the auditorium doorways, and they haven't done anything to protect the contents of the rooms." I came in as fast as I could. By the time I got there, the workmen had finished drilling, and the mess was incredible. There was a thick layer of cinder block dust on everything in the rooms. The music office looked like a moonscape, or like it had gone through a nuclear winter. Once more, a lack of respect. No one informed me of what the workmen would be doing. I spent the summer looking for a teaching position in another school, and although I was a finalist for a position on a couple occasions, I was unsuccessful in finding another position.

And so, I now had the stage set for my fourth year at Ansonia, in which all indications suggested an incredibly unsuccessful year. I wasn't ready to give up yet, but the situation looked bleak. The first issue was that it would be impossible for the band to participate during football season. I didn't feel right about coming to the games with a five-piece band. I felt it would be embarrassing for the students. However, combining them with the 7th and 8th graders was a tall order under these circumstances. The amount of rehearsal time I now had would not allow it. I lost a fairly large group of band seniors the previous year. The bulk of the band membership, which now totaled 17 students, was now largely comprised of students from the 7th and 8th grades, as well as a couple of students that attended the local vocational high school. That meant that the first hurdle I had was to find a way for the entire group to practice together. Finding a time during the school day was now impossible. Rehearsing after school was also not an option because the bus routes were not set up to accommodate it, and the school district was unwilling to make any changes in the school bus routes or schedules to make it happen. This wasn't just a lack of respect, it was a lack of support. That left evening rehearsals as the only option. However, the football season started before I could even schedule the first evening rehearsal. I did not like the idea of not fulfilling the performance obligations that the community expected of us, but I didn't have much of a choice. The level of support among 7th and 8th grade parents of band members was not strong enough for me to schedule more than one evening rehearsal a week, and even then, the attendance was spotty. That led to very slow progress among the students in the band, and it was clear that they would not be ready to perform anytime during the fall. The chances of doing a marching show were so remote, it was laughable. So as a result, the band ended up sitting out the football season. I felt bad for the remaining five high school students who had band as a daily class. I had to come up with a lot of alternative material for them to study. I did classes with them on music theory and music history, as well as individual lesson plans for them to follow. As far as band music was concerned, I only needed to rehearse band music with them once a week. Since they were generally the strongest players in the band, they usually went into the weekly evening rehearsal having mastered any music that I had planned to do. I tried as best I could to make the 3rd period class as interesting as possible for them. I think they appreciated that, but it still wasn't very satisfying.

At least the news wasn't all bad. The enrollment in the elementary grades had risen, and I now had about 40 students in the elementary grades. However, that was not about to last. The first problem was that I just didn't have the support among parents of the elementary students for an evening elementary band practice. I gave up on the idea after only two students showed up for the first evening elementary band practice. And then, one night in early January, I was out playing basketball with a bunch of guys. I went up for a rebound, landed on someone's foot and crashed to the floor. The result was a broken ankle. I was upset, but I figured "Hell, we'll just set the ankle in a cast and I'll have to deal with crutches for the next several weeks." Wrong! The doctor felt that the break was so severe, that he told me I had to stay out of work for at least a month. Again, I was concerned, but while that was a setback, I still felt I had an ace in the hole. There was a substitute teacher who was a graduate of the Hartt College of Music and was also an Ansonia alumnus. I called the principal and arranged to have this substitute teacher cover the band class and lessons. I spent the next several days sitting at home and working on my master's thesis, and as I was doing this, the most defining lack of respect moment occurred.

The idea of the auditorium being the base of band operations is something that goes back to when the building was built in the 1930's. One of the upstairs dressing rooms, that also served as band storage, had a closet that was made out of cedar. The cedar closet was designed to store band uniforms and functioned much like a cedar chest in a home would in terms of storing clothes. Unknown to me, the administration decided to discontinue using the substitute band teacher that I had requested a couple of days after they called him in. They suspended all band classes in the elementary schools. As far as the five high school band members went, they were sent to a study hall during their 3rd period band class each day until I returned. The problem was that no one had told the custodian of this, who continued to open up the auditorium, now unoccupied, each day, as he had always done. This meant that the auditorium was a totally open space that students could access without any supervision. And so, one afternoon, someone went into the auditorium, went to the upstairs dressing room/storage room, and set the cedar closet on fire. We lost the band uniforms, a sousaphone, and a couple of other instruments that were in the room.

I was furious. Not just because of the fire, but because I now realized that the damage to the band program due to the suspended classes would go far beyond what was lost in the fire. The fire, of course, was the result of stupid decisions and mis-communications by the administration. But even greater damage was done to the band program itself by turning away the substitute band teacher. It was a very poor decision, and as it turned out, a fatal one for the band.

After a month, and the doctor cleared me to return to work, my elementary band enrollment had dropped from 40, to about a dozen. I understood, because, after all, many parents would be unwilling to pay money for an instrument if their child did not receive lessons. I also had to wonder how many of the 5th and 6th grade instrumentalists would be willing to play with the high school band when they got older, considering the state that the program was now in. Damage was also caused to the situation of the 7th and 8th graders that were playing with the high school students, and I had to scramble to try to salvage something in time for the spring performances.

The insurance settlement was not just disappointingly low, but shockingly low. After they devalued the items that were lost, they employed a fairly large deductible. The result was an insurance settlement that was astoundingly pitiful. If it wasn't a crime, it should have been. The insurance money we received was so low, we couldn't even begin to replace what was lost.

In March, I was very depressed about how things were going, and on one particular Saturday night, I went to an indoor drum corps show. In those days, it wasn't unusual for a drum and bugle corps to hold an indoor show in the spring, where the participating groups would unveil at least some of their new repertoire for the upcoming summer competition season. This show was sponsored by the Connecticut Hurricanes, the local senior drum and bugle corps that had won a world championship the previous summer. Other groups that performed were some local junior corps, as well as a couple of out-of-state senior corps. During intermission, I sat in my seat with my crutches, which I still needed, at my side. I was completely miserable. As I was contemplating my situation, I was approached by a group of guys that used to march with the Explorers during the time that I was teaching them. I was really happy to see them, but I couldn't believe my ears as they outlined to me that they were involved in reactivating the Vagabonds drum corps in Torrington, this time as a senior corps. They told me that they were using my beginner guide to train their bugle section. My beginner guide – I had totally forgotten about that. I made up a beginner guide while I was teaching the Explorers that would help new bugle players in learning the instrument, as well as the elements involved in reading music. Not only were they happy with the results of using the beginner guide, but they wanted me to be the bugle instructor of the new corps, as well as arrange the music that the corps would perform. My mood brightened in an instant, and the following day, I immediately set to work on this new project.

In the meantime, Scott asked me if he could hold some jam sessions after school. Of the five high school band students, Scott was the one that I felt most bad for. A student with his level of talent deserved far better than the quality of program we were providing him. In order for him to do these jam sessions, he needed an adult staff member to supervise. He approached me as I was the most logical choice, and even though it would mean extra supervision time, I immediately agreed. At the first session, when I walked out of the music office and on to the stage, there was Scott with a couple of kids assisting him, and another 20 or so students seated on the stage who came just to listen. No question, Scott had a following. After the second session, I told Scott that he might want to think about some type of outcome that these sessions could provide, perhaps some type of performance. What we ended up doing was to set up a talent show to run as part of the Spring Concert. It made a certain amount of sense, since the band would only be able to perform three selections, and this was a way to bring in other students to perform. When Scott floated the idea to his friends, the reaction was very positive. So we set up a couple of work sessions and held auditions. The response to the auditions was not what we had hoped for. There was a duet, a girl and a guy, that sang the song "Endless Love", and there was another girl, Carolyn, that Scott had been working with, who was a pretty good singer.

The day of the Spring Concert came, and immediately there was a problem. Carolyn, the girl who had worked with Scott apparently decided to skip school that day and have her hair done in preparation for the show. It seems she was unaware of the school's policy that if a student is absent from school, he or she is not allowed to attend any after-school activities that day. The administration picked up on this almost immediately, before I was aware of it myself, and ordered me not to allow her to perform that night. A lot of students came to the show that night and were quite upset that Carolyn wasn't allowed to perform. There wasn't anything I could do. The administration would not waver. The band played as well as I think I could have hoped for, but I'm not sure many people noticed.

So the next hurdle on the horizon was the Memorial Day Parade. We were able to secure uniforms for the band to replace the ones that had burned in the fire. A local drum corps had ceased operations, and their uniforms just happened to match the school colors. There was also a parent who generously constructed a cart for the electric bass. Scott had picked up electric bass and was now playing it with the band. The cart was built to hold the bass amplifier, an automobile battery, and a power inverter so that the bass could be used with the band in a parade. I wrote a customized arrangement of "Yankee Doodle Dandy" focused on the exact instrumentation of the band, and the abilities of the players. The day of the parade came, and I was fairly confident as we started down the parade route, with the high school band leading the parade. About four or five minutes into the parade, there was a problem. The cord that Scott was using that connected the electric bass to the amplifier had gotten tangled in one of the cart's wheels. It took a long time to untangle it, but of course the parade had kept on moving. Several groups of parade marchers had passed us as we worked on freeing the bass cord. Once the cord was untangled, we finally had to run a significant distance to catch up with the band. Then, on a bridge that led to the downtown area, the drum section broke down, with players playing at different speeds, and I had to stop the band. Perhaps it was the problem with the bass cord, and now that I was all hot and sweaty, I was in no mood for a problem like a dis-functional drum line. I lost it and started yelling at the drummers. I felt bad afterward, because I realized that I wasn't really upset with them. I was upset at the circumstances that led to this. The drummers messed up because they were too inexperienced, and because they didn't have enough rehearsal time. I didn't say much to anybody as we finished the parade and got on the bus for the high school. I realized that this whole situation was starting to get to me, and I needed to leave it. I didn't want my career to be defined by my experience in Ansonia, and I knew that if I stayed, that was exactly what would happen.

So the school year ended, and I once again spent the summer looking for a teaching position somewhere, anywhere but Ansonia. I expanded my search area and ended up going to interviews in Massachusetts, Vermont, New Hampshire, New Jersey and New York State, but to no avail. Halfway through the summer, I turned in my resignation to the Ansonia school system, even though I had no other job lined up. Again, I was a finalist in a couple of places, but didn't get hired. An interesting thing happened at the next Ansonia school board meeting. They tabled my resignation and contacted me to set up a meeting. They didn't want me to resign and asked me to stay on. However, in my resignation letter, I stated that the reason I was resigning was due to limitations of the band program that were made through administrative decision. Even if they were to give me the scheduling and bus transportation support that I needed, the damage was done, and it would take several years to undue. I outlined several steps that they would need to take to preserve the program and make it more successful. However, I don't think they were prepared to support the actions that I outlined. The unspoken factor in all of this was the "Reduction In Force" policy that was in place in Ansonia, meaning that if a teacher resigned, that teacher was not replaced. In my case, it would mean the end of the band program in Ansonia. After the meeting, the band program at Ansonia High School was quietly ended, and for many years, the school went without a music program. About a year after the school board meeting, I was at the local mall, and I ran into one of the kids that assisted Scott with his jam sessions. He was upset. "Why did you leave?" he said to me, "Now we have nothing".

CATHOLIC MUSIC INSTRUCTORS (CMI)

As I said, I wasn't able to find a teaching position during the summer that I left Ansonia. Therefore, as September neared, the best I could do was sign up for substitute teaching in some of the local school districts. I subbed mostly for other music teachers, but I also subbed for English, Science, and Physical Ed. I wasn't really happy about what I was doing, but I held on, hoping that something would develop.

As it turns out, I caught an unexpected break. My one bright spot over the summer was working with the Vagabonds drum corps. The group was good and had many impressive performances in parades over the summer. When I started with the Vagabonds, I was pleased to see that a buddy of mine from my days at Western Connecticut State was involved in the corps. Jeff was a trumpet player in the WestConn Jazz Ensemble during the time that I played trombone with the group. He was part of our group from the Jazz Ensemble that would go to Bonanza Steak House for dinner after Jazz practice, every Wednesday night. Jeff graduated a year ahead of me, and I hadn't seen him since. But somehow, he found his way to the Vagabonds, and was a lead soprano bugle player and soloist with the group. It was great to be reunited with him, and with his extended range, I was able to fashion some arrangements with impressive soprano bugle parts.

I found out that Jeff was also a supervising teacher with Catholic Music Instructors. I had never heard of the group, but as it turned out, CMI was an independent group of music teachers tasked with providing music instruction for parochial, or catholic, schools. The group was based in New Jersey and had teachers in several parochial schools in that state. There were also some schools that they serviced in New

York, most of them on Long Island. However, in the previous few years, they had expanded into the Hartford Archdiocese, and now provided band programs in most of the 95 parochial schools in the Archdiocese. Jeff was also aware of the situation that I was in, and one night, he spoke with me at a Vagabonds rehearsal, offering me a proposal. It seems that several schools in the Archdiocese had just signed on to CMI to provide band programs for their schools, and now there were more schools that needed to be serviced by CMI than the current staff could cover. Jeff asked if I would be willing to work part time for CMI, teaching in some of these new band programs. I needed to go through an interview process, but in a couple of weeks, I was teaching at four schools in the Archdiocese. I was still able to substitute teach, but not every day. Of course, since the schools in which I was teaching had programs with small enrollments, I ended up teaching for CMI two days a week, two schools each day.

However, that situation didn't last long. A couple of weeks after I started teaching for CMI, I received a phone call from Jeff. One of the teachers on the CMI staff had resigned, and they were offering me full time employment with CMI. Not only that, but the additional schools that they wanted me to teach in had some of the more prominent band programs in the Archdiocese. Of course, what I was most grateful for was that for the first time in five years, I now had full time employment. The ironic part of this was that I was replacing a teacher who was also a graduate of Western Connecticut State, and played with Jeff and myself in the Jazz Ensemble. It certainly seemed to me that he didn't really want to leave teaching, but he had a young family, and the salary for CMI teachers as well as parochial school teachers in general was not very competitive compared to public schools.

So, the following week I started teaching in the three new

schools that were assigned me. The first school I walked into was the Sacred Heart School in New Britain. The school building itself was an older building, several decades old, and set behind the Sacred Heart Church, located in the factory district of the city. The school was nearly in the shadow of the Stanley Works, manufacturer of Stanley tools, which even today are carried in most every hardware store and known to just about every handyman. As I entered the lobby of the school, I began to wonder if I was in the right place. The lobby was filled with students and teachers, but I didn't hear a word of English. After a while, I figured out that everyone was speaking Polish. I must have looked totally confused, and after a few seconds, the school custodian came up to me and started speaking Polish to me. I really began to wonder what I had gotten myself into, but when I told him in English what I was doing there, he helped me find the Principal, and I was led to the room where the band instruction took place. It also put me at ease that everyone in the building also spoke English. I had never encountered a school in which there was such a tight-knit ethnic community. I found out later that Pope John Paul II had visited the parish years before, when he was a Cardinal in Poland.

Another school that I was assigned to was also located in New Britain. The St. Francis of Assisi Middle School was located on the other side of town, near the campus of Central Connecticut State University. St. Francis was a small school, grades 6-8, with around 80 or 90 students. The staff was friendly, and the place had more of a family atmosphere than the other schools that I taught in. The band numbered 21 students, which, considering the small student body, was really incredible. Of all the schools I taught in, St. Francis had the best teaching space for band instruction, an unused classroom. The remainder of the schools that I taught in were in the New Haven area, but the two New Britain schools were my favorites. Students in all of the CMI schools received both a class lesson on their instrument, and a band rehearsal, usually on the same day, once a week. Parents paid tuition to CMI in addition to what they paid for tuition at the school their children were attending.

I only had about 8 weeks to prepare the bands for their Christmas performances. Not every school in which I taught had a band capable of performing, at least not for Christmas. In one school, the band consisted of four flutes, and a trombone. Could I have forced them to perform? Yes. Would it have been productive? Probably not. In two of the schools I taught in, the band program was new, and the students were all beginners. If I had started at the schools in September, I probably could have put something together for a parent performance before Christmas, but the band programs in these schools started too late. The Christmas performances at the rest of the schools went well. I was pleased, and the parents and principals of the various schools also appeared pleased. After Christmas, CMI put on an Ensemble Festival, in which each teacher prepared a small group to perform. Since there were 14 teachers on the CMI staff at the time, and since some teachers prepared more than one ensemble, the Festival was a large event. In the spring, I turned my attention to the spring performances. Every year, the Hartford Archdiocese branch of CMI presented a series of Band festivals in the month of May, and every CMI school in the archdiocese was expected to participate. Bands from 5 or 6 schools performed in each festival, and each school would take turns playing for the audience. I'm not exactly sure how parents attending these festivals felt about their childrens' performances. I found the experience to be somewhat intimidating. Each time one of my bands would perform in a festival, I was always concerned about how respectable the performance of my band would compare to that of the other schools. For my New Britain schools, it wasn't a problem. They fared well compared with the other schools present at their festivals. However, for my beginner schools, I was worried. I arranged for the beginner schools to attend the same festival, and I combined the groups. I also composed a beginner level piece for them to perform which I called "CMI Rock". During rehearsal, I made a big deal of them premiering a new piece, and as a result, I felt their festival performance was much less intimidating, both for the students, and for me. As the school year ended, I started to think about ways in which I could use my orchestration skills to create some special pieces for some of the schools I was teaching in, especially at Sacred Heart School. I wanted to do something to celebrate the uniqueness of the school, the parish, and community. I asked the Principal to recommend some Polish Christmas carols that I might be able to orchestrate for the school band. I then started to work on a medley of these carols over the summer and began teaching it to the band the following fall.

What I didn't realize during that summer, was that the country of Poland was undergoing a transition where martial law had just been lifted. Eighteen months earlier, the Polish communist government had instituted martial law as a means of dealing with the trade unions and the Solidarity movement led by Lech Walesa. After, several weeks of escalating tensions, the Polish government declared martial law, and all of a sudden, the borders were sealed, airports were closed and road access to main cities was restricted. Travel between cities required permission. Curfew was imposed between 10 pm and 6 am. Telephone lines were disconnected. Mail was subject to censorship. All trade union and other independent organizations were de-legalized. Public administration, health services, power generation stations, coal mines, seaports, train stations, and most of the key factories were placed under military management. Broadcasters delivered the day's news on the only remaining TV station (which of course was a government station) dressed in military uniforms. As I started to teach the band the medley of Polish Christmas carols that I had written, the effects of this were still being felt by a large percentage of the students and their families, who had grown used to seeing their relatives in Poland on a regular basis. With all contact cut off for such a long time, things had looked grim. Even though the situation had improved, it was unsettled, and there was still a noticeable level of tension among both students and staff whenever there was discussion of the issue.

As Christmas approached, the school's Christmas Concert went on as scheduled. The students performed admirably, and the final selection of the concert was the medley of Polish Christmas Carols that I had arranged for the group. I wasn't sure what to expect, in fact I had considered pulling the piece from the program in light of the situation. However, I went ahead and did the piece with the band. When the last chord was sounded, I really was not prepared for the reaction of the audience.

At first, there was silence. Then the applause started and began to grow exponentially. I had the students stand for the applause and then turned around to take a bow. I stood there dumbfounded by what I saw. Most of the audience were standing and applauding, but there were many folks scattered across the audience that were in tears. Many of them were men as well as women, and some of them so inconsolable that they were unable to stand or clap. I had been able to stir the emotions of an audience through music before, but nothing like this. It seemed ironic to me how a seemingly insignificant collection of what to most people would be obscure Christmas Carols, written for a group of young, developing instrumentalists could have such an emotional impact on an audience as a masterwork might by one of the great composers. A cynical person might say that by doing the piece, I played on the emotions of the audience and students. I disagree. Performing the piece wasn't just a statement of pride in one's heritage. Here were Christmas Carols that had been in existence for not just years, but centuries. By performing the piece, the students made a statement to their elders that traditions would not die, and they were able to make that connection on a very personal level. One could see the pride in the beaming faces of the students after the performance, and I believe that the piece spoke to the fact that despite all of its recent problems, Poland would endure. That evening remains one of my proudest moments as a music educator.

After Christmas, I had a couple of disturbing experiences in the CMI organization. To begin with, I was given some new teaching assignments in some schools with a very low level of administrator support. One school, in particular, was a catholic high school newly signed on to CMI. We ended up doing the same CMI format that they used with elementary schools. This meant that I would only teach at the high school one day a week, certainly not a formula for success at the high school level. There was no opportunity given to me to make contacts with the students. Even though the school had a music room, they had me teach in a storage room in a remote part of the school. I could only work with students if they could get excused from their study halls, which didn't happen every week. As a result, I had a band of eight students that I saw once a week, if they could make it. I found out later that the administration of the school had complained to the CMI management that the band program wasn't growing to their expectations. To put it mildly, I wasn't amused. This high school was in a city with a very successful public high school band. It seemed that the reason they brought in CMI was so that they could offer a comparable music program to the public high school. The only problem was they didn't appear willing to give the necessary support to allow such a program to be successful. The public-school band met as a class every day, and had the necessary scheduling, budget, and facility support. My band of eight students had one band rehearsal a week, after school, and no budget, facility, or scheduling support. I was appalled at the expectation by the administration that somehow a comparable band program could be developed under those circumstances.

While this was going on, the administration of Catholic Music Instructors., which was based in New Jersey, announced to us that we were going to put on an honors festival, featuring an honors band of the best players in the archdiocese, based on a similar event that they held each year in New Jersey. I don't remember if I was asked, or if I volunteered to run the festival, but somehow, I ended up as the chairman for the festival. From the beginning, a series of things occurred that raised red flags with me. To begin with, I viewed the video tape of the New Jersey festival. I wasn't all that impressed, and I felt that I could provide a more memorable event for the students and their families. However, the New Jersey management was insistent that the festival be run like the New Jersey event. Almost every decision that I made that wasn't consistent with the New Jersey event was countermanded. They changed the rehearsal schedule that I had developed, scheduled the rehearsals in schools other than the ones that I had recommended. They made changes to the repertoire and logistics without telling me. The most interesting part was that as the festival chairman, I was supposed to conduct the National Anthem at the start of the festival concert, and in the end, the CMI management ended up having another teacher conduct instead. I wasn't happy, and I complained to Jeff about it, who was very understanding, but there wasn't much that he could do. There were also some other issues at some of the other schools I taught in. At one point, I had a major argument with the school secretary in one school, who wouldn't allow me to copy music for the students on their copier because she didn't consider me part of the school. At another school, I used the faculty bathroom, but neglected to put the toilet seat down. Since the school had an all-female staff, this didn't go well. The school not only complained to the CMI management, but also requested that they not assign me to their school the following year. I couldn't believe it. Here, I was essentially being fired from a school because I left the toilet seat up!!! When the spring band festivals came, I was fairly happy with how my school groups performed, but the Director of CMI found reasons to criticize my programing choices. When she met with me at the end of the school year, she told me that she was pulling me out of the high school I taught in, and a couple of elementary schools as well. However, she was not going to assign me to any additional schools to take the place of the programs that she was taking me out of. Essentially, I would be a part-time employee of CMI.

I wasn't about to accept this, so I updated my resume, dusted off my reference papers, and spent the summer job-hunting again. This time, I started out with a wide search area, attending interviews in New York, New Jersey, and the six New England states. Jeff gave me a good written reference, and I applied to nearly every high school band opening I could find, from large urban high schools to small rural ones. Toward the end of July, I applied for the high school music teacher position in Lisbon Falls, Maine. They called me for an interview, and I drove up from Connecticut with my friend John, who I had taught with in Ansonia. On the surface, the interview looked to be an intimidating experience. There was an entire panel of what seemed like a dozen people interviewing candidates including the principal, elementary music teacher, the president of the music boosters' organization, and a significant number of parents. John waited outside during the interview and told me later that the candidate that interviewed before me left the school looking rattled. However, all I did was relay to them my experiences, and how I felt those experiences would help me in providing the students with as successful a program as possible. I did another interview in Connecticut the following day, but when I returned home, there was a message waiting for me from the principal of the high school in Lisbon Falls. They were offering me the position. It was time to go back to Maine.

MOVING ON TO LISBON

Lisbon High School is located in the Lisbon Falls section of the Town of Lisbon, Maine. I spent a long time teaching in Lisbon, twenty-two years, in fact. Over that time, things in the town changed considerably. When I first started teaching there, the town was split into sections- Lisbon Village, Lisbon Center, and Lisbon Falls. There was a streak of independence, sometimes rivalry, among all three sections of the town, and it showed in a number of ways. To begin with, each area had its own post office. There were separate fire departments, one in Lisbon Falls with red fire trucks, and the other in Lisbon village with yellow fire trucks. Each year, the town held a Memorial Day Parade in which was held jointly by the VFW post, as well the American Legion posts in both Lisbon Village and Lisbon Falls. The Lisbon Falls segment of the parade would be held first, after which, the entire parade would board school buses to take them to Lisbon Village for the second segment of the parade. Each year, there were citizens who would attend the town meeting in order to vote against the school budget, because thirty years earlier, the two high schools, one in Lisbon Falls, and one in Lisbon Village were merged into one. Lisbon High School's most famous alumnus is writer Stephen King, who as I understand it, was also a member of the chorus.

Changes didn't just occur with the new teaching position I now had, but I also experienced changes on the drum corps side of things as well. I have heard it frequently said that when one door closes, another one opens. I experienced this my first day at Lisbon High School, as I was making preparations for the opening of school. The office called me on the intercom and told me that a man was looking for me. As I was headed to the office, I happened to come across this person on the stairway that was looking for me. "Are you the music teacher?" he asked as I approached. I told him I was, and we started a conversation that I did not expect, nor did I believe the good fortune that had come my way. Besides leaving my family again, the one other thing that I hated to leave behind in Connecticut was the drum corps I was instructing, the Connecticut Vagabonds. The man that I met on the stairway introduced himself to me as Jerry. I turns out that he and his brother, Jim, had started a drum and bugle corps in Waterville, a little more than an hour north of Lisbon. The corps was just finishing its first year in competition, and Jerry sought me out to see if I had any students who might be interested in marching with the corps the following season. Of course, I had no answer for him since I had not yet met with any students. However, I was aware of the corps, the 20th Maine Regiment, and had followed the progress of the group in the drum corps publications that reported the results of various drum corps contests, including the ones in the greater Boston area, where the 20th Maine Regiment competed. I told Jerry this, and then went on to outline my experiences in drum and bugle corps. Now it was Jerry's turn to be surprised. "The corps spent most of this past summer without a bugle instructor" he told me. "We promised the kids in the corps that we would find a bugle instructor for them for next year." I told him I would be interested, and a couple of weeks later I signed a contract with the corps as a bugle instructor for the following season.

As the school year began, there were several issues concerning the music program at Lisbon High School that I was not prepared for and ended up having to adjust to on the fly. The first issue was that I was replacing a music teacher whose probationary contract was not renewed, meaning that he basically was fired. A number of the students liked him, and the parents liked him as well. I imagine that was probably why there were so many parents on the interview committee. Although everyone treated me with respect, I did get the impression that there was some resentment simmering under the surface. The major indication of this occurred at the September meeting of the music boosters' organization, which called itself the "Friends of Music". Although they all seemed like nice people who were concerned about the quality of the music program that their children were a part of, I felt really uncomfortable because the majority of the meeting was spent discussing strategies they could use to convince the administration to change its mind about terminating the contract of the previous music teacher.

As time went on, I began to understand the reasons why the previous teacher's contract was terminated. It seems that he was a decent music teacher, well-liked by students and parents, but he made some very unwise decisions. The first day of band, I went down the line of students, 23 in all, asking them what they played, how long they had been playing, and what they liked most about being in band. The responses were fairly predictable, but what really threw me were the final two students. When I asked the first student what he played, he said, "Nothing, I set up lights for the concerts." I then moved on to the second student and asked him what he played. He said "Nothing, I'm the greyhound!" The greyhound was the school mascot. I was astounded. Here were two students receiving academic music credit for reasons that were neither academic nor musical. One of them did nothing more than set up lights for the two or three performances over the course of the school year, while the other simply donned a greyhound costume for the four football games that the band played at. I couldn't believe it. How could one assign a fair grade to these students in comparison to the other band students, let alone justifying academic credit for what they did?

When the first football game came, I ended up excusing the kid in the greyhound costume mid-way through the first quarter of the game. It was a fairly hot day, and the costume was heavy, and certainly not made for warm weather. I was concerned that he could pass out. Nor do I think he was missed very much. The headpiece of the costume was homemade and was made rather poorly, much wider than I think it was intended. With the out of proportion headpiece, he looked more like an elephant than a greyhound. A couple

163

of weeks later, he ended up dropping band as a class, mostly at my urging. The student that set up lights also dropped a few weeks later.

The band itself was pretty good, even though it was small. The most impressive players in the group were Brian and Bruce, twin boys of the elementary music teacher. Brian played trombone, and Bruce played tenor saxophone. When I say these boys were impressive, that's an understatement. To this day, they remain the two most accomplished players I think I've ever had. Both went on to become instructors at the university level. From the beginning, I knew that they were great players, but at the time, I had no idea how great. My first indication occurred during the All-State auditions. Brian had been the highest scoring trombone player in the Maine All-State auditions the previous year. I didn't realize that this created a sort of following for him. On the day of auditions, I was walking down the hallway of the school where the auditions were being held, only to come across a group of three or four students from other schools who were apparently trombone players. They had snuck into the wing of the school where the auditions were being held and stood just outside the trombone audition room and listened. Why would they risk getting into trouble for being in a restricted part of the school? The answer is they went to listen outside the room where Brian was auditioning. That isn't the only time that Brian impressed me. Over the course of the year, he was not only accepted as lead trombone to the Maine All-State Orchestra, but he was also accepted as lead trombone to the MENC All-Eastern Orchestra, an honors group made up of the best players in the northeastern states as well as Washington D.C. He was also accepted to the McDonald's All-American Band, again as lead trombone, one of two students from the state of Maine. He also won the High

School Soloist competition held by the Bangor Symphony orchestra. In this case, the only problem was that he wasn't allowed to play the solo with the orchestra, as was custom, because the conductor was unwilling to have the orchestra play a piece for a trombone soloist. I thought it was incredibly unfair. Had Brian played piano, or flute, or violin, there would have been no problem being able to play with the symphony. He did receive a scholarship for winning the competition, but the fact that he was not allowed to perform with the orchestra as any other winner of the competition would, is a sore spot with me that has remained to this day.

Bruce had his list of accomplishments also. He studied classical saxophone literature, but he was also into jazz, and took lessons from a prominent jazz saxophone player in Portland. He also was accepted to the Maine All-State Band, and the MENC All-Eastern Band. However, when his saxophone instructor set up a concert in Portland with special guest, jazz immortal Clark Terry, Bruce was invited to come on stage and perform with the group. When Clark Terry heard Bruce play, he awarded Bruce a scholarship on the spot to the summer jazz camp for high school students that he ran in Kansas.

The twins were exceptional, of course, and there were also many other good players in the band. Although, as you might expect, there were a few players that were not that good. That is what I thought at first about a Swedish exchange student who played the oboe. When I first heard her play, I didn't know if she could be a contributing member of the band. When she played, she had a lot of difficulty controlling the instrument. Many of her notes were out of tune, and her tone was scratchy. I tried working with her, but my knowledge of the oboe was limited, and I didn't know if what I was hearing was the result of her playing technique, or a poor instrument.

I wasn't about to give up though. One good thing that the previous band director had done was that he had managed to have some funds set aside in the music budget for clinicians, professional players from the outside who could work with the students. I decided to make use of this budget line and called an oboe player from the Portland Symphony. I arranged for her to come into the school to work with my Swedish exchange student. It is one of the best decisions I could have made. After listening to her play, the clinician took the reed from the student's oboe, picked up a knife she had brought with her and proceeded to trim parts of the oboe reed. This continued for a while, Each time, after trimming the reed, she would give it back to the student to play some more. She would listen to the sound, and then take the reed back and trim some more of it. She also worked with the student on playing technique, and after about 45 minutes, I could not get over the transformation that had taken place. My oboe student was playing with a full tone and nearly devoid of all indications that she was having difficulties. She went on to become a valuable member of the ensemble.

In the meantime, rehearsals had started with the 20th Maine Regiment. At the first rehearsal, I learned that I was going to be the assistant bugle instructor. They had decided to appoint Terry, a band director from the Portland area to be the primary bugle instructor. I didn't mind. After all, I had experience being an assistant instructor with the Explorers, and I had learned how I could be effective in such a role. The kids in the bugle section were fantastic. They had spent the summer with no bugle instructor, and now there were two on the instruction staff. They were highly motivated, and set a goal for themselves to be a bugle section that could achieve at the same level as the leading drum corps in the Boston area circuit that they competed in. We introduced them to several warm-up exercises and technique exercises. The increase in their skill level was impressive. About a month into rehearsals, we found out that the 20th Maine Regiment had been selected as Maine's representative to march in the Presidential Inauguration Parade in Washington DC. President Ronald Reagan had been re-elected for a second term, and as was custom on Inauguration Day every four years, a band, or other type of musical unit from each state was chosen to march in the parade, representing their state.

As the fall was proceeding into winter, I was very pleased at how the band at Lisbon was progressing. All-State auditions results had come in, and three Lisbon students were selected, Brian and Bruce, of course, and Scott, a friend of the twins who played Bass Clarinet, as well as electric bass. The Christmas Concert went off well, (yes, in those days we called it a Christmas Concert) despite the feeling that I was under a lot of scrutiny from the parents.

After Christmas, my attention turned to the Presidential Inauguration Parade, and the 20th Maine Regiment. A couple of weeks before the event, CBS sent a news crew to a rehearsal of the corps, for part of a news report showing the preparations we, and other groups across the country, were making for the parade. Two days before the event, the corps boarded two motor coaches, and headed for Washington DC. Now of course, many of you may remember that in all of history, there was only one Presidential Inauguration Parade that was canceled due to weather conditions, and this parade was it. A major blast of arctic air moved in to Washington that weekend, and on Sunday night, the night before the parade, we were told that the parade had been canceled. Apparently, the officials felt that the cold weather was too severe to hold the parade in safety. To try to make up for it, for all of the bands that had traveled to Washington, they quickly put together an indoor event for the groups, to be held the day of the inauguration at the Capitol Center in Landover, MD. I thought it was nice of them to put together an event like this for the music groups. President Reagan and Vice President Bush spoke at the event, but for me, the most memorable part of the afternoon took place as the 20th Maine Regiment was entering the arena. A television news crew took one of the members of the corps aside and began to interview him. When they asked him for his reaction to the canceled parade, he told them that he didn't agree with the decision, and that we should be marching in the parade. The reporter then asked him what state he was from, and he answered "Maine". Upon hearing this, the reporter signaled her crew to stop recording, and walked away muttering "It figures!".

So, I didn't get to march in Washington DC, but there were other things I wanted to accomplish, and not a whole lot of time to do it. Shortly after the inauguration, I hosted an honors festival at Lisbon, which in those days was known as the Seacoast Music Festival. The fact that Lisbon was hosting the festival is probably one of the reasons I was hired. I remember being asked about my experience in running a festival during my interview. I outlined the things I did when I ran the honors festival in the Hartford Archdiocese, leaving out the problems I had with the Catholic Music Instructors management, and apparently what I told the committee was satisfactory. The festival required extensive planning, setting up rehearsal space, arranging for meals, making sure we had all the necessary equipment, etc. The first day of the festival occurred on a Friday. Rehearsals started on time, and it looked like things were coming together quite well. During the afternoon rehearsals, there was a meeting of the music teachers of the various schools involved. It had started snowing, and the forecast for the following day, when the festival concert would be held, was questionable. The consensus was that I would make a decision the following morning based on the updated weather forecast, whether to proceed or not with the second day of the festival. I got up at 5am the next day, Saturday, checked the weather forecast and called all of the music teachers. I told them there would be a small amount of snow that morning, but that we probably should go ahead with the festival. The error I made was that I used the local forecast and didn't check beyond the Lisbon area. In some of the other locations where there were participating schools, the situation was different. About 50 miles or so up the coast, many of the participating schools in that area were experiencing heavy snow. When I arrived at the high school, I started getting calls from the schools in that area whose school buses had been grounded because of the snow. Only about half of the students in the festival actually arrived for the second day. I was at a loss as to what to do. I had tried to prepare for any problems that might occur, but I certainly did not anticipate this. I called together the music teachers of those schools that did make it, and we tried to arrive at a consensus as far as what to do. In the end, we held limited rehearsals, had the student groups perform for each other, gave everyone lunch, and sent everyone home. It was upsetting when I returned to my apartment after closing up the school, and the sun was shining.

After the festival, we then entered into a time that many music teachers in Maine refer to as "Jazz Season". Many high schools across the country have jazz bands, but in Maine, there is a series of regional competitions, followed by the state competition a few weeks later. At the beginning of the school year, Bruce had asked me if I would be willing to organize a jazz band. I said I would, and in the fall, we started with weekly jazz band rehearsals. However, one of the things I did that was different from the previous band director was that I organized the group as a jazz combo rather than a jazz band. For those unaware of the difference, the standard jazz band, or jazz ensemble, is based on big band jazz. Big band jazz was prevalent during the 1930's and '40's including the Duke Ellington, Count Basie, Woody Herman bands, etc. Such groups usually have a trumpet section, sax section, trombone section, as well as a rhythm section that includes piano, bass, drums, and sometimes guitar. Combos have only a few players. There is a rhythm section, but only a limited number of horns, or lead instruments. In the case of Lisbon, there was a piano player, bass player, and drummer that made up the rhythm section, but for lead horns, I only had Bruce on tenor sax, and Brian on trombone. With such strong players on lead horns, it was a simple case of developing and coordinating the rhythm section to properly back them up. When the day of the District 3 Jazz Festival came, I was nervous, but confident. The performance was outstanding. Brian and Bruce were almost flawless, and the rhythm section was more than up to the challenge. The results were as good as I could possibly hope for. The Lisbon jazz combo was awarded a "Superior" rating, and easily qualified for the State Jazz Festival. But it was more than that. The previous year, Lisbon performed as a jazz band (big band Jazz). They did not do well and didn't qualify for the state festival. Now, all of a sudden, out of the blue, here was this jazz combo from Lisbon, and they were astoundingly good. When I looked over the judges' sheets, and checked for their comments, on one sheet, the judge wrote one word - "Wow!". A few weeks later, Lisbon's jazz combo competed in the State Jazz Festival, winning second place. It wasn't as good a performance as the District 3 jazz festival, but it was still strong. What I found interesting was that rhythm section received as much attention as Brian and Bruce. At the state Music Educators Conference in May that year, I attended a conference session on jazz rhythm sections. The clinicians covered the various roles of the drummer, bass player, and keyboard or guitar players with a cohesive rhythm section. At one point, it appeared that the clinicians were fielding multiple questions about what the piano or keyboard player should actually play, and how they should interact with the drums and bass. One of the clinicians recognized me and pointed to me saying, "Lisbon is an example of how to do this properly. If you get a chance to see their combo, you should. They do it right!". I couldn't help but feel proud.

Shortly after the jazz festival, the high school band at Lisbon was invited to play at the State Capitol building in Augusta. The local state legislator was eager for the band to play there. I didn't really understand why, but I wanted to accommodate his wishes, and it would be a great experience for the students. So on the appointed day, I brought the band to Augusta. We were a bit late because I was tracking down some missing students. One girl refused to go because she had a test in one of her classes that day. A couple of others were not properly dressed, and I refused to allow them to go. When we arrived, the first thing I was asked to do was set the band up in the rotunda on the top floor. This apparently is an acoustically desirable place to perform. Even if there isn't much of an audience there, the sound of the band reverberates from the rotunda throughout the building. In a way, the state house operates a lot like a high school. There are bells going off at all different times to call legislators to various events. So when performing, one has to try to ignore the bells going off. It was distracting, but that's how the legislature operates. The band performed really well in the rotunda, but with all the activity going on, I wasn't sure anyone noticed. We played for about 45 minutes, and then the band was moved into the legislative observation gallery. There, we awaited the start of the legislative session. First, the session was called to order, followed by a prayer by an invited minister. After that, the band played the National Anthem. After we were finished, I had the students put their instruments on the bus, and they were allowed to observe the session. A week or so later, I received a letter from the Clerk of the House. For the most part, it was pretty much a form letter, thanking the band for performing. However, at the bottom of the letter was a hand-written notation by the Clerk, who served in that position for nearly three decades. The notation read: "This was the best 18-piece band to play at the State House in my memory". I posted the letter for the students to see and left it up until all of the participating students graduated from Lisbon.

As the end of the school year neared, I was starting to get fairly excited about the 20th Maine Regiment. It had been several years since I had been involved in drum and bugle corps field shows, and it was great to return to it. The corps traveled to the Boston area every week or two for competitions. They did well, although they scored several points below the leading corps. At the beginning of August, the corps embarked on its first tour. The first day was a travel day, and we stayed at a youth center in Pennsylvania. The corps arrived late, after 10pm, and the kids were animated and restless after spending so much time on the road. A bunch of them pleaded with me to allow them to take out the equipment and practice. It seemed as if the youth center was in a downtown area, and not really near any residences. So, even though it was now after 11pm, we ended up allowing them to practice in the hope that it wouldn't disturb anyone. Wrong! After about five minutes, a call came into the youth center. "Do you people know what time it is?" said the voice at the other end. We apologized and quickly shut things down. The following day was also a travel day, and we arrived in Marion, Ohio for the US Open Drum and Bugle Corps championships. All of the traveling must have taken a toll, because the performance at the US Open was less than stellar. The tour continued, and we headed for Madison, Wisconsin for the DCI World Championships.

We arrived a couple of days early and went into intense rehearsals to prepare for the prelims day. The 20th Maine Regiment competed in what was then known as the A-60 class, meaning that the total membership of the corps did not exceed 60 members. At Madison, they would be competing against other class A-60 corps from all over the country. All A-60 corps would compete in the prelims, and the top five corps would advance to the finals. We rehearsed every spare minute, even at 7am the morning of the prelims. The corps did well, but fell just short of making the finals, placing sixth, just a few tenths of a point behind the finalist corps. I was devastated and concerned. Over the years, I had seen situations in a number of corps that barely missed the finals where the membership became disheartened and did not return to the corps the following season leading to its breakup. I feared the same thing could occur with the 20th Maine Regiment. It really was bothering me as we started on the long bus trip home. However, something happened on the way home that gave me some hope for the situation. After traveling the first day, the corps stopped at a youth club in Cleveland to spend the night. Some of the neighbors apparently didn't care for us being there and vandalized our bus. This incident had an unexpected effect on the kids in the corps. They seemed to bond together as I had never seen the entire season, and it gave me hope that everything would be all right.

As I returned to Lisbon at the start of the school year, I was greeted with some news that I had strong mixed feelings about. My trombone player, Brian, had been awarded a full scholarship to the Interlochen Arts Academy. For persons who may be unaware, Interlochen is a fine arts boarding high school in Michigan where some of the best high school musicians in the country (and beyond) come to study. I was happy for Brian. After all, this was an incredible opportunity. He would get the chance to establish himself as an aspiring professional musician, which I had no doubt that he would become. On the down side, I would be missing from my band a student who was one of the best high school trombone players in the country. Brian had caught me by surprise my first year at Lisbon. I had no idea he was that good, and to perform any literature that would challenge him, and be playable for the band was a major challenge. I was determined that I would not let that happen the second year. I had a lot of plans to be able to spotlight Brian his senior year. I had even started sketching some pieces for band with him in mind. Now, all that planning had been for naught. Of course, I still had his brother, Bruce, and I had in mind some ideas with the Jazz combo that I felt he would enjoy. But my first project was to teach the band a field show for competitions. I had a good concept for a field show, but for some reason, teaching the band was painfully slow, and I ended up having to modify the show and "dumb down" the remaining music and drill for the show. The first marching band show we went to was a very difficult performance. Some students forgot a section of their music, and the band ended up getting really lost in the middle of the show. To make matters worse, one of the buses that brought us to the show developed a broken radiator hose as we arrived. The driver was unable to reach the mechanic back in Lisbon, and when the band show ended, we were stuck in the parking lot. We stayed there for a long time, and when we finally reached the mechanic, he ended up driving another bus from Lisbon to transport the students. But when he arrived, well after midnight, he insisted that the buses not leave until he fixed the broken radiator hose. The final result was that we pulled into the parking lot in Lisbon well after 2am. Several families had been waiting almost four hours for the band to arrive, and they were quite unhappy. But during this pre-cell phone era, contacting parents was difficult from the road.

The rest of the year went a lot like the first year, although an incident occurred that has bothered me to this day. The band at Lisbon was pretty good for its size, and I had no problems were working with them to achieve respectable performances. However, when I started at Lisbon, the chorus had basically crashed as an ensemble. The year before I arrived, there apparently were several skilled choral students that graduated, so when I took over the chorus, very few of the underclassmen of the previous year were still involved with the Chorus. My first year at Lisbon, the Chorus consisted of four students. I had to do a lot of alternative programming since there was no way that a group of four could actually function as a Chorus. The following year, I had built the group up to 10-12 students, but I was still not happy with the progress I was making in building the group up to its previous levels. When that year's Seacoast Music Festival took place, I decided that I needed to seek out advice from some of the experienced choral directors whose students were also participating in the festival. I went to one of those directors and asked what I might be able to do to help enhance the membership in my Chorus. Her answer took me aback. She said, "What you need to do is step aside and let a choral major take over your Chorus. You instrumental guys don't really know how to instruct a choral group well." I was stunned. I knew that I could instruct chorus as well as a lot of choral majors. My experience at Fryeburg proved that. So I really wasn't sure how to respond to a choral director who was so dismissive of my abilities. To this day, it has bothered me, to the point where I have even taken extra summer coursework in the choral area.

When we got to jazz season, I was really confident in what the jazz combo might be able to do. The rhythm section was back, and so was Bruce. I had a couple of new horn players that were interested in playing with the group, and I managed to work them in as well. But for one tune, I spotlighted Bruce with just him and the rhythm section playing John Coltrane's "Giant Steps" which as any fan of jazz would know is not just a jazz classic, but a difficult jazz classic. Bruce worked hard on it. I thought he did well, but the judges did not. It was disappointing, but sometimes that happens.

The rest of the school year went without incident, and I found myself looking forward to a second summer with the 20th Maine Regiment. The corps had a strong winter of rehearsals and membership growth, and for the oncoming season had made the jump from Class A-60, groups with 60 members or less, to Class A, meaning the membership exceeded 60 members. In addition, the group was now undertaking two tours. The first was a one-week tour going south, as far as Atlanta, and the other was a two-week tour going out to the mid-west, and the DCI World Championships. At first, the corps started its season with fairly mixed results. The judges in the Boston area circuit that the corps competed in seemed unwilling to recognize the improvement in the corps from the previous year. Once the corps was on tour, scores in the shows the group competed in seemed to reflect the strength of the corps that all of us instructors believed the corps could exhibit. Although the corps had experienced a lot of success on tour, I knew that the success of the season would hinge on how well the corps did at the DCI championships. I also did not want to speculate on how things would go in what, of course, would be considered the ultimate competition of the year. However, 20th Maine Regiment was awarded 2nd place at a DCI Regional competition just prior to the championships, which I thought was a good indication. On the day of the championships, 20th Maine was the second corps to compete in the prelims, and I sat on pins and needles the rest of the day, waiting to see if the 20th Maine score was enough to get the corps into the finals. As it turned out, they had the fourth highest score of the day, and so was one of six corps accepted to the finals. I was both ecstatic and proud. True, I was just one of a staff of instructors, but I had spent many years trying to get here. Three times, groups that I had instructed won state parade or circuit titles- the 20th Maine Regiment, the Vagabonds, and the Yankee Peddlers, but never had I taught a corps that was a DCI finalist. Even though Class A was a step below the World Class corps in those days, I still considered it a significant achievement. I didn't just spend 10 seasons as an instructor to arrive at this point. I also spent a lot of time observing countless rehearsals of other drum corps. I would watch high profile instructors work with some of the top corps always trying to pick up on some procedure or technique that these instructors used with their groups. Now, I was an instructor of a DCI finalist.

The finals took place in what seemed like the blink of an eye, and in some ways, it was a surreal experience. The corps entered through a back gate of Camp Randall Stadium at the

University of Wisconsin where the championship finals were held. They stayed on the running track of the stadium waiting for the previous corps to finish its performance. The corps stood rigid, as they waited for their turn on the field. No one in the corps moved. To their credit, they were like statues as they waited. I, on the other hand, paced nervously. Many times I had seen where a corps performed brilliantly in the preliminary competition, only to have multiple things go wrong in their finals performance. The corps went on and performed quite well. As far as I could tell, the bugle section performed well, at least by my vantage point. At some point, Terry and I figured out that the bugle section presented itself differently at the field level as opposed to the press box level in a performance. Errors that one might hear observing at the field level were not heard up near the press box, and vice versa. So as a result, each time the corps performed, one of us would station ourselves near the press box, and the other would observe at the field level. We would then compare notes later. In the finals, I didn't think the corps performed well enough to move up from their 4th place finish in the prelims, but it was still a very satisfying performance.

As the performance ended, the corps marched off the field and toward the back gate of the stadium. Once through the back gate, we halted the corps to give the kids a rest before putting away equipment. At this point, a group of men approached the corps. The leader of the group introduced himself as Jay Wanamaker. Wanamaker is a giant in the percussion world with multiple percussion pieces, books and articles to his credit. At the time, he was the percussion instructor of the University of Southern California Trojan Band and was a clinician for Yamaha. The gentlemen with him all appeared to be Japanese and wore business suits. That caught me by surprise. Who wears business suits to a drum corps competition? No one that I was aware of, that's for sure. It turns out these gentlemen were executives from Yamaha Corporation. Yamaha was looking to break into the marching percussion market that year and had introduced its first line of marching drums. The 20th Maine Regiment had purchased a new set of marching drums that spring, Yamaha drums, and therefore was one of the first groups to use this new line of drums. The executives fanned out among the drum line, asking the kids just about every conceivable question about the drums. How good was the response of the instruments? Were the carrier harnesses comfortable enough? How did the drummers feel about their design innovations? What about the durability of the drums? How well did they stand up to an entire season of use? As these conversations went on, one of the 20th Maine snare drummers complained that the drum heads could not stand up to the increased tension of the drum. Like most drum and bugle corps, the 20th Maine set the tension of their snare drums fairly high, in comparison to the average marching band, and throughout the season, the corps went through a significant number of drum heads that would tear apart under high tension. As the drummer pointed out this problem, we heard a voice nearby saying, "I can help with that!" The voice belonged to Bill Ludwig, president of the company his father founded, Ludwig Drums. Now, for those who may not be familiar with Ludwig drums, I should point out that at one time, Ludwig was the foremost manufacturer of drums in the world. Numerous recording artists played on Ludwig drums including Ringo Starr of the Beatles, Karen Carpenter, and Buddy Rich, just to name a few. Ludwig walked over to his van, which was parked nearby. He reached in and grabbed a handful of drum heads. He walked back to the drum line and presented the drum heads to the drum instructor.

"Here," he said. "These heads are a new design. They should solve your problem".

As I suspected, the placement of the corps did not change from the prelims. They still placed 4th in the finals. But during the retreat ceremony, when scores are announced, and awards presented, I don't think I ever felt prouder. This moment had been years in the making, and I wanted to enjoy every second of it. After the contest, the corps returned to the school where we were staying, just outside of Madison. It is standard procedure for drum corps on tour to stay at schools or community centers, using sleeping bags on the gym floor. The kids went directly to sleep. After all, it had been a long day. However, no matter how hard I tried, I couldn't go to sleep. I was just too excited over the evening's events. I got up and went to the cafeteria. The doors had been left open, so the evening summertime air could circulate through the building. The downside of this was that a multitude of flies had made their way into the cafeteria. Since I was bored, yet wide-awake, I took it upon myself to grab a fly swatter and spend the rest of the night trying to rid the cafeteria of flies, while running the events of the last few days in my head. As I was hunting flies, I was feeling exhilarated, and yet sad. At this point in time, my wife and I were starting a family, and I didn't know if I would ever get a chance to tour again with a drum corps. As things turned out, I never did. The 20th Maine Regiment Drum and Bugle Corps disbanded shortly after the season was over, and the staff members went their separate ways.

I began my third year at Lisbon, hoping for the best, but as the year began, more disappointment. During the summer, I designed what I considered to be the most sophisticated field show yet for the band. However, it seems some of the band members didn't appreciate the effort, and at each of the three field shows that the band participated in, there were kids missing. What was the point in designing challenging formations if they looked like Swiss cheese because of missing students? I'm sure some of the kids enjoyed the experience, even with the attendance problems, but I did not. I started to second-guess myself. A total reexamination of my approach to this aspect of the band was warranted.

The rest of the year went on with no problems, that is, until the spring. One of the kids in band was working on becoming an eagle scout. A particularly important boy scout event was being held on Memorial Day weekend, and I excused him from the Memorial Day Parade. This started a chain reaction among the remaining members of the band, and one by one, nearly all of the band members requested to be excused from the parade. Alarmed, I went to see the Principal, and it was decided that if a student brought in a parent note to excuse their child from the parade, we would need to honor it. Nearly all of the students brought in notes from their parents excusing them from the parade. I knew most of the "excuses" were bogus, but there wasn't much I could do. It was easier to take a count of those students who WOULD make the parade. It turned out to be a total of six students. Making a band out of six students was not an option. There were only two possibilities open to me: 1) cancel the appearance of the band in the parade all together, or 2) organize the six students into a drum line, so that the veterans would have at least a percussion cadence to march to. I went with the 2nd option and on the day of the parade, my six drummers represented the high school, and marched the parade providing a drum beat for the veterans. In all honesty, I have to say that I need not have bothered. The fallout among the veterans was swift and loud. As it was, I was upset with how the situation turned out. Some of the veterans complained to the school board, and at the town meeting, where all of the town budgets are approved, including the school budget, one of the veterans suggested that the music program be eliminated. Although I was dismayed at this reaction, what really bothered me was a prevalent attitude that was voiced several times. "Our tax dollars fund this band, and we have a right to get something for our tax dollars" was a comment heard more than once. This attitude was downright annoying. If I had a chance to debate the issue, I would have challenged them to identify just one other department in the high school where they would expect to "get something for our tax dollars". The function of a music program is to provide a music educational component for students, just like every other subject that is taught in the curriculum. The wood shop doesn't make furniture for the town. Neither does the metals shop. The home economics classes don't make meals for the town, and the high school business classes certainly don't do anyone's typing. Certainly, the band plays a unique role in civic events of this type. After all, it's hard to imagine a math class marching down Main St. on Memorial Day chanting algebra equations. Unfortunately, this was a case of not recognizing music as an educational program, and as an important part of a student's overall education. When summer came, I didn't have a drum corps to teach. The 20th Maine Regiment had been struggling all of the previous summer financially, and things fell apart before they could put together a corps for the following year. We did have a meeting of the 20th Maine instructors at Terry's house in the fall to start preliminary planning for the next season, but shortly after that, the corps filed for bankruptcy. I felt lost. There was plenty to keep me busy, with my wife expecting our second child in July that year, but I was constantly lamenting over my first summer without drum corps in a long time. I missed being on tour, and all summer it just felt that there was this major hole in my life.

In my fourth year at Lisbon, some developments led to a decision on my part to no longer participate in marching band competitions. To begin with, the school budget was cut considerably, and the cuts were spread over all departments. I don't remember how much exactly that I had to cut, but it was more than a thousand dollars. I looked at all my options and decided that the budget cut would have to be met through elimination of the marching band competitions. Eliminating the contest fees alone would save almost $ 1000. The busing costs would save nearly as much. In addition to this, the band was considerably smaller than the previous year. I had lost several seniors to graduation, and only had two incoming freshmen. There were other would-be freshmen of course, but a number of them opted to go to a nearby private school. It was something that I just didn't understand. If music was a major part of a student's life, then why would that student choose to go to a private school that didn't have a music program? As a result, I started the year with a smaller, but more balanced group. I simply concentrated on how the band would sound at football games. I didn't do a field show with them. Too few students, and I wasn't going to count on all of them being dedicated enough to show up at all of the games. For some, even knowing that they would receive a grade penalty did not deter them from simply skipping out on some of the games. Although there was some grumbling among the football fans, it turned out to be a good decision. The band sounded good, and they gave a good presentation from the stands. At one point, a local newspaper sports reporter came to write an article about the Lisbon football team, that had made an impressive turnaround that year. Although the article was mostly about the football team, he wrote: "(at Lisbon football games) ... The band numbers eight students, sometimes more. It is very good. The concept of quality over quantity still holds true."

The school year went on, and as we began jazz season, my jazz combo was doing well, but as the festivals approached, I knew the group would be against stiff competition. They went into the regional festival, and easily qualified for the state jazz festival. As we traveled to the state jazz festival a couple of weeks later, I felt that I had prepared the group as well as I could, but I still wasn't expecting much in terms of how they would finish. I was less confident in the warm-up room, as we spent an awful lot of time in the room while the festival was being held up. The judges stopped the festival while they considered the legality of a piece of equipment that the school performing ahead of us was using. In those days, there were a lot of new advances in music technology, and some of these new electronic instruments were classified as illegal in the festival rules. The school performing ahead of us apparently was using such an electronic instrument, and our group had to wait in the warm-up room while the judges had to determine if this instrument was or was not allowed, according to the rules. This made me nervous. It has been my experience that when kids are ready to perform, but the performance is delayed for some reason, the kids become nervous and don't perform as well. Eventually, the judges ruled on the questionable equipment, and the school performing ahead of us completed its performance. My students took the stage and set up for their performance. Fortunately, I didn't sense any extra nervousness on their part, although they obviously weren't happy at having to wait through the delay. They performed well, and I was happy with the performance. I complemented them on the job they did. I had them put their equipment on the bus, and I then went to view some of the other groups. I wanted to delay our departure for an hour or two so that the students would take the opportunity to view the jazz groups from other schools. About an hour after I had them put the equipment on the bus, I was sitting watching a performance when the kids came up to me. "I think we might be in the top three!" they told me. "We're still listed on the board". The board they were referring to was the leader board. In those days, with 80 or so jazz bands of various types involved in this one-day festival, the procedure was to list all of the categories of jazz bands, and for each category list the three highest scoring bands in each of the categories. If a school that performed later in the day scored higher than one of the top three groups in their division, their name was added to the leader board, and the school with the lowest score on the leader board was dropped.

I immediately left my seat and went with the kids to view the leader board. Sure enough, there was Lisbon listed in the top three in the combo division. At the end of the row where the top three were listed was the word "final", meaning that all of the combos had performed, and the three schools listed were the top three finishing schools. When I confirmed what they were thinking, the students were elated. I was very glad that I had told them a few days before the festival that if they placed in the top three, that they would need extra money to stay for supper in order to attend the evening finals, where they would receive their trophy. Of course, when I told them that, I wasn't expecting them to place. I expected us to finish fifth, which would allow us to go home early. But now, we needed to stay for the finals in the evening. We had supper at a nearby pizza restaurant and returned to the school for the evening finals. When the combo winners were announced, Lisbon was announced as the third-place winner. I stayed in my seat while I allowed the kids to go up to the stage to receive their trophy. As far as I was concerned, it was their award, not mine. Plus, it was something I totally did not expect. One might classify it as an upset over two of the groups that I expected would do better than us. When Lisbon was announced, the students strode up the aisle to the stage. Their celebratory mood might have caused one to think that they had won 1st place rather than third. No matter. Trophy in hand, we boarded the bus for a triumphant trip home.

In the meantime, I had managed to convince the administration to adopt a clinician program to teach instrumental lessons. I was now teaching both the high school and middle school band, and I wanted to find ways in which we could maximize the instruction options that we were able to deliver to students. There were several advantages to a clinician program, in which we would bring in instructors from the outside to instruct. To begin with, we would seek out professionals on various instruments to instruct the students. A professional trumpet player, for instance, would have a greater knowledge of technique than I did. In addition, it would be cheaper to pay clinicians to instruct as opposed to doing it with music faculty. This then would free music faculty to instruct in other areas of the curriculum. Therefore, the following fall, we instituted a clinician program. That first year, I did not see a lot of progress from kids in the high school band, but that was not something that I had been expecting. The strategy was that I was looking for a greater evidence of progress from the middle school band members, and in that area, I was not disappointed. The plan was simple. The clinician program would not have a big impact on the high school musicians, but as the middle school students moved on to the high school, freshman band members would come into the high school band with a more advanced skill set. I only needed to hang on and hope that the administration would be patient enough until the program would be able to bear fruit. That particular year, I was more optimistic about the middle school band than the high school band. I had lost a good senior class, and was looking at, to put it mildly, a rebuilding year. My jazz group consisted of almost all beginners, and I knew the previous year's success would not be duplicated. The group did score high enough to qualify for the State Jazz Festival, but there was no success beyond that. As it turned out, it snowed on the morning of the State Jazz Festival. Not a lot, just a couple of inches, but it was enough so that the Director of Transportation would not allow the school bus to take us to the festival. It was a major disappointment. Hours upon hours of work by the students, and they didn't get a chance to perform. A few weeks later, a band director friend of mine said "It's too bad your group couldn't be there. They would have cleaned up." The rest of the school year was fairly normal. As the Spring Concert approached, I was optimistic about how the kids would perform. On the night of the concert, my wife came with our two small children, seating them in the front row, just a few feet from where the students were performing. I held the concerts in the school cafeteria in those days for a couple of reasons. First, the acoustics were a lot better than the gym. On the gym stage, there was about a half-second delay in hearing sounds made on the other side of the stage. Also, the cafeteria location made for a lot less moving of equipment, and since the setting was less formal, I could announce pieces to the audience without needing a microphone or sound system. Toward the end of the concert, my son needed to go to the bathroom, and so my wife took him, leaving my daughter seated in the front row. As I was announcing the next piece, I felt something grab my leg. I looked down. I saw my daughter, who was not yet two years old, had left her front row seat, walked up to me and started hugging my leg. It was nothing short of adorable. I picked her up, and several flash bulbs went off. As I took her back to her seat, I said, "You better behave, or I'll tell your daddy". It was one of my most treasured moments as a parent.

SMELLING LIKE A ROSE

Towards the end of the school year, we found out that the middle school choral teacher was leaving. With this in the works, the high school principal decided he wanted me at the high school full time. I was fine with that, but I worried about what would happen with the middle school program. As it turned out, a teacher's aide in the elementary school applied for the middle school music position. I was skeptical. Why would a person certified in music education be spending their time as a teacher's aide? There were several elementary music teaching positions open in the general area, and yet, this person wanted to teach music at the middle school level. As it turned out, this person did a marvelous job of selling herself in the teacher interview, although I was not part of the hiring process. She managed to convince the administration that she would do a wonderful job in the position. They ended up hiring her, and although I was wary, I decided I would give her the benefit of the doubt.

The first couple of days of the school year for teachers, are usually filled with faculty meetings and presentations prior to the first day for students. We had a few conversations as a music staff, and this new middle school teacher struck me as highly confident, but I wasn't convinced. I asked her a couple of probing questions, and all of a sudden, she snapped at me saying, "You shouldn't have any doubts about me being able to do this job. I can be just like you, stepping in it and coming out smelling like a rose." I was taken aback. Red flags went up immediately. No question, she intended the comment as a put-down, but I didn't get upset. She obviously was unaware that I had to turn a lot of lemons into lemonade in order to "smell like a rose". But as I considered this incident, one question bothered me. Here was a teacher highly confident that she would be able to craft a successful music program. If she was going to do such a marvelous job, then why get defensive like that? Clearly, I needed to watch the situation. I made it a point to stop by for a visit when I had free time. It seemed my free time just happened to coincide with the middle school band rehearsal. The first time I stopped by, she said to me "Good, you're here. Would you mind showing this student how to play a high Eb?" as she motioned to a nearby clarinet player. This did nothing to allay my doubts. Any music major should be able to know what the fingering is for a high Eb on the clarinet. The second week, no sooner had I arrived then the teacher was called to the office for a phone call. She left, and I was faced with a room full of students, most of them were mine the previous year, but now, no longer. It felt awkward, and I hesitated as I considered how to engage them in a supportive conversation, and then an 8th grade sax player moaned, "Please come back!" It was as if a big, black cloud had engulfed the room. I really didn't know what to say, although I tried to put as much of a positive spin on the situation that I could. After my third visit to the middle school, I was called in to my high school principal's office. It turns out that this teacher filed a complaint with the superintendent about my visits to the middle school, saying they were "intrusive". The principal asked me not to make any more visits to the middle school, and I complied. I didn't see the music teacher, or the middle school kids until their Christmas Concert. The night of the concert, I sat in the back of the middle school gym, not saying anything to anyone. I watched pre-concert preparations. When the concert started, the middle school band sounded OK, but I don't think the kids were challenged very much, and it occurred to me that the probable reason for the easy music was so the teacher would feel comfortable conducting it. However, her Waterloo came in one of the last pieces of the concert. This particular selection included pick-up notes at the beginning of the piece, and when she started the piece, she tried to bring the band in without any preparation. Her conducting wasn't that clear, and the different sections of the band came in at different times. After a few beats of music, she had to stop them. They simply were not playing together. Some may call it a rookie error, but I'm not sure she had the conducting technique to pull it off. She started them again, and again the same result. I could see the embarrassment in the kids' faces as she tried to start them a third time. Again, they didn't start together, but this time as least, they were close enough to continue playing. To say I was distressed was putting it mildly. I left the concert before it was over, because I didn't want to get into any conversations with parents. I tried to contemplate how I would approach my principal in the morning to express my concerns. As it turned out, when folks came into the middle school that following morning, they found a note from the music teacher taped to the music room door, announcing that she had quit.

All well and good, but now we were faced with the fact that there was another half-year left of school, and we had no middle school music teacher. We conducted a round of interviews, but the middle school administration was not happy with any of the candidates. Finally, we decided to use the clinicians to cover the classes for the rest of the year. Our sax and clarinet clinician was a retired high school band director. He had the time, and clearly I was confident that he could fulfill the role. The year went on, and things ended quite satisfactory.

The following school year, another woman was hired to fill the vacant position at the middle school. If the middle school administration had been wise, they would have advertised the position in the spring of the previous school year. Instead, they waited until August to advertise the position, and the crop of prospective candidates was fairly weak. As the year started out, I decided that I would stay away from the middle school, although I wasn't any more confident in the prospective success of the middle school program for the new year, than I was with the other teacher the previous year. This teacher didn't have the bluster of the previous teacher, but clearly she did not have the skill set to teach music at the middle school level. At the high school, I was experiencing the first crop of freshmen band members trained by the clinicians, and I realized my experiment was going to work. However, things in the middle school were not going good, and one of the clinicians complained to me that several kids wanted to drop band because the music teacher did not appear to be able to lead the group. I didn't know what to do. I wasn't a music department head, so I had no authority over the situation, but clearly, it appeared that this music teacher was going to undermine the progress that had been made with the clinician program. I was hoping the middle school administration was wise to what was going on and perhaps would not renew her contract, but no; it seemed they were totally oblivious to what was going on.

BUDGET WOES

However, as the end of the school year approached, a major budget issue arose in the Lisbon schools, which would impact me and the music program considerably for several years. The State of Maine had determined that their state revenue projections were way off, and the state budget would most likely incur a major deficit. In order to balance the state budget for the coming year, the Governor announced major cuts to state school aid. Lisbon was a high receiver of state school aid, and the result was a major budget crisis for the school system. I don't remember the exact amount of the cut, but in Lisbon, the cut amounted to the laying off of six teachers, as well as a multitude of components of the school budget. One of those components, as it turns out, was the music clinician program. Also, it was determined that one of the six positions to be eliminated would be either an Art of Music teacher. As teachers, we were left to go into conferences to recommend to the school board where the teacher cuts would be. I sat down with the Art staff. They were fully prepared to argue that the teacher to be cut should not be an Art teacher. I sat, and at first did not say anything. The Art teacher that had the least amount of seniority was a young mother, and really did not deserve such a fate as being laid off. I said to them, "The middle school music teacher has the least seniority of anyone, so the music department should absorb the cut". And so began a very dark portion of my time in Lisbon.

As the next school year began, I found myself with a schedule where each day I would spend the first half of the day teaching in the high school, and the other half at the middle school. The clinician program had worked. I now had a lot of freshmen and sophomore band members that were becoming monster players, and the band itself had grown to almost 30 members. The sad part was that I knew that because there was no longer any clinician program, the effects of the that program at the high school was now at its high-water mark and would probably be viewed by most as a flash in the pan, if it was noticed at all. I did my best at the middle school, but without clinicians, instrument lessons were more problematic. Because of time constraints, I had to teach lessons in large sectional groups as opposed to small groups like the clinicians were able to do. As time went on, things settled into a routine, and I was able to at least keep the music program respectable. At least things were stable. It wasn't like Ansonia, where I had to try to hold a program together with scotch tape and happy thoughts.

Fast-forward three years. The music program at Lisbon was still stable, although there was a threshold that the kids could never seem to exceed. It was at this point in time that I made my first presentation to the school board to restore the music teaching position that was cut during the budget crisis of three years previously. For those three years, the music program had operated short-handed. I had to split my time between the high school and middle school, not being able to give either building the all the attention that was needed. In the school district, there was one remaining music teacher who covered all the music classes in the elementary grades. As a result, music class schedules in the elementary grades had been cut in half. Students in the elementary schools now only received music classes once a week for one-half of the school year. This was disheartening. In music, everything that occurs in the rest of the school district is directly tied to the quality of instruction that kids receive in the elementary grades. I had also been dismayed that of the six teaching positions that had been eliminated three years earlier, all had been restored except for the music position. I thought carefully about how I would fashion this school board presentation. I didn't want the focus to be on me or the portions of the music program that I was responsible for. That could have been interpreted as whining. So I made the focus of the presentation on the elementary grades.

I decided to pull from some of the things I had learned in a course that I had taken the previous summer. The course was in Music Learning Theory, about the processes involved in kids learning music. The instructor of the course, Edwin Gordon, was a nationally known researcher and writer about this topic. Besides focusing on how kids learn music, a major segment of the course involved the development of musical aptitude. In a manner of putting a punctuation mark on that topic, Gordon gave all of the students in the class a music aptitude test. We didn't write our names down on the test paper, he wasn't interested in that. Overnight, he corrected the tests, and gave us a sheet with the results the following day. No names were listed on the sheet, just the test scores in descending order. I looked at my test sheet, and then looked at the score sheet. My score was at the top of the list, placing in the 95th percentile on the music major scale (meaning of all the tests completed nationally by folks who were music majors). In the general population, I was ranked in the 99th percentile. The rest of the scores of my classmates were mostly in the 60's and 70's percentiles, even a couple scores in the 40's. I was all set to claim victory as having the highest score in the class, when someone spoke out "Wow, that 95% score is impressive!" The instructor nodded, and then said, "Yes, but I have to say that someone who receives this score probably should not be teaching music. This person should be in Hollywood, or New York, pursuing music as a commercial musician or composer!" All of a sudden, I didn't much feel like crowing about my high score. It did make me think about what I was doing. Obviously, I wasn't in a very satisfactory place in my teaching career at this point in time, but the fact was I loved teaching, and couldn't see myself being a commercial musician. However, what I learned from the experience was the importance of musical aptitude in the pursuit of music, and I knew that the best way to structure my presentation to the school board was to focus on aptitude. For my school board presentation, I asked one of the art teachers to draw a silhouette of the head of a student from the side view. In the middle of the student's head, I had her draw a beaker halfway filled with liquid. This was a critical visual aid in my presentation to the school board. When I showed it to them, I explained that the beaker symbolized aptitude, while the liquid within signified achievement. Although in the upper grades, the focus is on music achievement, I explained, the focus in the lower grades should be music aptitude. It only makes sense that a person's achievement level is largely a reflection of his or her aptitude. In a young child, I said pointing to the beaker, aptitude is pliable, meaning that if a child receives supportive instruction and experiences, we can expand the beaker of aptitude. However, without such support, the aptitude beaker will shrink. When a child becomes older in the upper elementary grades, I explained, the size of the aptitude beaker becomes permanent, and from that point forward will not change. From a logical standpoint, if we are to encourage high levels of achievement in the upper grades, then we need to maximize the growth of aptitude in the lower grades. "It is extremely difficult to do that," I said, "when the elementary grade students receive only a half year of music classes, as they currently do." The school board members thought it was a wonderful presentation, but they didn't restore the lost music teaching position.

A few weeks later, I received a call from the commander of the local VFW post. The Lisbon VFW post was going to host the annual state VFW convention. As part of the festivities, there would be the state VFW parade, and would the Lisbon High School Band be able to participate. I told them we would, and the very next band class, I spoke at length about how important it would be to have everyone present that day for the parade. Unfortunately, a few days before the parade, I received a call from my mother that my grandmother had passed away. And when was the funeral scheduled for? The day of the parade, of course. I spoke with the principal, and he was agreeable to the suggestion that a parent or parents, could be placed in charge of the band that day, seeing as how the performance was in town. A couple of parents stepped forward to volunteer, and I went to the funeral in Connecticut hoping that everything would come together for the parade. When I returned to school, I found out that the parade had gone quite well. In fact, as I understand it, as the band was packing up after the parade, one of the parade officials approached them and awarded them the 1st place trophy for musical units. Now, when I was growing up in drum corps, the VFW and American Legion organizations held a state championship event at their state conventions in most places. Many times, the state championship competition was in the form of a parade, while in other states, a field competition was held. When I marched with the Explorers, I participated in several American Legion state convention parades, and the winning musical unit of that parade was always considered the Connecticut state champion. The Explorers had a very impressive collection of trophies from various parade and field competitions, but the largest of all the trophies, and the one placed most prominently in the collection, was the 1st place trophy the corps won at the state American Legion parade a number of years previous. Now, so many years later, my band had won the state VFW title. I'm not sure how much of a victory it was. After all, there were only one or two musical units that the band competed against. However, I told the band that as far as I was concerned, this was a state title. In fact, I kidded one of the parents that supervised the kids at the parade that day. I said "Wow! I can't believe it! I've been teaching music for almost 20 years, and none of my groups have ever won a state title. You were band director for one day, and the band wins a state championship. What's your secret?"

Fast forward another two years. It was now five years in total that we were operating the music program short-handed. In the meantime, I took the chorus to the State Capitol to perform for legislators as part of Music In Our Schools Month, a national initiative. It was part of a program adopted by the Maine Music Educators Association to promote music education in the schools with legislators. After the performance, the chairperson of the event sent me a survey regarding our experience. I sent the survey in with a mixed assessment on the event. I notated some issues and difficulties that I saw with the event, and also made some suggestions. A couple of months later, at the MMEA State Conference, I was approached by the State President of the Maine Music Educators Association and offered a seat on the MMEA Executive Board as chairman of Advocacy and Music In Our Schools Month, which of course included being the coordinator of the State Capitol performances. I accepted the position and served in that capacity for the next two years.

In Lisbon, I went and talked with the school board again, but we now had a new superintendent who had no interest in restoring the lost position. The elementary music teacher retired, and now it seemed like I was the only one who had been around when the music position was cut, and probably the only one who understood what that meant for the students. Not that the band and choir were bad. They were respectable for the small groups that they were. I took them to an out-of-state festival, and the head judge was amazed at how well the group performed. "There's no place to hide in this group!" the head judge said. Large bands may have three of four people, maybe more, on a part. However, in my band, almost every student had a singular part that they were responsible for. I rewrote parts as necessary so that every line in the conductor's score was being covered. In an interesting sidebar, as I was planning to take the band and chorus to this out-of-state festival, I heard rumors that some students were planning to travel along with the band and chorus, following the bus in their car. In contrast to my experience in Ansonia, when the principal heard of this, he brought the students involved to his office, and told them in no uncertain terms that if they interfered with a school field trip, they would face disciplinary action. After the students were told this, I heard no more rumors, and did not encounter any problems on the trip, such as I did with Ansonia.

The following year, the superintendent ran into some difficulties. To begin with, she had made some very questionable decisions, and several teachers were openly critical of the direction that the school district seemed to be taking. She had also run up large legal bills because she was consulting with the attorneys for the school district on a very frequent basis. She ended up leaving the school district in the middle of the school year. In most school districts, when this scenario occurs, the normal procedure is to hire a temporary superintendent, a person, usually a retired superintendent, to fill in until a new permanent superintendent is hired. It just so happened that a retired superintendent, who was also a former State Commissioner of Education, agreed to be the temporary superintendent in Lisbon. It was obvious that the temporary superintendent had to immediately deal with a considerable amount of negative feelings both within the faculty, and within the community. His solution was to set up an independent group of prominent citizens, which he called the "Blue Ribbon Commission". This commission was tasked with talking with parents and citizens of the community, as well as interviewing the teachers in every department of the school district. At the end of the process, they were to produce a report that would outline suggested changes and policies. I thought the whole idea was promising, but I had no idea if folks would take the findings of the commission seriously. However, when it was time for the commission to interview the music department, I was ready. I gave a comprehensive outline of what had transpired in the music department of the last several years, since the music teaching position had been cut, and the difficulties of trying to adequately serve the students in music with only two staff members. The commission members listened intently, asked a few questions, and thanked me for sitting down and talking with them. I left the meeting feeling pretty good about what transpired. At least I had managed to get my thoughts on the record. When the report of the commission was released, the restoration of the music teaching position that had been cut several years earlier was listed as a priority. I was pleased, and I noticed that teachers, parents, and community members were taking the report seriously. The situation created what seemed as a groundswell of support for restoring the lost position, and the following year, a new music teacher was hired, and we were now a three-person department again.

It was also at about this time that I was contacted by the National Board of Professional Teaching Standards. They sent me an invitation to participate in a pilot project to develop a system for national certification of music teachers. Ever since the "Nation at Risk" report during the Reagan administration, there had been calls for some type of national teacher certification program. In the late 1980's, the first type of national certification was announced for music teachers by MENC. This was a case where the music educators were leading the rest of the teaching profession. Other areas of education were still getting their act together in terms of this goal, but the music educators were the first to implement it. There were two levels of music teacher certification initially offered by MENC. The first level was referred to as "Nationally Registered Music Educator" in which candidates needed to show certain credentials such as advanced degree or coursework. The second level was referred to as "Nationally Certified Music Educator" and required more evidence from candidates. I opted for the "Nationally Registered" status and ended up being one of four music educators in the state of Maine given MENC certification status the first year it was offered. I earned a "Nationally Registered" pin, which I wore on my jacket at performances and conferences. After several years, the MENC certification program was discontinued for what seemed like political reasons, although the issue was never fully explained. Now, ten years had passed since MENC first offered national certification, and the National Board of Professional Teaching Standards had decided to offer a system of national certification for music teachers. I sent in my application for their pilot project, and in a few weeks received the materials and instructions. Many of the tasks were "reflective" activities where I was supposed to reflect upon what I did in class. In the end, I completed all of the required tasks for the pilot project, but I never applied for the NBPTS music teacher certification once it was offered. I just didn't see the point. Having the MENC "Nationally Registered" status didn't open any doors for me, nor give me any kind of advantage. Why would the NBPTS certification be any different?

In the meantime, my term as Music In Our Schools Month Chair on the Maine Music Educators Executive Board was coming to an end. However, I remained on the Executive Board when I was elected Chairman of MMEA District III. In the Maine Music Educators Association, the state is geographically divided into seven districts. Each of the districts holds events for the schools in their respective districts on a regional basis. For instance, in order to qualify for the State Jazz Festival, my jazz group has to score high enough to qualify at the District III Jazz Festival. I held the chairmanship of District III for four years. In that time, several innovations were introduced to District III activities, and one could make a valid argument that District III be considered the top District in MMEA.

I also started experimenting with a spring trip for band and chorus. It had been several years since I had done such a trip, and I wasn't eager to face the same problems that had occurred on those overnight trips. However, a day trip was something I had been willing to try. The whole thing started at a festival where I had a conversation with one of my fellow music teachers in District III. The teacher, John, was the music teacher at the Islesboro Central School. Islesboro is an island just off the coast by Lincolnville, which is near Rockland. The school itself is quite small. It is the only school on the island and has only about 100 students in grades K-12. John had a great desire to find an activity to bring his students to the mainland. By the time spring arrives, and his students have spent the entire winter on the island, finding a reason to go to the mainland is very desirable. On the other hand, I thought it would be really cool to bring my students on the ferry to the island school to see how the different life on an island was. We got together with a couple of other schools on the mainland and set up a two-phase combined concert featuring the bands and choirs of the participating schools. Phase one would take place at one of the mainland schools, which would give John a chance to give his students a trip off the island, while phase two would consist of a combined concert on

Islesboro. All of the participating schools cleared the dates with their administrations, and the music teachers collectively chose a concert program for the combined groups. The phase one concert took place at a nearby school on a weeknight. We had the students rehearse in the afternoon, and supper was provided for the students. The concert went fine, and I found myself looking forward to the concert on the island of Islesboro. About a week later, it was time for phase two. I arranged for the bus to leave at 6:15 in the morning, figuring that the trip to the Lincolnville Landing, where we would catch the Islesboro ferry would take about 90 minutes, which would give me about 15 minutes to distribute tickets and have the kids transport equipment from the bus. The Islesboro ferry is not a very large boat. It can hold maybe a dozen vehicles, and there are two passenger cabins on each side of the boat that can hold perhaps 50 or so passengers. I instructed the band kids to bring the equipment to the passenger cabin on the port side of the ferry, where we would sit for the trip. The ferry cast off as we were securing the last of the equipment, and I noticed several students were missing. I silently cursed myself. I was giving all of my attention to the band kids in getting all of the equipment on board and secured, I had neglected to give any guidelines to the chorus kids. I knew that everyone had boarded, so that indicated that these students had either gone to the other passenger cabin or were on the deck of the ferry with the vehicles. I did a quick attendance and found that 15 students were not in the cabin. I quickly descended the stairs to the main deck and found my missing students. The first thing I noticed was that 12 or so of the students, all chorus members, and all girls, were right at the bow of the ferry. Now, larger ferries may have a door or some other barrier where vehicles disembark. However, the Islesboro ferry didn't have anything like that. When the

Islesboro ferry pulled in to the landing, vehicles disembarked via the bow of the boat. However, while the boat was moving, the only thing separating the vehicles from the open front of the boat was a single chain. When I spied my chorus girls near the bow, they were pressing against the chain, the only thing stopping them from falling into the water. Oblivious to their own safety, the girls were spaced across the bow, arms extended straight out, just like the movie "Titanic". It was cute, but I felt I needed to move them away from the chain just a little bit. I then surveyed the rest of the deck and found the remaining three or four chorus girls. They were crowded around a pick-up truck on the deck that contained a construction crew, obviously on their way to the island for a building project they had. The guys in the construction crew were trying to pick up the girls. I wasn't worried that they would succeed, but just in case, I meandered over to the pick-up truck. Upon seeing me, the girls walked away from the pick-up without me having to say a word. The guys in the construction crew didn't seem happy, but nobody said anything to me. The rest of the trip went without incident. A short time after we arrived on the island, a bus from the school came to pick us up. The Islesboro Central School is a very unique place. The central part of the building is a former stone mansion that was built atop a seaside cliff. Many years before, the mansion had been donated for use as a school. There had recently been an addition constructed adjacent to the school that contained a gym and a kitchen for preparing student meals, things that the original building apparently lacked. We spent a couple of hours rehearsing the combined groups, and then presented a concert just before lunchtime. The audience consisted of the student body of the school, and about 25 or so island residents. The concert went well, and after it was over, we boarded a school bus for the trip back to the ferry landing. However, there was a delay prior to departure, because we had to wait until the kindergarten students were excused. Two of the five kindergarten students needed to ride the bus with us and be dropped off at their homes before the bus brought us to the ferry landing. The trip was very successful, and John and I repeated the trip with our students, and the other mainland schools, for the next several years.

RESTORING THE CUT AND THE BICENTENNIAL

As the next school year started, the teacher that was hired was a new teacher right out of college. She was a choral major, and therefore it made sense for us to take advantage of that. We now had three teachers, but we had four buildings to cover. We decided that I would continue to cover the high school classes as well as middle school band. The second teacher would cover the general music classes in one elementary school, 5th grade beginning band in both elementary schools, and some of the instrumental lessons at the middle school. The new teacher would teach general music classes in the other elementary school and be the chorus teacher at the middle school. The arrangement worked quite well, and I finally felt that we were able to give adequate instruction in all of the buildings.

In the meantime, we received an email from the superintendent stating that the Town of Lisbon would soon hold its bicentennial celebration, the 200th anniversary of the founding of Lisbon, and each teacher as asked to involve their students in the celebration in some way. For me, this was easy. I composed a march that I titled "The Lisbon Bicentennial March" for the students to perform. I composed the march on two levels, one for the middle school kids, and a more challenging level for the high school kids. I scheduled the "premier" of the piece for our "Lisbon Music Night" concert. Each year, the music teachers prepare performances for their students for this annual concert, in which students of the elementary, middle school and high school perform. The objective was that I had to write it in such a way that the students in both the middle and high school bands could function without rehearsing it together. It wasn't possible to schedule rehearsal time for both groups together. As a result, the first time anyone would hear the full version with all the students present would be the concert itself. When the night of the concert came, I had placed the "Lisbon Bicentennial March" as the last selection on the program. When we played it, there was a small glitch in the percussion section at the beginning, but the rest of the march worked out just fine. The reaction from the audience was wonderful. A lot of townspeople expressed their gratitude for writing the march. What I didn't expect was that the piece would take on a life of its own. A local community band came to Lisbon as part of the bicentennial activities. I was asked to conduct the march with this group. I was a little embarrassed since the march was composed for school kids, not adults. However, the performance went well, and everyone was appreciative. In the summer celebrations, the Maine National Guard Band came to town to do a concert. Unknown to me, the Bicentennial people passed out the music to the march and asked the band to play it. It's good that I wasn't there. I probably would have wanted to crawl under a rock. I'm guessing that the bicentennial folks didn't explain to the band, which included several music teachers that I knew, that this was intended for kids. In addition, the parts were hand-written and my handwriting, be it words or music, is not all that easy to read, especially to sight-read. I never received any comments from the folks that I knew in the National Guard Band, but in an interesting footnote, the bicentennial folks decided to include a copy of the march in a time capsule that was buried at the end of the celebration. I can't even begin to guess what the reaction will be when it is dug up years from now.

As the following school year got underway, I was optimistic. The band was performing quite well, although it was still small, one of the "effects" of teaching short-handed all those years. The Lisbon football team was pretty good that year. Not only that, but I was impressed with the dedication the kids on the team showed. There were several afternoons in the late fall when I ended up working until the supper hour. As I was walking to my car, I could hear the team still practicing. At that point in the afternoon, darkness had fallen. I couldn't see anything, but I could hear them on the practice field, running drills in complete darkness, no lighting of any kind. So it was no surprise to me when the team made it to the state championship football game. However, on the last Saturday before Thanksgiving, which was supposed to be the day of the championship game, there was a major snowstorm. The game was called off and rescheduled for the following Monday afternoon. I wasn't looking forward to this game at all. The weather forecast was not encouraging. There would be no additional snow, but the temperature was expected to drop considerably. When we arrived at the game site, I was alarmed by the situation. The temperature was in the teens, with a significant wind chill that made if feel below zero. In addition, there was 9 inches of snow on the ground and in the bleachers, the snow hadn't been cleared. Once we had figured out where the band would set up, the next task was how to set up a drum set on 9 inches of snow. Some of the kids started jumping off the side of the bleachers from the 3rd or 4th row in order to pack down the snow where the drum set would be set up. Once that was done, the rest of the band set up, but I was still worried about student safety in such cold weather. I arranged for the driver of the band bus to stay with the bus and keep it running with the heater on. Throughout the game, I kept shuttling groups of kids back and forth to the bus to warm up. After half-time, I sent all of the kids to the bus for about a ten-minute break, which I would normally give kids anyway at a game. I shut off the electric bass amplifier, since it would not be used for a while. To their credit, most of the band members returned on time after their 10-minute break, and we were ready to play as the next time-out occurred. I switched on the bass amplifier and played a note. All I heard was a pop from the speaker, which had apparently frozen during the 10-minute break. Lisbon won the game, and I was happy for the kids, but this wasn't an experience that I would ever care to repeat.

A few weeks later, I was summoned to the nurse's room along with four other teachers. The nurse sat us down and started explaining to us about a new student that was transferring into the school. She continued to explain that this student, a girl, apparently was attacked by a teacher at her previous school. The nurse told us that she felt we needed to have this conversation because it seems that the teacher that attacked her had a beard and wore glasses. I looked around the room. All five teachers present were men who wore glasses and had a beard. The nurse went on to explain that this student was placed in all of our classes because of our physical resemblance to the teacher that attacked her, at least as far as glasses and beards were concerned. I was both annoyed and concerned at the same time. Not caring about sparing anyone's feelings, I said, "Who's the genius that came up with this idea?" We were told it was an administrative decision that came from the Special Services office. I was unimpressed. It seemed to me that having this girl in our classes so that she could, in effect, "face her attacker" in five classes a day wasn't just stupid, it was cruel. A couple of days later, this girl entered my chorus class for the first time. About halfway through the class on her first day, she asked to be excused to go to the nurse, and I wrote a pass for her immediately. As it turned out, she never came to my class again, and left the school within the week.

As time went on, things in the middle school took an unfortunate turn. The new choral teacher only stayed a couple of years. She was replaced by another choral major, and even though I thought things were working out great, this teacher only lasted a year. What happened was that in the meantime, the voters of Lisbon approved the construction of a new elementary school to take the place of the two elementary schools that were showing their age and proving to be inadequate. Like all the other departments, the music teachers sat down with the architect, and we made suggestions in terms of what the music facilities should look like in the new building. In the meantime, we also had a new superintendent, and we were unsure of her attitude toward music education. I was disturbed by a speaker she had brought in to give a presentation to teachers. This speaker started making some disparaging remarks about art and music in the curriculum. I called the speaker on it, and I'm guessing the new superintendent wasn't happy about it. Anyway, the new superintendent presided over a celebratory ceremony that was held at the end of the school year since the foundation for the new school had been recently poured. The event included music performed by some elementary students and middle school students. When the ceremony was over, we were encouraged to view the concrete foundation of the new building. I went with the other music teachers to look at the foundation. When we found the spot where the music classrooms would be built, the choral teacher became really distressed. The space allowed for music instruction was considerably smaller than what we thought it would be. The choral teacher's distress turned to panic. "I can't teach in a space this small!" she proclaimed. A few weeks later, we were informed that she had taken another position in another town. The second music teacher also ended up taking a new position in another community.

HAVING DOUBTS

The elementary principals asked me if I would be involved in the interviews to fill both music positions. The first teacher we hired was just out of college, and I was pretty confident that she could do well with both the general music instruction as well as the band program. In the second situation, the choral instructor, I had doubts. This teacher was also just out of college and assured the elementary principal and myself that she could handle the middle school choir. The teacher handled the interview really well, but I had been down this road before, and I was skeptical. The major thing that bothered me in the interview was that this teacher would not admit to having any weaknesses or shortcomings. When I asked her how she would handle a cambiata singer, which is a pre-teen or early teen boy singer whose voice is in the midst of changing. She did not know what a cambiata was, but she assured us she could handle it wonderfully. After the interview, I told the elementary principal that I wasn't totally on board with this candidate. However, the elementary principal was suitably impressed with this teacher, and ended up hiring her.

It didn't take long for problems to start once the school year got underway. Almost immediately, it was clear that this choral teacher was not suited to teach middle school chorus. Students were complaining to me, but I wasn't sure what I could do. In the meantime, this teacher started complaining to the administration that her teaching schedule was too difficult. I knew that this was hogwash, and I checked with other music teachers in the area to compare our elementary class schedule with theirs. In all cases, the Lisbon elementary music teacher schedules were the lightest of all the schools in the area. However, this teacher kept complaining that her schedule was too difficult and managed to convince her principal of this. A couple of weeks later, the superintendent handed down a decision that removed the choral teacher from teaching middle school chorus, and of course, who was commanded to take over the middle school chorus? Me, no surprise, and with no relief to my teaching schedule. Middle school chorus was simply added onto the schedule I already had. I complained to the middle school principal, who was in her first year. She was a musician herself, and I think she understood when I explained that we would now have to compress the middle school band lesson schedule due to the superintendent's decision.

Meanwhile, at the high school, things were going well. I received a flier from the University of Maine announcing a clinic day with a special guest composer. The guest composer was David Shaffer, a nationally known band composer. The guidelines specified that each participating band would play a piece of their choice, and a piece composed by David Shaffer. Mr. Shaffer would also act as a clinician with each group. I really wanted my band to have this experience, but the small size of the band would compromise the experience. Clinicians tend to make their judgments on how well the band is able to replicate the music in the full score of the piece. Because of the incomplete instrumentation of my group, a lot of the parts in the score would go unplayed. However, I wasn't prepared to give up on this idea so quickly. I contacted the band director at the University of Maine and asked if it would be possible for university students to sit in with my band covering the parts that the band wasn't able to play. For instance, there were three trumpet parts in the piece, but I only had two trumpets. I also had no tenor saxophone player, no bass clarinet player, no baritone horn player, etc. When I explained what I wanted to do, the UMaine band director was

212

agreeable, and I started making preparations. I chose the David Shaffer piece "Bravada Esprit", and the Bach Prelude and Fugue in Bb as my two pieces. On the day of the clinic, I brought the band to the University of Maine where the students spent the morning in master classes on their various instruments. After lunch, the band performances began. I watched the first band perform. The judges were fairly hard on the band, and I started to wonder "Hell, what have I gotten into?" After the first band was finished, it was time for the Lisbon band to go into warm-ups. I knew I had only a limited time of 20 minutes or so to facilitate everyone being comfortable playing together, both my 25-piece band, and the additional 15 or so university students covering the rest of the instrumentation. I spent a lot of time explaining to the university students my approach to the music, and my interpretation and style expectations. At the end of the warm-up time, we were escorted to the auditorium, where we performed for Mr. Shaffer. When we were finished, I tried to appear as the vision of equanimity, in order to hide my concern that I might hear a string of critical comments. To my surprise, Mr. Shaffer made no negative critical comments about the performance. In fact, he told us a story that when he performed "Bravada Esprit" with his band at a festival, one of the judges was very critical, saying that the tempo that Shaffer conducted the piece was too slow. "How can it be too slow?" Shaffer argued with the judge, "I wrote the piece!" As we started packing up, one of the university students that played with my band took me aside. He said "Thank you for doing this today. There were 90 kids in my high school band, but I have to say that I learned more from you today than I did in my four years of high school". I was surprised by this comment, but extremely pleased. It made all the aggravation that I had to put up with, worth it.

A few weeks later, several of us on the MMEA Executive Board went to the State Capitol for what was called a "Music in the Schools" Day, and distributed leaflets to legislators. As we were finishing up, the State President, who was in the last year of her term, took me aside, and said, "I just wanted you to know that you are on my short list for State President. It's something I want you to think about".

Meanwhile, as the year progressed, the middle school principal appeared to be taking my concerns to heart. At first, I thought this was a positive development. I had no idea it was going to backfire on me. She developed a plan to comprehensively change how music instruction was done in her school. At that point, I was spending about a third of my teaching time in the middle school, while the elementary band director covered a few other classes each week. That amounted to the comparable teaching time of about a half-time teaching position. The plan of the principal increased this to a full-time position. This was a pleasant surprise. I knew this principal wanted a successful music program in her school and this would certainly help. I was even more impressed when she shared with me the details of her plan. Many years before, when I first started working with band students at the middle school, a trend emerged in education called "middle school concept". The idea behind it was that most middle school and junior high schools at the time were simply duplicating the approach of high schools in their class formats. Middle school concept believed that the format structure of classes could be adjusted to better serve students of that age group. On paper, it seemed like a good concept, and I was willing to approach it with an open mind. However, as I watched other schools around me implement middle school concept, a very disturbing trend emerged. Performing groups such as band and choir were not taken into

214

consideration in the development of this concept. In fact, I became alarmed when it appeared that middle school concept had the effect of decimating membership in performing groups. Many schools saw the membership in their bands and choirs drop by 50% or more when their school adopted middle school concept. The head of the middle school principals' association waived off such concerns, saying that the needs of musicians could well be met in general music classes. In fact, he stressed the general music classes were more important than band or chorus because they served all of the students in contrast to band and chorus, that served only a percentage of the students. Now, I don't know who came up with this idea, but they should get a medal for stupidity. To best study music, one must be an active participant in it. Music has to be pursued as the discipline that it is. You can't get that from listening to a recording in a general music class. It's like trying to coach a baseball team by having the players only watching videos. Steering students away from band and chorus into general music makes for a neatly packaged class schedule that serves the administrators well. However, the students are short-changed. So, I spent many years teaching middle school students, but being totally unimpressed with middle school concept. What was so impressive about the middle school principal's plan in Lisbon was that music would be grouped with other classes into what can be best described as an elective course block. Rather than limit their instruction in a class to a few weeks of the school year, such as was the case with exploratory courses such as art or health, classes in the elective block would run the entire school year. I had been advocating for a plan such as this for many years, but my ideas fell on deaf ears. Now it appeared that this could become a reality. The superintendent seemed unimpressed however. I never saw any indications of her support for this plan, one way or the other. It appeared that the responsibility of "selling" this plan to the school board and the community fell to the middle school principal. However, she was more than up for the task, meeting with the school board, she first managed to get their support for the plan. She then took to the floor at Town Meeting, where the school budget is voted on, and explained her plan to the town's voters, who also voted in favor of the plan. I was elated. Now, I thought, we would have a full-time teacher in the middle school addressing the needs of that building, while in the high school, I could expand my course load to cover classes that we had long been neglecting due to my time at the middle school. However, that's not what occurred. The superintendent came up with a ruling that while the middle school music position would be full time, the high school music position would not. At the same time, she announced that she would pursue a policy of building based instructors and minimize the number of teachers that taught in multiple buildings. The effect of this was that I was offered a "choice". I could take the full-time teaching position at the middle school or be a half-time teacher in the high school. This, of course, was no choice. I had a family with kids in high school, looking at college, and being a half-time teacher wasn't an option. I have long wondered what prompted the superintendent to make these rulings. In the short time that she had been in Lisbon, she had acquired a reputation among the teachers for vindictiveness. The middle school principal had messed with "her" budget, at least partially on my prompting. She well could have blamed me for the whole thing. In some ways, her ruling didn't make a lot of sense. One should always place their teachers where they are at their strongest. At this point I had almost 20 years experience in teaching high school. The high school level was my teaching strength. My time teaching middle school was a mere fraction in comparison. In addition, to expect a half-time teacher to adequately address all the needs of the high school program seemed at best, a reach. I tried to impress this upon the superintendent in my meeting with her. She waived it off saying, "Call me optimistic". And what about the elementary music teacher that caused this mess in the first place? She left Lisbon after one year, taking a similar position in a nearby town. When I talked to friends of mine who also taught in this town, they told me that in no uncertain terms, that as a music staff, they sat her down, and set her straight when she tried to pull the same whining about her schedule there.

It now appeared that I would be destined to be the middle school music teacher. As the school year was ending, many high school staff members expressed their sorrow at my leaving, saying they would miss me, and how unfair the situation was. After the high school graduation, the high school principal came up to me and expressed similar feelings. "I've seen you get blood out of a stone" he said. In a short time however, something interesting developed. The high school in the town where I lived, and where my children attended school, had an opening for a high school band director. Wouldn't it be cool, I thought, if I taught in a school where my own kids were in the band program. I had already updated my resume and references, so I applied for the position. The interview was not a typical interview. I knew most of the people on the interview committee, so it wasn't a case of having to show that I could do the job. The question was more along the line of how well I could fit in with the staff, and the academic climate of the school. The interview went all right, although not as well as I had hoped it would. I did not get the position, but later, I found out why. Now it must be understood that this information that was given to me was at best third hand. However, as I understand it, I was one of two finalists for the position. The other finalist was a woman from a school district some distance away. I'm told that after the interviews, the committee struggled to reach a decision. At that point, it seems that a member of the committee, who was the assistant principal, and former music teacher, stated that for more than a hundred years, there had been a band at this school taught only by male band directors, and she felt that perhaps it was now time for a female. It was very disappointing. I never mind losing out to a more qualified candidate, but to my knowledge, this was the first time I ended up not being hired for a position because I'm a male.

THE DIRIGO EXPERIENCE

Toward the end of the summer, another opening for a high school music teacher developed. I knew I had a very good shot at this position because the band had participated in the state marching band competitions for the last several years, and it seemed that bringing in a director who could continue this practice appeared to be a priority. The name of the school was Dirigo High School. For those unfamiliar with the name, Dirigo is Maine's state motto. It is Latin for "I lead". I attended an interview and was offered the position. Unfortunately, I wasn't able to accept. There were two major problems that were non-starters for me. As I went through the interview, I learned that although continuing the marching band program was highly desirable, the band itself was very small, just 11 members. After asking a few probing questions I found out why. Whenever one sees a small high school band, the problem is rarely with the high school itself. The problem is usually with the program infrastructure in the lower grades. In this case, the middle school band program was structured in a very poor manner. Students could only receive band instruction once a week, when they could be excused from their general music class. I told the interview committee that quite frankly, there was no way that this could make for a successful program. However, the middle school principal, who was a member of the interview committee, displayed no willingness to change the situation. The second issue was a non-musical one, but also important. The teachers of this school district were not enrolled in standard health plans, but instead needed to subscribe to an HMO. My wife, the nurse, found this to be completely unacceptable. It was unfortunate, but there was no way to make this work. However, in the course of the interview, I found out that the students were engaged in pre-season marching band rehearsals. Even though they had no band director, even though the band had a fairly unsuccessful last few years in competition, the kids were in rehearsals, led by a couple of college kids, giving up summer vacation time in order to prepare for the new marching band season. I had to admire the dedication of these kids, but another thought came to me that seemed foreboding. Without a band director, would these kids even be able to have a season? Also, even if they attempted to compete, how successful could they be? That prospect really shook me, and I couldn't stop thinking about it. Then a thought came to me. What if I could direct the group on an after-school basis? If I could convince the school principal to hire me on what is called a co-curricular basis, this could work.

When I talked to the principal, and outlined this idea, he agreed. There were two college kids that instructed the color guard, but I also needed a percussion instructor to round out the staff. I contacted Rick, a drum instructor who had worked with me at the 20th Maine Regiment and invited him to be part of the staff. And so, two days a week, after school got out in Lisbon, I would get in my car and drive to Dirigo, where I would run a three-hour rehearsal.

In the meantime, my first couple of weeks in my new position of middle school music instructor, it was a struggle. It was difficult to adjust to middle school kids, having taught high school for so many years. I found the kids to be immature and mouthy. Then came September 11. The day started out quite normally. I didn't find out about the terrorist attacks until lunchtime. The principal decided to share information with staff members only on an "as needed" basis, so as not to alarm students, or disrupt classes. As I was in the lunchroom, and various staff members were discussing what was going on, the Spanish teacher entered the room. This teacher was just out of college, and in her first year of teaching. She knew her stuff, was fluent in multiple languages, and the kids really liked her. I remember being impressed when I saw her sharing tips with the other foreign language teacher, who was a veteran of several years. The Spanish teacher listened to the conversation, obviously the first she heard about the events in New York and Washington, as she did what most teachers do during this time, checking her mailbox and preparing her lunch. All of a sudden, she froze, completely, and it was obvious that something was wrong. "My parents are flying today" she said in a quiet voice, and she quickly left the lunchroom. The following morning, we did not start classes immediately. The principal had assigned two teachers to every classroom, so that we could help students deal with what had happened. I was paired with an 8th grade math teacher in one of the classrooms as the principal started the day speaking on the intercom, giving an overview of events, and informing everyone that our Spanish teacher had lost her parents in one of the plane crashes. We talked to the students. Some of them had comments, others had questions. During this process, we were not music teachers, or math teachers, or English teachers, etc. We were just teachers, trying to help kids cope with a frightening event.

The next evening, at Dirigo, there was some talk about 9/11, but not a lot, although I heard from another band director that his marching band rehearsal at his school became completely disrupted when a military jet, that was obviously on patrol, flew at a low altitude over their practice field. At Dirigo, no such incident took place, and the kids were responding really well to me and my approach. Unfortunately, I faced a problem. One of the college students that had run the summer rehearsals was also writing the marching designs for the show. It was now the week before the first competition, and we still did not have the final charts to finish the marching show. I decided that enough was enough and composed a set of formations on the spot to finish the show. This gave the group a completed show going into the first competition. This didn't always happen with some bands, and at Dirigo, starting the year with an unfinished show was historically a frequent happening. At the school my kids attended, where I was passed over for Band Director, their band had to drop out of the first competition because their show was not finished yet. But with parent help with key issues, Dirigo was ready. Parents took on such roles as fitting the kids for their uniforms, helping to transport and organize equipment, and acting as additional chaperones on the bus. The community support was evident. On the day of the first competition, there was a spaghetti supper held for the band at the local firehouse before they traveled to the show. When we arrived at the show site, parents and students took the equipment off the bus, and we began preparations for the show. I did a music warm-up with the students, as well as a marching warm-up. Dirigo was the first band to perform. I sent the kids out on the field, and I sat in the bleachers. I wanted to be able to observe the band from the time they first came into sight, until they left the field. I had a lot of confidence in the kids that they all knew what to do, I just wasn't sure the judges would appreciate it.

The kids performed, and the show went quite well. I was fairly satisfied as I watched the band leave the field. I headed out of the stadium, and toward the bus parking area. As I approached the bus, I noticed a number of parents standing around the bus. Several of them appeared to be crying. "Oh Hell!" I thought. "It's only the first show of the season and already there are problems!" When I got near the bus, the parents noticed me, walked over to me and started hugging me. What I thought were tears of distress were actually tears of joy. They told me that in their memories, this was the first time that Dirigo went into the first competition with a completed show. Not only that, but they told me that they had never seen the band perform so well. They continued to thank me for instructing the students. I was awed by this outpouring of thanks and support. It may have only been an 11-piece band, but to those 11 kids and their parents, it was a big deal. The marching band circuit had made some changes in their scoring system that year. Instead of scoring bands from 1 to 100 in head-to-head competition, the judges instead gave ratings to the bands. Bands were rated from one star to four stars in several categories, marching, music, color guard, drum major, percussion, and general effect. Dirigo received a rating of two stars in every category that night. I was extremely pleased. When judges start off their season, and the band performing first in the opening show of the season is an

11-piece band, and yet the judging panel gives them a two-star rating across the board, that's significant. Judges are historically careful at the beginning of the season to keep their scores on the low side. Bands will improve throughout the season, and it only makes sense that judges don't score bands too high in the beginning of the season. Otherwise, as bands improve, judges will have "boxed their numbers in", and be unable to have their scores reflect the true growth of the bands as the season goes on. And there's no question that Dirigo would improve. It was just a question of how much. I also received a number of compliments from other band directors as the season went on. When Terry, the bugle instructor that I worked with at 20th Maine Regiment saw the band, I'm told that he commented that he didn't think it was possible to produce a better presentation for an 11-piece band than what we were able to accomplish with Dirigo. Another band director, Tom, who was a judge and also heavily involved in drum and bugle corps, also commented along the same line. Judges who were long time veterans, with service not just in years, but in decades, told me that I was doing all the right things. At the final show of the season, conveniently known as "the finals", bands were awarded gold, silver, and bronze medals to reflect their scores. Dirigo was awarded a silver medal, and individual silver medals were distributed to all the band and color guard members, as well as the staff. Unfortunately, that was the last of my involvement with Dirigo. During the marching band season, the school district hired another music teacher to take over at the high school, and this teacher was not interested in continuing the marching band tradition there. However, my silver medal from the finals hangs at my bedside, where it has been ever since the medals ceremony. I smile every time I see it.

THE MIDDLE SCHOOL SAGA

In the meantime, I was getting a better footing at the middle school. I was impressed at how much progress I was making with the band, now that I was seeing them every day as a class. Hell, this was better than a clinician program! Not only that, but my jazz band in the middle school was turning out to be an excellent group. When it was time for the jazz festivals, I went out and purchased special T-shirts for the jazz band. We went to the District III Jazz Festival and stunned everyone. The band then performed at the State Jazz Festival, receiving a standing ovation. While things were going really well in the middle school, things were not going so well at the high school. For one thing, the half-time teacher that took my place in the high school refused to do several of the offerings and activities that I carried out when I was there, that apparently many students and staff took for granted. He ended up resigning halfway through the school year. The problems that I had predicted when I talked to the superintendent were coming true. So much for her "Call me optimistic" comment. Now, the high school had no music teacher, and the high school principal was calling me, asking me if I would please take over the high school jazz band through the jazz season. My first instinct was to say "no". The superintendent had set up this situation, and it would only be fitting for her to lie in the bed that she had made. But then, I thought through the situation some more. Now that things had turned out the way that I had predicted, the stage was set. It was going to be necessary for the superintendent to ask for the high school music position to be increased from half time, to full-time. I thought that perhaps my jumping in and helping with the high school jazz band might create some goodwill when it came time for them to hire for the position. Plus, the students in the jazz band had been my students the previous year. I didn't want to see them fail when they entered the jazz festivals. And so, I went ahead and took over the high school jazz band. I had high hopes for them at the State Jazz Festival. However, during their performance, one of the kids skipped a section of the music, and the group was in disarray while they struggled to get everyone on the same page. The rest of the performance went well, but the damage was done.

As the end of the year approached, the superintendent went into the town meeting with the proposed school budget. One of the increases that she was asking for was the funding to increase the high school music teaching position from one-half time, to full-time. As justification for asking for the additional funding, she outlined a plan where the high school would establish a music requirement for graduation that each student would have to satisfy. During discussions, one of the voters raised his hand asking why it was necessary to establish a music requirement for high school students when there wasn't one for middle school students. The point was well taken. Band and chorus were offered in the middle school, but they were elective courses. I was not at the town meeting, but from what I'm told, the superintendent was caught by surprise by this question. However, after a short pause, she announced that there would be general music classes at the middle school the next year. Her budget passed, but that created a dilemma for me. I was hoping I could be transferred into the now full-time position at the high school, but if that didn't work out, I would be faced with creating a 6th grade general music class with no budget, no curriculum, no equipment, no textbook, etc. When it came time to fill the high school position, the superintendent ruled that I had to go through the interview process, just like everyone else. This was incredibly unfair. I had seen other teachers receive transfers within the school system simply by asking. I didn't understand why I was the victim of this double standard. I applied for the position anyway and was passed over. The union saw the unfairness of this and launched a protest. Unfortunately, the protest went nowhere, and I now faced another year of teaching in the middle school. However, there was one bright spot at the end of the year. I was elected President-Elect of the Maine Music Educators Association.

The following year started out ok, but I just couldn't shake a feeling of foreboding that I felt. I had fashioned a curriculum for the 6th grade general music classes, and things seemed to be going well. There was one student in the 6th grade general music class that I noticed was getting into major discipline difficulties in other classes, but in my class, he was fine. However, it seems that in other classes, he was proving to be a fairly difficult student. He was sent to the office from other classes on almost a daily basis and was suspended from school on multiple occasions. When Parents Conference night came, I took a break about halfway through my conferences to go to the bathroom. As I was walking down the hallway, I heard someone call "Mr. Judd!" I turned, and saw a father with his son, the 6th grade student that had been in so much trouble in his other classes, but not in mine. The father said to me "You may not remember me, but I had you for guitar class when I went to high school." He was right. Although he looked familiar, I couldn't remember his name. He then said, "I told my son that you were the coolest teacher, and that he better behave in your class." I assured him that was the case, and he started talking about his experience in my guitar class years before when he was in high school. He described the class in very glowing terms, and I was starting to become very impressed with myself. I then said to him "So, you got a lot out of my class then?" "No," he replied, "You flunked me!

but I deserved it. I was really goofing off in those days." I thanked him and went off to do the rest of my conferences.

In the meantime, the middle school principal appeared to be under a lot of pressure. She was very professional and did not share any of the details of her difficulties, but it was clear that something wasn't right, and it was real easy for me to assume that the pressure she was experiencing was coming from the superintendent. Toward the end of the fall, she announced that she was leaving for an assistant superintendent position in a nearby town. I was sorry to see her go. On the basis of the changes that she had made that had benefited the music program, I nominated her for the MMEA administrator of the year award. She was not chosen as the winner, but I considered my nomination of her to be an acknowledgment of the good that she had done for my program. The only problem now was whether her successor would appreciate that work as well. One could not argue with the results. The middle school band membership was now up to 55 students, and they sounded great. It was a far cry from all those years when I had to struggle with a pull-out program where kids could only attend band rehearsal if they gave up their recess. The middle school jazz band was just outstanding, and I was looking forward to the jazz festival season. The principal was succeeded by the new assistant principal, who had just gotten into administration, and who I found to be fairly unimpressive. However, I was willing not to be judgmental and have an open mind as the school year continued.

However, I didn't spend a lot of time dwelling on the situation in light of my new duties as MMEA President-Elect. The major issue in those days, was that it was the responsibility of the President-Elect to plan and run the Maine All-State Music Festival. This was something I had to learn on the fly. Fortunately, the previous experience I had running

227

festivals served me well. In the All-State festival structure, there is the Festival Director, which was me, as well as Managers of the various performing groups, the All-State Band, All-State Chorus, and the All-State Orchestra. A lot of the planning is done along with the State President, who in those days was responsible for running the annual MMEA State Teachers Conference, a series of clinics and master classes for the music teachers that ran concurrent with the All-State Music Festival. As we were in the midst of planning for the festival at the MMEA Executive Board meeting in the winter, the All-State Orchestra manager brought up an issue with that group. It seems that the percussionists in the orchestra only had music assignments for one of the Orchestra pieces. The remaining pieces on the Orchestra program had no percussion parts. The Orchestra manager was concerned about the percussion players coming to the All-State Festival and only performing on one piece. Not only was it an under-utilization of their abilities, but it would leave them with a lot of time doing nothing during the two days of rehearsals. The Orchestra manager asked if it would be possible to include some percussion ensemble music in the program so that the orchestra percussionists would have a chance to perform on an equal basis with the rest of the musicians, and still remain active when they were not needed in the Orchestra rehearsals. The Executive Board agreed to extend the performing time of the orchestra an extra 10 minutes at the All-State concert for the percussion ensemble music. However, at the Executive Board meeting a couple of months later, I became alarmed as we were updated on plans for the percussion ensemble music at the festival. This project now appeared to be taking on a life of its own. I found out that a conductor had been hired for the percussion ensemble music, and that the music that this conductor had chosen contained multiple percussion parts way beyond what three percussionists could handle. The Orchestra manager suggested that teachers be utilized for the remaining percussion parts. As far as I was concerned, this was all well and good for teachers who wanted to improve their percussion skills, but clearly, this wasn't something that I voted for or approved of. As the festival approached, I didn't think much about the percussion ensemble issue. There were some improvements in the registration and organizational process that I was looking to implement. When the day of the festival arrived, I was ready. Things went relatively smooth. An added bonus was that my daughter, now in high school, made the All-State Chorus, and would be singing in this festival. As the festival proceeded, there were a few glitches, but nothing that anyone would have been able to anticipate. On the last day of the festival, the schedule was cut and dried. The performing groups would rehearse in the morning, and there would be concerts in the afternoon and evening. The afternoon concert started out ok, but then several things occurred that threw the schedule off. To begin with, the conductor of the All-State Band insisted on announcing each band selection during their performance. His talking was excessive, and what should have been a 25-minute performance ended up being stretched to 45 minutes. Then the All-State Orchestra performed, with the percussion ensemble music added on. What was supposed to be a 10-minute percussion ensemble presentation turned into a 30-minute performance. I wasn't happy, and we ended up having to delay the start of the evening concert in order to give everyone a chance to get supper.

In the meantime, an interesting situation was taking shape in Lisbon. Every year for as long as I had been in Lisbon, the music department held what was known as "Lisbon Music Night" every spring. The event included band and choir performances by all of the groups in the elementary, middle, and high schools. Normally, the concert would start off with the elementary band, followed by the middle school chorus, band, and jazz band. Finally, the high school groups would perform, which was supposed to be the highlight of the evening. However, this time around, the evening did not play out that way. Now that I was working with the middle school kids for my second year with a proper middle school music class schedule, the middle school band was nothing short of impressive. The middle school jazz band was stellar also, but that created a situation where the high school groups could not eclipse the performances of the middle school. The audience was cheering the middle school groups, while the high school groups only received polite applause. It wasn't anything that I had intended to happen, it just sort of worked out that way. I knew the woman that was hired over me to fill the high school position. She was a competent music teacher and had met with success in other music programs. But while she needed to spend her first year developing relationships with the high school students and allowing them to get used to her teaching style, I didn't have to worry about those things, and I was able to take the middle school groups to a performance level that I believe had never been obtained before in the history of the school. At the Memorial Day Parade, the same issue occurred. The middle school band was impressive, looked sharp, and sounded great, while the same could not be said for the high school band.

As the new school year approached, my daughter came to me and told me that there was an opening for a percussion instructor for her high school marching band. I wanted to be able to say I was interested, but I was a bit concerned. After all, this was the band director position that I was passed over for a woman a couple of years earlier. If we could both get past that, it could work, so I decided to give it a try. Things didn't start particularly well. To begin with, there was some resentment from some of the drummers at my presence. I never knew what had prompted the previous percussion instructor to leave, but some of the kids were obviously having a hard time with it. In addition, I didn't care for the percussion assignments. There were too many snare drummers on the field, and not enough bass drummers. I made the appropriate changes immediately, which did not go over well with the drummers. They went to the band director, and to her credit, she defended me and told them that the change was my decision as percussion instructor, and she would honor it. As rehearsals progressed, the drum line was doing well, and besides addressing any mistakes that might occur in the music, I also helped work on their marching formations. The band went into their first competition and did reasonably well. One of the judges that night was Tom, one of the band directors who had been so complimentary to me for the work that I had done with Dirigo. In the judges' critique, which took place after the show that evening, the staff of each school was called in to the judges room, one school at a time, to allow the staff to ask questions, or to allow the judges to expand on previous comments. As one of the judges, Tom was talking to the band director that I was working with about various details that occurred during the band's performance in the show. As the critique was winding down, he said to the band director "There's one thing that I am strongly recommending that you do" With that, he took her by the hand, and led her over to me, where I was sitting off to the side. Pointing to me, he said, "Whatever this man tells you to do, do it!" As the season went on, the drum line improved as well as the band. At the state finals, the drum line seemed satisfied that their score matched the drum line score from the previous year.

Meanwhile, in Lisbon, I should have been happy, or at least optimistic. We now had a music staff of four full-time teachers, and we were covering more of the curriculum than we ever had. but I wasn't feeling that way. On the plus side, my activities with the Maine Music Educators Association proved to be a great distraction. I attended the MENC national conference as President-Elect of MMEA. Today, the music teachers' national professional organization for music teachers is NAfME, the National Association for Music Education. However, in those days, the organization was known as MENC, the Music Educators National Conference. At any rate, I attended several clinics and master classes at the national conference in Minneapolis. Observed a meeting of the MENC Eastern Division Executive Board, went to an open rehearsal of the Minneapolis Symphony Orchestra, and several other events. But the most significant event that I was involved with occurred when I was the Maine Delegate to the International Symposium of Music Education. I met several of the top experts in music education, had dinner with some of them and had some really great conversations. I found the symposium interesting in that I learned about how music is taught in all parts of the world. A lot of the focus was on the future of music education throughout the world, but I learned that while some countries do things better than we do in America, a whole lot of countries do things worse.

NEW PRINCIPAL, NEW PROBLEMS

While I had a great experience in Minneapolis, in Lisbon, not so much. I was concerned about the direction the school system seemed to be taking. Previous superintendents that I had worked under in Lisbon regularly sought teacher input, trying to reach consensus whenever possible. However, this superintendent had a top-down management style that I found troubling. I then noticed that this approach had worked its way down to the individual building administrators as well. In the middle school, the main problem that I had with this was that the new principal seemed compelled to act as one who knew all the answers, when in fact any teacher with moderate experience would know that this was just an act. The previous principal, the one that had implemented a full-time middle school music teacher, was a musician, was knowledgeable, and knew what kind of support a music program needed in order to be successful. Unfortunately, when it came to music education, this current principal was clueless, but he would never admit to it. He insisted on talking to the audience before each concert, but when he did, he never talked about the kids performing, or their achievements in music. Instead, he talked about upcoming school events and school issues. In the spring, as we were planning for the following school year, the principal informed me that there were going to be major changes in my schedule. The superintendent apparently commanded that all middle school students would be required to take French or Spanish classes during the elective course block. Since band and chorus classes were held during the elective course block, this meant that the band and chorus students would no longer be able to have daily classes, but that we would have to go back to a pull-out type of program for music that I struggled with for so many years. Clearly, the superintendent was manipulating me, but towards what end? That became clear when the principal informed me that the following school year, I would be teaching general music classes to the 7th and 8th grades. Of course, now I understood

233

what happened. The problem with top-down management is that many times the person at the top will make decisions that will make his or her life easier, while creating difficulties for those underneath them. In a normal middle school concept, the students attend "specialist" classes. In Lisbon, these classes were called "Exploratory" classes, and the middle school students originally attended Physical Education, Art, Health, and Computer classes as their exploratories, spending one quarter of the school year in each class. For instance, a student might possibly have Art classes every day for a quarter of the year. In the 2nd quarter, they might attend Health classes, Physical Education the 3rd quarter, and Computer class the 4th quarter. A couple of years previous, when the school district ran into some budget problems, the computer teacher was moved to the elementary school, and the middle school was left with only three exploratory subjects. This made things difficult for grading purposes, because the exploratories needed to be graded in trimesters in comparison to the other classes that were graded each quarter. The principal cited falling music enrollments in band and chorus for these changes, but everyone could see that this excuse was completely bogus. Assigning me to teach general music classes was his way to get back to four exploratory classes. His life would be easier, but the effects would be quite negative for the band and chorus students, as well as myself. The superintendent put her stamp on the plan with her French and Spanish directive, even though none of the teachers had ever made that recommendation, and in fact seemed puzzled by it. I'm guessing she was motivated to do this because it would become impossible to maintain the same level of excellence that I had been able to accomplish with the band and chorus over the previous three years. The music groups would not be able to perform as strongly, and whatever embarrassment she may have experienced after the mess she made at the high school would erode, thereby making her life easier.

But there was more. It was decided that I needed to teach 5th and 6th grade general music classes at the elementary school. I don't know why this was necessary, after all, there were two full-time music teachers at the elementary school. In addition, they scheduled me to teach a 1st grade general music class. Now this was tantamount to educational malpractice. I hadn't taught a first-grade general music class since I was a junior in college. I pointed this out, but my protests fell on deaf ears. In a related development, the Lisbon High School principal did not renew the contract of the high school music teacher, thereby firing her. I interviewed for the high school position once again, but, no surprise, I was passed over again. Clearly, I needed to leave Lisbon, but the number of opportunities appeared to be dwindling.

I applied for a lot of positions, but I didn't get a lot of interviews. The reason for this was obvious. By this time, I had taught music for almost 30 years. That would put me near the top of the pay scale in most school systems. The sad truth was that most school administrators either did not value music enough to hire a teacher of my experience or did not have the financial resources to do so. However, there was one band director opening that I thought I had a good shot at. I was invited to interview for a high school band director position in a town on the Maine coast. Tom, the band judge who told the band director from my daughter's school that she should do whatever I said, had been the band director at this school several years before, and there was a very respectable program still in place at the school. I went to the interview and did quite well. I got the impression that I was their top candidate. As I was leaving, the principal told me to stay near my phone that afternoon, which was when the successful candidate would be notified. So I sat by my phone, but no call came. I found out later that a member of the school board commanded the principal and interview committee to set aside their choice, and for budgetary reasons, hire a teacher just out of college.

When the next school year started, there certainly was cause for me to be miserable. Instead of teaching music at the high school, it seemed as if I was headed in the opposite direction. I was now teaching grades 5-8 general music, as well as a first-grade music class. The band and chorus at the middle school had been relegated to nothing more than window dressing, with rehearsals being held in the morning, a couple of times a week, for about 30 minutes. However, there was another side of me that viewed all of this as a challenge. Other music teachers might fall to pieces with such a shift in their jobs, but I was determined not to. I consulted with Jonathan, who was a new elementary music teacher in Lisbon. Now, I should mention that Jonathan had studied extensively with the national leading experts in early childhood music education. He went on to be quite an expert himself and presented seminars at many state music educator conferences in several states, including Texas. I was quite rusty when it came to teaching elementary students, but Jonathan knew the most recent trends and approaches in teaching young students. With his help, I developed a comprehensive set of lesson plans for the 5th and 6th grade classes. As for the middle school, I decided that a hands-on approach would be the most effective for the general music classes. I found a relatively low-cost electric piano sold at Radio Shack, that had an on-board sequencer. A sequencer digitally records what is played on the keyboard and has multiple tracks so that one can produce an entire orchestration. I wanted to use the keyboards to teach a unit in music composition to the students. The principal, however, would not approve the budget request to obtain enough keyboards and earphones for the class, so I used the money from the music fundraisers in order to purchase the keyboards I needed. I also asked for additional electric outlets in the music room to accommodate the instruments. This was also denied. Apparently, the principal felt that general music classes should simply consist of my putting on a record and telling the class to be quiet. How out of touch could an administrator possibly be? Fortunately, the Radio Shack keyboards could also be operated on batteries, so I purchased enough batteries for all of the keyboards. As might be expected, once classes got underway, a number of students did wonderfully well with the keyboards, while others struggled. I realized this was a process that I would have to refine as time went on. As to my 1st grade class, I decided just to have fun with them and see where things led. The 5th grade classes went fairly well, but I experienced a lot of difficulties with the 6th grade classes. It seemed only logical that if I had to teach elementary general music, it made the most sense to teach classes in the older grades because I was more likely to relate to kids in those grades as compared to younger kids. Of course, the flip side of this issue is that the most discipline problems are likely to occur with the older grades. In this case, there were several 6th graders that were quite good at creating distractions in class. Now, I don't expect every kid to like general music class, however, I do expect everyone to behave. I sent more kids out of class and to the office for behavior reasons, than any place I had ever taught. The problem was that the issue was not confined to my class. Many times, I would send a student to the office due to behavior, only to have that student return to my class a few minutes later. The reason? It seems that there were times when there were so many 6th graders sent to the office for bad behavior from other classrooms, that there was no room in the office for them all. Subsequent misbehaving kids were simply sent back to class. As was expected, the middle school band and chorus were running smoothly, but the progress the students were making was not anywhere near the progress they were making the previous year, when they had a full class schedule. When performances came, however, their performances were still quite respectable. The middle school jazz band was still stellar, and if anyone thought that the program would fall to pieces because of the severe reduction in class time, they were quite mistaken.

MR. PRESIDENT

Once again, Maine Music Educators Association presented a welcome distraction for me. I was now in my first year as State President. When making such a commitment to MMEA, a person has to serve two years as President-Elect, two years as President, and two years as Executive Vice-President. Along with the duties of the office, the State President also serves on the MENC Eastern Division Executive Board. The MENC Eastern Division consists of all the northeastern states, as well as the District of Columbia, and Europe. Why Europe? There are several American music educators that teach in schools on military bases, and American-run schools throughout Europe. That group of music educators is also represented through the MENC Eastern Division. The Eastern Division oversees activities for its members such as an Eastern Division teachers' conference, and an honors festival for students that is known as the All-Eastern Festival. The Eastern Division Executive Board meets three times a year, in the spring, summer, and fall. The spring and summer meetings were generally held in conjunction with conferences, but the fall meeting was held within the Eastern Division, usually hosted by one of the member states delegations. During my first year as President, the site of the Eastern Division Executive Board meeting was in Europe, at a military base just outside of Venice. Not only was MMEA paying the cost of my travel, but the President of the European delegation asked me if I would give a presentation at their conference, which was scheduled during the same time as the Eastern Division Meeting. It seems that many of the bands in the American schools in Europe are fairly small, and most of the music programs there utilize an electric bass with their bands because they have no tuba player. When the European President found out that I was a bass player, he asked me if I would give a clinic on electric bass at the European conference. I spent several hours working on the clinic presentation. I was certainly looking forward to this trip. I also purchased a ticket for my wife, who has always wanted to go to Europe. Unfortunately, the week before the trip, I noticed that I was becoming fatigued rather easily. By the end of the week, it got so bad that I couldn't walk from my car to the school without having to stop to catch my breath.

On the Friday before the trip, I mentioned it to my wife. She immediately took me to the doctor, and he immediately admitted me to the hospital. I was diagnosed with Congestive Heart Failure. The doctor ordered no traveling, meaning that my European trip was off. I was really disappointed, but even more, I felt really bad for my wife, who ended up staying home with me.

When I returned to school, there was a Letter of Reprimand waiting for me. It seems that the principal had been documenting what he considered to be infractions on my part, no matter how minor they were. Some of it may have been legitimate. I certainly was late for class a couple of times that he had documented. One day, I was uncertain of where a faculty meeting was supposed to be and went to the wrong site. That was documented as well. He also said that the condition of the music room was unacceptable, which certainly was a matter of opinion. In addition, he insisted that I document my after-school activities. I received a stipend each year for time spent outside of class. Groups that met after-school, such as Jazz Band were included. Also included were times that I spent outside of school, such as supervising kids at festivals, performances at night or on weekends or holidays (such as the Memorial Day Parade). Of course, the reason behind all of this was that I wasn't really responding to his leadership, and I guess to a certain extent, I was not. I had resigned from all after-school faculty committees that I had previously been on, and I made it no secret that because I was teaching in the middle school that my talents were being under-utilized. I didn't care for the way he manipulated my schedule in order to give himself a fourth exploratory class, and I highly resented the way he acted in that he felt he had to appear that he knew more about teaching music than I did, simply because he was a principal. I'm guessing that he also did not appreciate that I had fashioned a way to teach 7th and 8th grade general music, using the electric pianos, that he disagreed with. It appears that he arranged to have the school district Curriculum Coordinator observe my class. Now, it should be said that this Curriculum Coordinator was a young woman and was very pretty. However, her knowledge of curriculum appeared to be questionable. I had heard of heated exchanges that had taken place in other department meetings that she had attended. As far as my class was concerned, I knew that she had no music background, and therefore would not understand what I was doing in my class.

I'm sure she was there for just one reason, to discredit what I was doing in my class. The class that she attended happened to have several 8th grade boys, and certainly, having a beautiful young woman observing their class had its effect on these kids. The boys had problems staying on task, and one boy in particular was incredibly obnoxious. After class, the Curriculum Coordinator said to me that the real problem was that my class was not exciting enough. Then, as if a light bulb went on, she said, "What you really need to do is include hip-hop dancing in your class." I couldn't believe what I was hearing. Dance experts at that time didn't even consider hip-hop to be a legitimate form of dance. In addition, I was a music teacher, not a dance teacher, and I had grave concerns about teaching dance in my classes. The idea struck me as being quite stupid. I continued on, teaching my classes as I had envisioned them, and I never heard anything more about teaching hip-hop.

Unfortunately, the principal wasn't done yet. When time for the school budget hearings came around, he informed me in a department meeting that he was planning to move all band and chorus classes to after school the following school year. This, of course, would have a devastating impact on membership in these organizations. Students would have to make decisions on participation in music, or sports, or other co-curricular after-school activities. I was extremely upset, not only because of the serious enrollment impact implications, but because as a result of his decision, that the most important part of the music program, for which we had developed a curriculum and was listed in the state standards, would now be relegated to an after-school, co-curricular activity. Additionally, I couldn't escape the feeling that this wasn't an educational decision. It seemed that this was personal, and he was coming after me. Through all of this, I had to wonder where he was getting these ideas. Like most administrators in the area, this principal regularly attended conferences sponsored by an organization called the Maine School Management Association. I wasn't able to tell if this organization was the source of these types of ideas, but now that I was president of the Maine Music Educators Association, I was receiving phone calls and emails from music teachers from throughout the area complaining of similar types of administrative moves and proposals, mostly in middle schools. After this principal told me of his plans to move band and chorus to after school, it wasn't long before I started hearing from other middle school music teachers that were facing similar situations.

In my case, I told the principal that I would inform parents of these plans, and that there would most likely be a negative fall-out as a result. He told me not to notify parents, and I responded "Baloney! I'm a teacher fighting for what's best for his students. Of course I'm going to notify parents." A few weeks later, the school board held its hearing for this particular section of the budget. The entire room was flooded with parents, students, and even some alumni, former band and chorus students of mine from when I taught in the high school. I learned from my years in music education that the most important part of building a successful music program is the strength of the program infrastructure. The band program in the elementary, middle school, and high school must function properly, and that includes giving proper access to students for proper instruction. I had turned down the position at Dirigo because their middle school did not do this. As a result, I realized that so long as their middle school situation wasn't fixed, that the goal of building a successful program in Dirigo would remain elusive. It now appeared that the middle school principal in Lisbon was looking to create a similar situation. When the school board questioned me on how his idea would impact the music program, I simply told them that this setup would blow a hole in the program infrastructure that eventually would affect the music program from elementary grades through high school. The eventual result would be minimal enrollment for band and chorus at all grade levels. When it came time in the hearing for public comments, the public comment time had to be extended because of all the parents, students, and members of the community that wanted to speak. Parents, who over the years had been supportive of the music program took the principal and the school board to task for even considering this type of plan. In the end, the school board would not approve the principal's recommendation. However, the principal managed to get back at me when he set up the schedule for the following school year. He reduced the weekly rehearsal time for band and chorus from 60 minutes to 40 minutes. Perhaps he thought I would panic at the time reduction, and perhaps would not be able to sustain quality performing groups. However, there are times when young administrators underestimate the resourcefulness of veteran teachers. Yes, the rehearsal time reduction would hurt the growth of kids, but I wasn't the least bit worried about maintaining quality. The whole thing was a classic example of clueless leadership.

Toward the end of the year, the Art teacher, Laurel, came to me with a proposal. I had worked with Laurel ever since I had started teaching full-time at the middle school. Her son played in the band, and she was probably the most supportive music parent that I had. However, in this case, she suggested that we take a summer class together. The Portland Museum of Art had received a grant from the National Endowment of the Arts, through the Massachusetts Arts Commission to offer a class to teaching teams. Each team was to include an Art teacher, and the second person would be a teacher at the same school. The idea was that they would teach in parallel and that their classes would be coordinated around a central theme. In this case, the central theme was "invoking a sense of place". The subject of the central theme was the Winslow Homer painting "Weather-beaten", a famous ocean scape painting that hung in the museum. Of all the teams taking this seminar, Laurel and I were the only art/music team. Other teams consisted of an art teacher and another subject area teacher, such as English, Science, or Special Education. The focus of the seminar was to explore ways that the teaching teams could offer coordinated lessons revolving around "Weather-beaten" with their students and focusing on the "sense of place" theme. The activities were varied. They included a trip to Winslow Homer's oceanside cottage, located in nearby Scarborough, that had recently been acquired by the museum. Here, we saw Homer's work area, as well as the oceanfront, that he used for a number of his paintings including "Weather-beaten". I was stuck by imagining an 70-year-old man, sketchpad in hand, jumping from rock to rock in a fierce storm, knowing that he could easily be swept away by a rogue wave. We also looked at work from other artists who used the scenes in and around Portland for their subjects. We took a ferry ride to Great Diamond Island, just off Portland, and went to a place called Diamond Cove, a place where several prominent artists produced paintings that hung in museums. We also embarked on another field trip to Tenant's Harbor, near the seaside town of Rockland. Here, we visited with an artist in his studio where he painted large paintings, seven or eight feet in diameter. It was interesting, but the most interesting event of the day happened when we left for lunch. We all stopped at a lobster pound along the road for lunch. At first, it was just our group from the Portland Museum of Art ordering lunch and being seated at the various picnic tables. Not wanting to sit in the sun, I chose a table in the shade to have my lobster. As I was sitting down, I noticed that another group had arrived. This group was from the Farnsworth Art Museum in nearby Rockland. It struck me as interesting that groups from two different art museums would choose the same place at about the same time for lunch. As I was contemplating this, a gentleman approached and took the seat across from me at the table. Now, I am certainly no expert in art. I can't even draw a straight line. My knowledge of painting doesn't go beyond what the primary colors are. However, even in my diminished state of knowledge, I wasn't so dumb that I didn't recognize the man that had sat across from me. The great Andrew Wyeth, one of America's most famous artists, whose world-famous painting "Christina's World" hangs in the Museum of Modern Art in New York, had chosen to sit at my table. Perhaps it was because he also wanted to sit in the shade, or perhaps he needed a respite from being the center of attention of the Farnsworth group. After all, he was in his advanced years, and I imagine he would find events such as he participated in with this group from the Farnsworth, where many of his paintings hung, to be physically demanding. I didn't say anything to him because I wasn't sure he would welcome a conversation with someone like myself, who was basically a layman when it came to the art world. Laurel, however, was a different story. She came over to the table and was as giddy as a teenager as she talked to Wyeth, hugging him, and telling him that he was her inspiration to become an art teacher. She insisted that I take a picture of her and Wyeth together, and I complied. As it turned out, Wyeth's grandson, Jaime, a prominent artist in his own right, came over to rescue

245

his grandfather. It certainly wasn't something the Portland Museum people planned, nor was it expected in any way, but for me, it certainly was the most memorable moment of the seminar.

When we returned to school in September, Laurel and I had a plan in place. She would work with the kids on the elements and structures of paintings such as "Weather-beaten", while I would work with kids on creating soundscapes and musical themes that might go with a scene from an ocean storm such as was captured in "Weather-beaten". I did not have the time to teach kids advanced music composition components, but I fell back to a type of music that I studied in college called "Music Concrete". It is a French term that basically means to make music out of environmental sounds. Traffic sounds, the sound of people walking, animal sounds, the wind, and of course the ocean, are all legitimate sounds for Music Concrete. The keyboards that I had selected for the general music classes had extensive sound banks, which included many environmental sounds. Many of the students fashioned compositions that included Music Concrete mixed with musical themes inspired by "Weather-beaten". Some of them were really good, and I couldn't wait to play some of them for a fall follow-up session of the class in Portland. When Laurel and I went to the follow-up, and I played some of the music pieces that students composed, the instructors and staff of the seminar became really excited. They asked if some of compositions could be placed on the National Endowment for the Arts website, since that organization and the Massachusetts Arts Commission were the overseeing entities of the seminar. When I told the principal what had occurred, he said, "That's nice", and that's as far as things went.

A few weeks later, I was informed that I was being placed on a "teacher action plan". Apparently, the principal felt that I was a teacher "in need of improvement", and this so called "action plan" would help me improve. I felt the plan was hogwash. This was the type of plan that weak teachers were placed on as a stepping-stone to firing them. I was insulted and appalled. At first, I was planning to refuse to cooperate with this stupid idea. However, after talking to the union folks, they convinced me to comply, at the very least in order to defend myself against these so-called "deficiencies". So, throughout the year, I would meet periodically with the principal, union representative by my side, to discuss these issues. I thought it was a total waste of time, and that was confirmed when we had a discussion over one of the principal's complaints. The issue had to do with the stairwell leading to the music room. He felt the students were making too much noise when changing classes, and that there were some students being unruly on the stairwell during this time. I almost always had students come to me with questions or other issues every time class ended, so being able to police the stairwell wasn't something that I was always able to do. The principal, however, was insistent, so I offered a solution, although it would run into some money. I suggested that a closed-circuit camera be placed on the stairwell to monitor the kids. After all, there were closed circuit cameras in other parts of the building, what was one camera more? To my surprise, the principal agreed. However, weeks went by, then months went by, and no camera was ever installed. The message was clear. The principal didn't really have an interest in improving the situation. It seemed as if he was only interested in expanding his documentation on me. This whole thing was taking a toll on me. The anxiety about my job was overwhelming, not because of how well I could do the job. I had no doubt I would do it well. I just wondered if it would matter. Unfortunately, this situation was on my mind every waking hour. I even refused to turn on the radio in my car because I felt it would distract me from trying to anticipate whatever difficulties the principal or superintendent might throw at me. The radio stayed off for almost the entire year. I realized that I needed to do some serious thinking. I still had a very strong desire to return to high school teaching. However, it seemed that the opportunity to find such a position in Maine was dwindling. If I couldn't succeed in finding this type of job in Maine, then perhaps the situation in another state might be more promising. I expanded my job search to other states. I paid close attention to job openings in New Hampshire, Vermont, Massachusetts, parts of New York, New Jersey, and even Florida.

THE SALT LAKE CITY CONFERENCE

I also spoke to some county music supervisors from Florida when I attended the National MENC conference in Salt Lake City. This conference was something that I consider memorable for several reasons. To begin with, in the months prior to the conference, MENC announced plans for a music educator's chorus as part of a gala concert in collaboration with the Mormon Tabernacle Choir. The national MENC office informed all of the state presidents that this music educator's chorus should consist of two teachers from each state, one male and one female. When I put out the call to the MMEA board members and District Chairs, I had several female teachers respond, but no males. I sent out another memo to board members and District Chairs outlining the situation and requesting that if no male music educators came forward, that I would be willing to be the male singer from

Maine. Again, when no male music educators indicated any interest, I sent in my name, and one of the Maine female teachers to the MENC national office.

The night before the concert was the dress rehearsal, and I arrived a bit early, but the whole scene seemed surreal as I entered the auditorium. To begin with, the auditorium was huge, perhaps the largest I've ever been in. The audience capacity of the facility was 21,000 people. There were large projection screens on either side of the stage with state-of-the-art remote operated video cameras. If the facility itself wasn't impressive or surreal enough, on stage, the Oak Ridge Boys were in the middle of their rehearsal. On the balcony above the stage, members of the Mormon Tabernacle Choir started drifting in. When the time came, after some staging directions, the rehearsal started, and just singing along with this world-famous choir was an awesome experience. However, the following evening, the concert itself took things to the next level. Sharing the stage and performing alongside of the Mormon Tabernacle Choir, the Oak Ridge Boys, and the US Army Herald Trumpets was overwhelming.

The next morning of the conference, a meeting of the MENC Eastern Division Executive Board took place. This particular meeting was to be the pinnacle of four years of struggle between the Eastern Division Board and the National Office of MENC. In my first year as president-elect of the Maine Music Educators Association, I started attending Eastern Division Board meetings in anticipation of being a member of the board when I became state president. From that first meeting, I became aware of this struggle. The Eastern Division Board was unhappy with various decisions made by the National Office that affected the Eastern Division. As part of past practice, the National Office set up and ran division teacher conferences across the country, including the Eastern

Division. As part of the Eastern Division Conference, a high school honors festival was also held, which included the best students from the Eastern Division. The festival was also run by the MENC National Office. Over the years, making All-Eastern was a significant achievement. I remember when I participated in the All-Eastern Orchestra in Atlantic City as a high school senior, and it was the defining event of my high school career. However, at this point, several members of the Eastern Division Board began to question policies, finances, and procedures of the National Office in setting up Eastern Division events. I honestly did not participate much in these discussions at first, although I noted that several folks had very strong feelings about what was going on. However, when I became president of MMEA, I experienced first-hand some of these issues. To begin with, the National Office assigned the job of running the All-Eastern Festival to a staff member who apparently did not have very much experience running a festival. I started receiving a lot of complaints from Maine high school music teachers when the list of accepted All-Eastern students was released late. I received more complaints when the All-Eastern music came out late. In addition, the participation fee for All-Eastern students seemed abnormally high. Several board members charged that the MENC National Office was setting high participation fees to gain significant profits from the All-Eastern Festival. As state president, I was aware that in many cases, the participation fee was not covered by the schools of the students, and the families of the students ended up paying the participation fees. In Maine, it was common practice to keep festival expenses as low as possible because we knew that in many cases the families of festival students were paying fees. I was not amused by what seemed like MENC making profits on the backs of the families of participating students.

For four years, I witnessed this clash of wills, and now I was beginning to see why so many of the Eastern Division Board members were upset with the National Office. So when I attended my last Eastern Division Board meeting as a state officer, this whole issue had come to a head. Since the National Office seemed uninterested in pleas from the Eastern Division to modify the way it ran Eastern Division events, that could only mean that the Eastern Division had a decision to make. Should it allow Eastern Division events to continue under the policies and procedures of the National Office, or to break away and run Eastern Division events under the direction of the Eastern Division Executive Board? As the meeting unfolded, the Eastern Division officers brought everyone up to date on the most recent discussions with the National Office. It appeared that no progress was being made, and now the Board needed to determine a course of action. It was now time for someone to make a motion for the Eastern Division Executive Board to run Eastern Division events. Silence descended upon the room as no one spoke up. It seemed like a very long pause, and I couldn't believe it. The Eastern Division Executive Board is a fairly large group, which includes the presidents of eleven states, District of Columbia, and the European contingent. Many of the board members spoke as passionately as anyone I have ever heard arguing the need for the Eastern Division to take over these events. Now, when it became time to act, these people were sitting on their hands. In my mind, I did a quick debate on whether I should speak up or not. As strange as it may seem, my answer came from *Star Trek*. Now, I'm not what you would call a "trekkie", although I am a Star Trek fan. I have seen most of the Star Trek TV programs and movies. In the interim, I also have read several Star Trek paperback novels. In one of those novels, I remembered a quote from a star ship captain, not Captain Kirk, but the Captain of another star ship. The quote is "Sometimes, you have to assess a situation and say to yourself 'Dammit, it's me or nobody', and if you can't live with nobody, then you have to act". The way was clear, no one was speaking up, and I had come to the conclusion that I couldn't live with nobody. My biggest motivation was that the All-Eastern Festival of the previous year had been operated like amateur hour, certainly not up to the professionalism that it deserved. I had fielded multiple complaints from Maine music teachers about the way things were handled by the National Office, and I didn't want to see all of that repeated the next time around, so I raised my hand, and said I would make the motion if folks would be willing to help me formulate it. After several minutes of wordsmithing, we finally arrived at a motion with wording that most everyone could agree to. I made the motion, and the president of New Hampshire, who was seated next to me, seconded. The motion passed easily. Now, the Eastern Division would run its own conference and All-Eastern high school festival. I had acted, it was done, and even though some of the MENC staff were not happy with what I had done, and made mention of it to me, I still felt that I had made the right choice and acted in the best interest of students, teachers, and families throughout the Eastern Division.

THE BIG STOMP

When I returned home, the next project that I needed to turn my attention to was the fifth and sixth grade end-of-the-year performance. I had about seven weeks to prepare the kids for the performance, which sounds like a long time. However, if you consider that I only see each class once a week, that meant that I only had seven classes to prepare them. Once again, I turned to Jonathan, the other elementary music teacher, for help. After some discussion, we decided to pursue a theme based on the Broadway show "Stomp!" All of the teachers in the area towns had access to a resource that was called the "Share Center". The Share Center was set up to help local teachers by collecting items from local businesses that were no longer used. I, myself, had been to the Share Center, and had been able to procure items such as unused file cabinets, discarded computer disks, and storage bins. All of it had been donated to the Share Center by various local businesses and all I had to do was sign for them. As a teacher in one of the local towns, there was no cost to me.

After deciding on the "Stomp!" theme, Jonathan and I went to the Share Center, and managed to find several items that we could put to use. We found what appeared to be pipe fittings made out of a very dense cardboard. We also found a bunch of cans, and other items that we thought could be utilized quite nicely. In addition, Jonathan had a connection with a parent who was able to get us about a dozen highway construction barrels that were unused. Jonathan then played for me several albums that he had that featured African and Caribbean drumming. As we were listening to the recordings, I wrote down several of the rhythms that I felt could be useful in preparing a program for the 6th graders. I taught six different 6th grade classes, so I assigned a type of instrument to each class. The construction barrels would be the most popular item, so I assigned those to the class that had given me the least amount of discipline problems. It was kind of a reward to them for being so attentive. I then assigned the other "instruments" to the other classes. One class played on the cardboard pipe fittings we had gotten from the Share Center. Another class played on cans, others on wood blocks and so on for the remaining classes. Since we didn't have enough mallets for all of the students, I ended up spending a couple of evenings in my garage cutting and shaping about nine dozen wooden dowels. Now, I didn't have a lot of experience teaching elementary general music, but there were a couple of things that I did know. First, these kids, for the most part were not involved in band, did not study an instrument, and therefore had no ensemble playing skills. That would mean that the most difficult issue that I would have to deal with is getting them to play complicated poly-rhythms together on the same beat. Second, I would not get the chance to rehearse them before the performance. The only time we would probably hear what the entire presentation sounded like would be the performance itself. Six classes of kids, one hundred twenty-five students in all, would play six different poly-rhythms simultaneously, and I could only guess at what it was going to sound like. In addition, each class would be spotlighted, and in that spotlighted segment, the students would also play several poly-rhythms at once as a class. It began to seem as if this was a disaster waiting to happen. There were plenty of places where things could go wrong. However, I had a feeling I could pull it together so long as I had a strategy to prepare all the classes. I spent the next seven weeks working with each class on the rhythms assigned to them and teaching them to follow my conducting. I set up a system of auditory cues for them to move from segment to segment and developed rhythm "tags" that would allow them to segue from section to section. There were some struggles over the seven weeks, but as the day of the performance approached, I felt we would be ready. On the day of the performance, Jonathan managed to set up some rehearsal time for the full sixth grade. The kids filed in to the cafeteria, and we pulled out all of the "equipment". I quickly reviewed all of the procedures with the students, and we began to rehearse. I was amazed at how quickly everything came together. They sounded like a polished group that had been rehearsing with each other all along, certainly not like a group that had just been put together. I had to stop them three or four times to go over procedural details relative to the entire group, but all in all, I was very pleased. A few minutes later, everyone filed in to the gym, and the performance began. The Kindergarten, first and second grades had all previously performed in evening events set up for parents and presented more like a demonstration of class activities as opposed to an actual performance. As a result, the performances on this day began with Jonathan's third and fourth grade students. Classrooms and some combined classrooms took turns performing in front of the rest of the school. They were followed by my fifth-grade classes, which mostly performed on Orff instruments, small xylophones and such. They were very successful, and then it was time for the sixth grade to perform. The younger students may not have noticed, but I think the teachers and a handful of parents that attended may have sensed that this would be unlike any of the previous performances. The first thing that was different was that the entire sixth grade was setting up on the gym floor. Then there was the array of "instruments" that we were using. We set the row of construction barrels up front and arranged the remaining classes in a semicircle behind. I took my position in front of the group and did a quick check to see that I had everyone's attention. I tried not to look tense, but I also didn't want to appear to be too informal. The rehearsal had gone very well, but that was no guarantee of what would happen in the performance. I gave the first auditory cue, and 125 students started performing. The acoustics of the gym made the sound of the full group even more impressive than the rehearsal in the cafeteria. The performance flowed from full group to classroom #1 that was playing cans. After their segment, it was back to the full group followed by classroom #2 playing wood blocks. It was then back to the full group, and we continued to circulate among all the sixth-grade classes, giving each one a spotlight segment. I kept waiting for something to go wrong, some kid not paying attention messing things up, or some kids making a wrong entrance, but none of those things happened. The performance was nearly flawless. When everything ended, the sixth grade received an enthusiastic round of applause, and everyone went back to class. As the last of the equipment was put away, I sat down, fairly satisfied with how things had gone. I hadn't done much teaching on the elementary level, and this was the first significantly successful performance that I experienced with students of this level. I had a proud sense of accomplishment, but that didn't stop me from going to the post office after school and mailing four applications and resumes to school districts with open high school teaching positions, including two in New Hampshire.

FINDING NEWFOUND

In a few weeks, we were into the middle of the summer, and the phone rang. A very pleasant secretary from a high school in New Hampshire was on the other end, inviting me to an interview for their music teacher position. Her demeanor was so positive, I wanted to drop everything and go to the school right then and there for an interview. Of course, I had to wait a few days for the actual interview, but I also asked my wife if she would like to go with me and we could make a nice day trip out of it. She agreed to go with me, and on the appointed day, we traveled to New Hampshire and to Newfound Regional High School.

The interview was nothing like I was expecting. I had grown used to going to interviews with panels of people asking various scripted questions. The problem with that scenario is that this type of format doesn't do what it is supposed to do. One might consider it logical that the candidate most able to answer these scripted questions would be the most successful person to teach in the position. However, it has been my experience that the person who gets hired in these situations are simply better at navigating these scripted questions. Once teaching in the position, their effectiveness in the classroom is never assured. I had been a victim of this on several occasions, situations where I knew beyond a doubt that I was the better teacher, but the other person simply managed to handle the interview better, and so I lost out.

That is why my interview at Newfound was so refreshing, no panels of people, no scripted questions, just the principal and I sitting down and talking about music education. Before I knew it, we had been talking nearly 90 minutes. He then showed me the music facilities, and I was impressed, to say the least. The music room had a high ceiling with skylights and several practice rooms on the periphery. In the front of the room, there was a movable wall that opened up to the backstage of the auditorium. The equipment all appeared to be high quality, including a baby grand piano. All I could think was "Wow!" In thirty years of teaching, I had never taught in a room that was actually designed for teaching music. My music room at Fryeburg was an old one-room schoolhouse. At Holy Cross, I taught in several different rooms, none of them music rooms. At Ansonia, I taught on the stage of the auditorium, that was basically a cave. When I taught for Catholic Music Instructors. in the parochial schools, most of those schools had me teach in storage rooms or common areas. In Lisbon, I taught in the cafeteria, while at the middle school in Lisbon, their music room was a double sized classroom that had been added on to the blueprints of the building as an after-thought.

The interview being concluded, I bid farewell to the principal, and my wife was waiting for me in the car.

As we started the trip back home, I said to my wife "This interview went really well. I think there's a chance that they may offer me this position. If they do, what do you think? Should I accept it?"

This was an issue that I wanted to get out of the way immediately with my wife. I was half expecting that she would protest my taking the position because it would mean moving. I once before turned down an interview for a position that I thought I had a good shot at because of her protests that accepting such a position would have meant moving to a location that she deemed undesirable. It seemed to me that she might be agreeable to moving if it were a location she liked, and we both liked the lakes region of New Hampshire. If she had said to me that she did not want me to consider the position at Newfound because it would have meant moving, then I would know to turn down the position should it be offered to me. But in this case, I didn't hear any protest.

She simply said, "Well, if you think you would be happy teaching there, you should take the position."

"Great!" I thought, and with that issue out of the way, I began my wait to find out the results of the interview.

A few days later, on a Sunday, I brought my wife and my parents to see a concert in which my son participated at the summer high school music program at the University of Maine. After the concert, we went to a Chinese buffet restaurant.

When I opened my fortune cookie, it said, "Good Luck is coming your way."

"That would be welcome," I said. "I can use some good luck."

And proceeded to tell my mom about the position I interviewed for at Newfound.

"I'll pray for you," my mom said.

A couple of days later, I decided I needed to contact Newfound to find out what happened. I called the principal and told him I wanted to follow up on my interview and get his thoughts.

"Actually, Ed," the principal, whose name was Mike, said. "I was planning to call you later. You're our guy."

I had to let this sink in for a couple of seconds. "Really?" I asked.

"Yes, I've been having a lot of conversations with other administrators, because after all, we don't hire someone with your level of experience lightly," Mike said.

The rest of the conversation was very pleasant, and when the phone call ended, I practically collapsed in my chair. The significance of this could not be understated. I was now able to leave a school district where the administration had no respect for my abilities or efforts, and where they actively opposed me and treated me as a target. All of the stress that had accumulated over the last several years was lifted all at once. I couldn't wait to tell my wife and found her in the bedroom.

"I just spoke with Newfound," I told her. "They just offered me the position."

"They What?!" she replied, anger building. "You took the position without talking it over with me?"

"We did talk it over," I reminded her. "In the car, on the way home from the interview."

"No we didn't," she said. "We never discussed it!"

And so, the conversation continued to go back and forth the entire morning. Normally, my wife has a pretty good memory. However, there have been lapses. I remember several years before, when I taught high school band at Lisbon, I found a newly released version of the "Pizzicato Polka" by Strauss. I remembered that my wife danced a ballet solo to this selection when she was a student in my mother's dance studio, and I thought it would be nice to surprise her by having the high school band playing it at a concert in Lisbon. After the concert, I asked her what she thought, and she told me she had no memory of ever dancing to "Pizzicato Polka". It occurred to me that perhaps our conversation in the car on the way back from Newfound was a "Pizzicato Moment". I realized that it was possible that she truly had no memory of the conversation. We continued to argue, although I think most of her anger was brought on by this perceived slight of my not discussing it with her. She wanted me to call Newfound and decline the position. I told her there was no way I was going to do that. Not only was I able to escape teaching in a place where I was miserable, but I knew that I could eventually take the music program at Newfound to levels I had never been able to attain anywhere else I had taught. Although she continued to argue with me vehemently, she could not dispute the fact that teaching at Newfound would be a major improvement over teaching at Lisbon. Slowly, it began to dawn on me why she was so upset. It was as if she thought that I expected her drop everything and move to New Hampshire with me. To tell the truth, I hadn't even thought it through that far. Then, I realized that she was fearful that I would simply go to New Hampshire and abandon her. I had actually seen that happen with a couple of music teachers that I knew in the past. With a lot of effort, I was able to convince her that this would not be the case with me. I didn't have any desire to take her away from her job, or her friends. As a nurse, she was very dedicated to the nursing home that she worked and was very attached to some of her patients.

That meant that some out of the box thinking would be required that would allow me to teach at Newfound but allow my wife to continue with her job in Maine. The answer came about a week later, when we took another trip to New Hampshire and Newfound. My wife dropped me off at the school where I wanted to start making preparations, while she explored the area. Once in the school, I started to unpack materials, inventory instruments, scan through files and the music library, etc. When I went to the copy room to make copies of some documents, there was a notice on the bulletin board announcing winter rentals at a lakeside condo. To make a long story short, there was a two-room apartment in the condo that I was able to rent. It was a financial sacrifice to do things this way. Besides taking a pay cut to come to Newfound, I also had the added expense of renting an apartment. However, I believed that in the overall view of things, the sacrifice was worth it. A number of years prior, before I was removed from the high school in Lisbon, I think I would have been content to spend the rest of my career there. However, that was before I ended up working under the school superintendent and principal from hell. Now, the stage was set for the next, and I hoped the most fulfilling, chapter of my career.

Newfound Regional High School, located on the edge of New Hampshire's White Mountains, is a high school of about 350 students, quite small by most standards. The students come from seven different towns, most of them surrounding Newfound Lake, which is a pretty and sizable lake, about seven miles long. The Music Department schedule is mostly taken up by band and chorus classes, two of each, to better give scheduling options for students so that they can schedule all the classes they need as well as their music class. If a student needs a special class that meets during the same time as a band class, there is another band class available during another class period that the student can choose. Once a month, the two classes rehearse together. It's not a perfect solution, but during my first few years at Newfound, it was rare to find a student that could not add band to his schedule because of conflicts with other classes. There were 63 kids in the band classes, the largest band I had conducted since my time at Holy Cross. In the chorus classes, there were 46 students, which was the largest chorus I had conducted since my time at Fryeburg Academy. Not only did I have a baby grand piano to teach chorus, but another music teacher in the district served as accompanist for the chorus and attended class two days a week. I had never had this much support in any other school that I had ever taught. The inventory of instruments was high quality, and the music room itself was a wonderful place in which to teach. As to the students, I sensed that some of them were disappointed that their previous teacher had left, and in their eyes, I might not be able to measure up to past years. I tried to impress upon them that my methods were not necessarily better than the previous teacher, just different. I think most of the students understood, although I couldn't escape the feeling that some did not.

I felt totally spoiled in band and chorus rehearsals. I wasn't used to having a band that was larger than any other high school band I've ever taught, and the band classes were a total joy. The chorus classes were decent also. It had been a long time since I had taught a four-part SATB chorus, and the boy's section at Newfound was really good. A few weeks into the school year, Mike, the principal, came in to do an observation of my class. His evaluation was very complimentary. He said, "Many times, I observe a teacher whose class is like a river a mile wide and a foot deep, but in your class you go into depth." Needless to say, I was very pleased. For the first time in many years, I was looking forward to coming to work each morning. Of course, on Fridays, I would get into my car after school and head to my home in Maine, to be with my family. My wife still seemed somewhat resentful, although she was supportive. On Sunday evening, I would travel back to my apartment in New Hampshire to get ready for school on Monday morning. It was somewhat tiring, but as far as I was concerned, it was worth it.

It was fair to say that I loved being at Newfound. Still, I could not escape the feeling that my presence at Newfound was not appreciated by some students and parents. A common event in most schools is the "Open House", which is usually held sometime in the fall. It's usually a pleasant evening when you get to meet the parents of the kids, and in my case it would be a great opportunity to begin a relationship with the parents of my students. However, that's not exactly how it worked out my first year at Newfound. It had a lot to do with why the previous music teacher left Newfound. I was told that the superintendent made some changes to the structure of the elementary music program, and that the high school music teacher became very upset. He ended up leaving Newfound, telling people that the music program was now in danger of collapse. As a result, when I met with parents at my first Open House at Newfound, I wasn't greeted with a whole lot of smiling-faced parents. Most of these parents looked very stern and asked very pointed questions about the welfare of the music program at this point in time. I tried to reassure them as much as I could, but to tell the truth, I had no prognosis on the future because I wasn't totally aware of what had taken place prior to my arrival at Newfound. The impression I got from most of them was that they would take a wait-and-see attitude toward the program. I really did not change anything in my approach to teaching the band and chorus, but I could sense that there would be a lot of scrutiny at my first concert at Newfound. I continued to work though the fall, making satisfactory progress with both groups. Things were going great in the band. The students were making great progress, and the only concern I had was the instrumentation of the band, which had a small brass section that wasn't always able to keep up with the woodwinds. In the chorus, the tenor and bass sections were quite strong, but the alto section was weak. It was the largest section of the chorus, but many of the kids in the section didn't sing well, if they sang at all. The soprano section was stronger, but their high range was limited. I had to be very careful about what music I would assign to them so that the notes in the piece would not be too high for them to sing.   However, as time went on, I was able to fashion a program for their first concert (the Winter Concert) that I was satisfied with. A few weeks before the concert, I received an email from Roger, who was at that time the chairman of District III of the Maine Music Educators Association, a position I held for several years during the time that I taught in Maine. Roger told me that the membership of District III voted to award me the District III Distinguished Service Award for the time I had spent as District III Chairman, as well as chair of the District III Jazz Festival, Solo & Ensemble Festival, Honors Festival Host, Auditions Chair, and Honors Band Manager. Roger told me that he and some of the District III Teachers wanted to come to New Hampshire to present the award to me at the Newfound Winter Concert. I felt quite honored, gave them directions, and told them I would very much look forward to them coming to the concert. When the day of the concert came, the weather wasn't very cooperative. It snowed on and off all day with more snow expected in the evening. Although it wasn't so bad that I needed to postpone the concert, I was pretty sure that at some point that my former colleagues from Maine would be in touch with me, telling me that they would not be able to make the trip. About a half-hour before the concert started, Roger, Sam and Ray, all teachers that I had worked with not only in District III, but on the state level as well, walked in the door. I was completely flattered that they made the journey, which in the snow amounted to a four-hour trip.

As the concert started, I was aware that I needed to allay concerns among some parents and community members that the high school music program could still be successful, despite the issues that were still swirling around the departure of the previous music teacher. The Superintendent of Schools was in the audience, as well as some school board members.

Yet, there was something reassuring about having the District III teachers in the audience, and I couldn't help but feel confident about how the evening would turn out. As principal, Mike gave me a wonderful introduction to start the concert, and we were off. The kids performed well, and I was happy with how things were progressing. About mid-way through the concert, the District III teachers took the podium. What I thought was going to be a short presentation, became considerably longer as each teacher took the microphone. Roger talked about my involvement with the array of activities that District III sponsors. Sam talked about my time as the District III Chairperson, and some of the innovations that were made during my time at the helm. Ray talked about my time as MMEA President, and the number of things that I was involved with in that capacity. The audience was warmly receptive, and when the concert continued, the students responded as well. At the end of the concert, the chorus gave an impressive performance, and the audience responded with a standing ovation. I couldn't help but think what a contrast this was to my time in Lisbon. I hurried back to the music room, hoping I could talk a little bit with Roger, Sam and Ray before they had to leave to go back to Maine. As we were starting to say goodbyes, the door to the music room opened, and in came Marie, the Superintendent of Schools. There was joy in her expression, as well as relief. She came up to me and gave me a big hug. "This is different" I thought to myself. In all my years of teaching, I had never received a hug from a superintendent. The following morning, Marie came into my first period class to talk to the band students and tell them what a great job they had done at the concert. Mike also appeared very happy with how things turned out.

Things were working out really well, but there were still a couple of challenges on the horizon that I had to take on. One was the annual music department spring trip. The spring trip was a tradition at Newfound, and I knew that I needed to design and implement a trip for music students. Spring trips for the music department ran on a two-year rotation. The trip for my first year at Newfound needed to consist of having the students perform at an out-of-state music festival. The following year, the spring trip would consist of taking the students to a professional performance such as a Broadway musical. There were notes from past years concerning music department trips to places such as Williamsburg, VA, Hershey, PA, Philadelphia, etc. I decided that at least for my first year, I should choose some place close to home that had previously been a Spring Trip destination. I decided that the trip should be to the "Music In the Parks" Festival at Six Flags New England in Massachusetts. On the wall of the music room, there were plaques from that festival, and it appeared that it was a somewhat frequent destination for Newfound music spring trips in the past. However, I had some new tools at my disposal since I last did music trips in Lisbon. In the late '80's the internet was still developing, and it was challenging to make trip arrangements for my band and chorus, but now, it was relatively simple for me to find a hotel web site. I entered my contact information, the date of the trip, and how many rooms I would need for my group. In a few days, I received more than 20 bids for rooms from various hotels in the Springfield, MA area, where Six Flags New England is located. I also now had spreadsheet software to keep track of student payments, which was a big help for keeping track of that information. I set up a system that a lot of schools use when doing trips such as this. First, I calculate the cost of the trip and break it down on a per-student basis. Students then register for the trip, and what they don't cover through fund-raising they pay out-of-pocket. Although fund raising is involved not all students take advantage of it. As a result, except in a couple of instances, I have never had a student earn enough money fund raising to totally defray their trip cost.

At any rate, the day of the trip arrived, and with a few parent chaperones to assist me, we boarded our coaches and left for Springfield area. The plan for the first day was simple. We left at the end of the school day, and after a two-and- a-half hour trip we would arrive at our hotel. We would then take the kids to a local shopping mall where they could get supper in the food court and do some shopping after. Finally, we would return to the hotel, allow the kids to do some swimming, and then send them to their rooms at curfew. It sounded simple, but it didn't work out that way. To begin with, the bus drivers decided to take a "shortcut" that wasn't all that short. As a result, we were behind schedule when we arrived at the hotel. I quickly checked in, passed out room keys, and told the kids to drop off their luggage in their rooms and get back on the bus so we could get them to the mall. As we entered the mall, we encountered another problem. We were met by security people who stopped us, and then a young woman who was a mall administrator appeared. It seems this particular mall had a policy that on Friday and Saturday nights, teenagers under 18 could not enter the mall without a parent, and of course, this was a Friday. I explained the situation to the mall administrator and pointed out to her that we had several chaperones with our group. After a few minutes of discussion, she reluctantly allowed our group into the mall. The first place that everyone went was the food court, since we had arrived well past suppertime. As I sat down, I couldn't help but notice several security people watching our group from a balcony above the food court. It was unsettling. While it was true that I had only known these kids since the beginning of the school year, I had never seen anything to suggest that any of them were thieves or displayed any other type of bad behavior. I had found them all to be trustworthy, something I could not say about other classes I'd had over the years. Still, I was on edge until we could get all of them out of the mall.

The following day was festival day, and the kids were excited. The band performed first, and they did okay, although there were some minor errors. The chorus performed next, and they did well, although they were very small. There were kids missing in all of the sections, especially the alto section, which I had been struggling with all year. The majority of them couldn't be bothered to make the trip. After the chorus performance, I checked the weather outside. The skies had been threatening all morning, and now a light rain was falling. I stood just outside of the front door of the school where all the judging was taking place. The last performance of the morning was supposed to be the band in the parade competition. I had been working hard with the band to prepare for parade judging. For me, it was something I had done before, and having that previous experience, I knew what all of the expectations were, and what the judges would be looking for. Explaining all of that to the kids and practicing for the parade competition format took a lot more rehearsal time than I anticipated, but now I had a decision to make. The band at Newfound does not have band uniforms. For concerts, the students wear concert clothes consisting of black pants and white shirts, with ties for the boys. However, for the annual Memorial Day Parade, which is the only marching performance of the year for the band, the kids wear t-shirts with a Newfound Band logo. The rain was heavy enough that I knew that the kids would be soaked with their t-shirt uniform. I realized I could pull them from the parade competition and then it wouldn't be a problem. As I was pondering this, about 20 of my band members came rushing by me on their way to the buses to get their equipment, 15 minutes early no less. There was no question, they were ready to perform in the rain.

"Decision Made," I thought.

As they were getting ready, I told everyone to forget about the t-shirts, and dress for the rain. I told them I didn't want anyone to catch a cold because they didn't dress properly. As they lined up for the parade judging, I was disappointed by what I saw. In many situations, proper judging for a parade usually requires at least one judge to evaluate the music, and one to evaluate marching. In other cases, an entire panel of judges evaluate the groups. However, in this case, it appears that one of the judges did not show up that day, so the parade judging was being done by a single judge. It is difficult for a single person to evaluate all of the components of a parade performance, and as a result, I doubted that the band had received a true evaluation on both the music and the marching judging sheets. Add to that, the band lost points because they were not wearing uniforms, and I just wasn't sure it was worth it for the band to compete in this category. However, everyone seemed to have a good time, and overall, I would have to classify the trip as successful.

The next challenge was to prepare for the Memorial Day Parade. I didn't have to do much with the high school students, because, after all, I had just spent a significant amount of time preparing them for the parade competition on the spring trip, only a couple of weeks before. However, at Newfound, the bands of the high school and middle school combine for the Memorial Day Parade, and the middle school kids were unaware of what the high school kids were doing. Another issue was that the band director at the middle school, who was also in her first year in the district, did not have any experience teaching marching band. Fortunately, when I explained the situation to Mike, the high school principal, he arranged for me to be able to go to the middle school a few times to work with the middle school students. On the day of the parade, the combined bands were awesome. They looked great, they sounded great, and they put in a superlative appearance. At the end of the parade, there was a ceremony in the town square. The band carried off all the protocols with no problem, and after the ceremony was over, the entire crowd applauded as the band marched away. In addition, once again, on the day after the parade, Marie, the school district superintendent, made it a point to come to my band class to tell the kids how wonderful they were.

And so, I would classify my first year at Newfound as an unqualified success. I spent the summer at home in Maine with my wife and turned my attention to the next school year. I decided it was time to pursue a project that I had been thinking about for a long time. When I taught in Lisbon, I held a concert close to Christmas time. The concert program consisted of a large amount of Christmas music, and as high school events go, it was pretty nice. However, something I had long wanted to do was produce a Christmas event that involved a large amount of adults as well as high school kids. However, with the high school concert so close to Christmas, my hands were full in preparing students, and there simply wasn't time to work with adults. Add to that, the fact that I wanted to use the event to expand my orchestration abilities, and fashion some home grown versions of Christmas classics for a singer, or group of singers, with a full orchestra. So, I was never able to pursue this project at Lisbon. However, now that I was at Newfound, the situation had changed. The Newfound Winter Concert was held in the beginning of

December, which would leave a small, but workable window in which to hold a major Christmas event. In addition, an opportunity presented itself that would allow me to build an ensemble worthy of such a project. In central New Hampshire, there is an orchestra known as the Lakes Region Symphony Orchestra. I had been thinking about joining the group for some time, so I started attending rehearsals of the orchestra. Eventually, I was able to recruit some players for an ensemble to accompany singers. In the meantime, I started putting other pieces together for a Christmas event. I surveyed parents, put out publicity for adult singers, and started making plans with other high school staff members who were also interested in putting on an event such as this. I started writing orchestrations and found some sheet music resources. I decided to call the event "Christmas at Newfound", and in my memo to recruit parents, I outlined my vision of an event where parents would perform with their children, making this an inter-generational celebration of music for the Christmas season. I started rehearsals with nearly 40 adults, which eventually settled to around 30. Some were experienced singers, and some had not sung in a long time. I made plans to perform four selections with a chorus consisting of the adults and the high school kids together. The remainder of the concert selections would be soloists or small groups of kids or adults. The hard part was crunching together two different sets of choral selections for the high school kids, one set for the high school Winter Concert, the other set for Christmas at Newfound. The Drama director was very supportive of this endeavor, and we discussed ways in which the drama department would be a part of the event. I shared my vision with her of a presentation based on the old concept of minstrel shows in which all of the performers are on stage throughout the presentation. However, instead of sidemen, we decided to use drama students dressed as elves for dialogue and introductions in between music selections. When we held dress rehearsal, there was a delay in starting, because we had to get creative in where to put everyone on stage. The concert itself was a great success. As an added touch, during intermission, there were tables set up in the lobby with refreshments, and students circulating throughout the lobby area offering various treats and goodies to the audience members.

It was great to see a vision take shape and become a reality, but I wasn't done yet. I went on to create two other events that year, both of which went on to become yearly traditions. One was an annual "Jazz Night" in which performances by both the high school and middle school jazz bands were featured, as well as a jazz group made up of local adults. That first year, the event was held in the auditorium, but in subsequent years "Jazz Night" conflicted with dress rehearsals for the spring musical production, so we ended up performing in the cafeteria. To make the best of the situation, I had students rearrange the tables in the cafeteria so that it resembled a nightclub setting. Tablecloths were placed on the tables, and my wife was good enough to provide battery candles and green tinted goblets for centerpieces. I also arranged for a large coffee pot and sometimes cookies or other goodies as well. The audience has grown each year, and many folks continue to look forward to this event.

The other event that I initiated, was a concert that I christened as the "Student Music Project". Originally, I was looking to create a setting where students could take some leadership roles, and then I thought, "why not let students run the whole thing?" I sat down with a group of students and we discussed all of the components and roles that students would have to take on in order to run their own production. We drew up rules and procedures, and then I allowed the students to take over and start planning the production. Prospective performers for the concert were auditioned, and the student leaders assigned various jobs to those that volunteered for stage management, tech crew, publicity, etc. Over the years, this has been an interesting event to watch. Each year, a senior acts a chairperson of the production, and an underclassman, usually a junior, acts as an assistant, and then takes over the following year. Each student that chairs the project puts their own stamp on the production, and no Student Music Project concert is exactly the same from year to year. The principal, Mike, was very pleased with all these new developments, and I think he appreciated the new opportunities and experiences that I was offering students.

When I started my third year at Newfound, I was feeling more comfortable with the situation. For the most part, the group of students that were resentful about their previous music teacher being replaced had now graduated, and I now had a much more committed group of students in band and chorus. Once again, I did "Christmas at Newfound", and the other events that I had started the previous year. Again, some may look at this and say, "Why would you do so much extra work"? However, I continued to press on, and I made the refining of the procedures of each of the events my focus for the year. When it came to selecting a destination for the Music Department Spring Trip, I decided on the Music Showcase Festival at Jackson, NJ. Jackson is the location of the Six Flags Great Adventure Park. The itinerary called for judging to take place at a nearby school in the morning, after which the students would spend the afternoon in the amusement park. I thought most of the music students would jump at the chance to do this trip, and once again, to keep the student cost as low as possible, I made all the trip arrangements myself.

Unfortunately, the number of music students registering for the trip was surprisingly low. I wasn't happy, and I realized that I had to find a way to make this trip successful, because I didn't even want to think about the possible consequences if it wasn't. I didn't want it to be just a "fun" trip. I knew the key component to going to the festival was a successful music experience. I spent a lot of time studying music that could be utilized with limited instrumentation that I was expecting with the band. In the chorus, I chose music in three parts, soprano, alto and baritone as opposed to the standard SATB voicing. I also set up after-school band and chorus rehearsals with just the kids that would be going on the trip. I was pleasantly surprised that nearly all the kids in the ensembles made it to the rehearsals, save for athletic conflicts, and as a result, I had the unique opportunity to work with just those kids involved in the festival. That is what played a critical role in turning the situation around from what would have been a case of students struggling to perform music that was intended for larger groups than they were, to the band and chorus giving respectable performances in their own right.

On the day of the trip, I had no illusions about the situation. I was certain that the band and chorus performances would be respectable, and I would be satisfied with that. I told other staff members that all I really wanted to do was get everyone back in one piece. The following day, we arrived early at the school where the adjudications were taking place. The Newfound groups were scheduled to be the last groups performing, so we viewed some of the performances of other schools. I remember that I wasn't particularly impressed by any of the other schools with the exception of one choir that was very good. The thing is, I didn't really give the issue a lot of thought. The Newfound band and chorus performed as expected, and I was happy at how well they did. Off we went to Six Flags, and the kids spent the afternoon in the park. Around suppertime, the awards ceremony was held, and all of the groups from the performing schools crowded into a small stadium and awaited the announcement of the results. To begin the ceremony, all of the directors from the participating schools were called to the stage to be acknowledged, and to receive their score sheets. The first awards given were soloist awards, and three of my chorus members received awards for their solos. Next, awards were given for the best sections. At this point, I settled back and started looking over the score sheets, half-listening as best section awards were given to other schools. I scanned the chorus score sheet. Judges awarded them an "Excellent" rating, and I was fairly pleased with that. I then looked at the band score sheet and was pleasantly surprised. The group was awarded a "Superior" rating with a numerical score of 90.1 out of 100 points. This was unexpected. The kids performed well, but their instrumentation was thin, and the program I had them perform wasn't that challenging. As I was studying the score sheet, I heard the announcer say, "Best Trumpet Section – Newfound". My kids went nuts, and I sent my very excited trumpet section up to the podium to receive their award.

"Well, that's cool," I thought, but that wasn't the end of the story.

The announcer then said, "Best Low Brass Section – Newfound."

Once again, the Newfound kids went nuts, and all I could think was "Wow"!

It was now time for the group awards. In the mixed choir category, Newfound placed 2nd. As far as I was concerned, that was fine. Their evaluation was very good, and I don't think I could have expected much more from an SAB choir.

The awards for instrumental groups followed, with awards for jazz band, string orchestra, and then concert band. As good as the band's evaluation was, I held my breath. I was hopeful, but not confident.

The announcer then said "2nd Place in Concert Band…"

And then announced the name of another school. I smiled, knowing what was coming next, and the announcer said "1st place in Concert Band…Newfound!"

The kids cheered again, and I sent a couple of seniors to the podium to receive the award. The final awards were Overall Awards, to the highest scoring Choral and Instrumental groups across all of the categories. First, the overall choral award was given to the school that I had seen earlier, that had performed so well.

Then the announcer said, "Best Overall Instrumental group, with a score of 90.1…"

Totally zoning out, I said to myself, "90.1, That sounds familiar."

Just as it dawned on me what the significance of the score meant, the announcer said "Newfound!"

For me, it was almost beyond belief. All I had wished for was for both groups to have respectable performances, and here we were, taking home a Grand Champion trophy. It was a great bus ride home, and the publicity we received in the next several days was really wonderful.

ON TO THE STATE FESTIVAL

As we began the following school year, I decided it was time to take on another challenge. Like most states, New Hampshire holds a festival for the adjudication of bands, choirs, and orchestras. The judging follows a state rubric, so the judging can be consistent year to year, even though one might find a totally different judging panel from one year to the next. The festival is called the "Large Group Festival". To be honest, I wish the festival was called something different, but there doesn't seem to be any groundswell to change it. At this point, the chorus had improved to the point that I felt it was ready to enter such a festival. The band had always been ready, but I hesitated to impose a new requirement on band without a similar requirement for chorus. I had to make some adjustments to my lesson unit planning, but I had no problem making such changes. After another year of "Christmas at Newfound", I set the band and chorus on a new trajectory, to prepare for adjudication on the state level. I talked with Mike, the principal, about what I was planning. My feeling was that in this era of accountability, we test kids in math, English, and science, but little else. This was a chance to test our music students according to parameters set by the state's music educators. Mike agreed, and I went forward with my plans. When the day arrived for the festival, I put the band on one bus, and the chorus on another, and headed for the festival site. The performances for both groups went ok, but each group had difficulties with the sight-reading portion of their performance. In the Large Group Festival, each group performs pieces they prepare before a panel of three judges. After the conclusion of the performance, the group moves to a private room, known as the sight-reading room. Parents and the public can view the first performance, but not the sight-reading performance. In the sight-reading room, music that the group has never seen before is passed out face down on the music stands. When the session begins, students are allowed to turn over their music, and quietly talk among themselves about the piece they have to sight-read. The conductor is also allowed to study the score for a couple of minutes, and then can talk to the group about the piece for another couple of minutes. The group then performs the piece and the judge gives them a grade based on how accurately the students are able to perform it. The sight-reading grade is then factored into the scores the group received from the three judges in their first performance, and the group is given an overall Festival Rating. The overall Festival Rating grade differs from state to state. In this case, groups were given overall grades of A, B, C, or D. For their first experience with this event, both the band and the chorus were awarded a "B" rating. I found it acceptable for a first attempt, but I told both groups that we would return the following year, and I expected them to do better.

Of course, doing this festival along with all the other stuff I was doing is something I think some people might call foolish. I wasn't being paid anything extra to do all of this. I just did it because I felt it was in the best interest of the music program, and the students. However, as it turned out, there was a benefit to all that work that I did not anticipate. About the same time as I was preparing the kids for the

Large Group Festival, the school district was dealing with a budget crisis. It is about this time of year that the School District goes through its budget procedure. Public hearings are scheduled, and the voters go to the polls to decide what the budget for the following school year will be. In this case, the voters determined that the school budget would be exactly the same for all budget lines the following year. Of course, the difficulty with this is that there are always some costs in the budget such as heating oil, transportation, insurance, etc. that rise every year. Since the voters were not willing to provide the extra funds to address these rising costs, it became necessary for the school board to make cuts to the budget in other areas. All of the staff members held their breath waiting to see where the school board would make cuts. When the school board released its list of cuts, we could see that cuts were made in nearly all areas of the budget. In my case, however, the news was quite good. Every department in the high school suffered some type of cut, except for the music program. I found out later that some parents had spoken at a budget hearing and said that they considered any cut to the music program to be unacceptable. This was something new. In all of the other places that I had worked, if budget cuts were necessary, the music department took its lumps along with everyone else, more so in several cases. As a teacher, I knew that budget cuts were sometimes unavoidable. If the cuts were fair, that is to say that if the music department cuts were in line with cuts the other departments were experiencing, then I didn't make a big deal out of it. I only became upset when the music program was singled out or was the recipient of cuts to a greater degree than other subjects. But to be on the other end of this outcome, watching other departments deal with cuts while I had no change to my budget, was something I had never experienced. I felt lucky and honored at the same time.

The following year, I was blessed with some very good groups. The chorus was outstanding, and the band was exceptionally good. I was able to give them music that was particularly challenging, and they were able to handle it. When time for the Large Group Festival came, I was hopeful, that they could give the kind of performance that would warrant a superior grade. Again, I ordered two buses for the festival, one for the band, the other for the chorus. A much larger contingent of parents attended as opposed to the previous year. When we arrived at the festival, I gave the chorus kids some free time to watch some of the other performances, while I concentrated on getting the band ready for their performance, which would occur first. The band played well, so well in fact that I don't think I could have expected them to perform better. It was then time for the chorus to get ready for their performance. As kids were changing into their performance clothes, one of the boys in the chorus managed to tear his pants. He ended up borrowing a pair of black pants from one of the band members, and crisis was resolved. However, it ended up being a distraction for the whole group, and I wasn't able to give them the kind of warm-up I wanted to for the performance. As it turned out, it didn't really matter. The chorus performed brilliantly. In fact, I'm told that during the performance of "Lacrimosa" from the Mozart Requiem, several parents were in tears. The end result was that the chorus was awarded an "A" rating for their performance. I was thrilled, and so were the kids. I couldn't help but remember the time that I was teaching in Lisbon, and one of the other District III teachers told me I should turn my chorus over to a choral major, and that as an instrumental major I would never succeed as a choral conductor. That conversation haunted me for many years, and now that my chorus had been awarded an "A" rating, I could finally shake that burden off my back.

When I looked at the band score sheets, it was a different story. The band was awarded a "B" rating. However, as I was looking through the score sheets, something struck me as odd. The score sheets for this festival broke down each performance into multiple captions. Many elements were evaluated, including tone, rhythm, intonation, dynamics, etc. In all, each judge graded the band on 19 different captions, with each caption given a grade of A, B, C, etc. The rule was that the average grade of the 19 captions would be the overall rating of the group. However, when I looked at the score sheets for Newfound's band performance, most of the caption grades were A's. This was in opposition to what the festival rules were. According to festival guidelines, the fact that Newfound received A's in most of the judging captions would mean that their overall rating should be an "A". I contacted the festival chairman and explained the situation. I brought him the score sheets a couple of weeks later, and he ended up changing the rating of the Newfound band to an "A". The Music Department Spring Trip that year featured a trip to a festival in Hershey, PA. As with other such festivals, the students would perform for evaluation in the morning, and spend the afternoon in the amusement park. The first day of the trip was spent mostly on the road, approximately 10 hours travel time with stops. We pulled into our hotel around dusk. At about that time, I was approached by a student. David played alto sax in band, and guitar in the jazz band. "Mr. Judd" he said to me, "I forgot my saxophone and music at school". "Back in New Hampshire?" I asked, knowing that there was no other answer. I groaned. The only way to provide music for David was to copy the conductor scores of all the selections we would perform the next day, cut out the alto saxophone lines in the scores and tape them all together to make alto sax parts. It would be a lot of work, but with a borrowed alto saxophone, David would be able to perform with the band, and we wouldn't be missing any critical alto sax parts. I figured if that was going to be the only glitch on this trip, then I was getting off easy, but about 10 minutes later, my lead trumpet player, Matt, came up to me. "Mr. Judd" he said, "My trumpet is back in New Hampshire". Now, I had to piece together an alto sax part, and a trumpet part. I couldn't understand how these students, both seniors could be so forgetful. With the help of a very kind clerk in the hotel, I was able to get copies of the scores. I then spent the rest of the evening, and most of breakfast the next morning cutting out and taping together the alto sax and trumpet parts.

The judging for this festival took place at a high school that appeared to be fairly new. The facilities were impressive, and I couldn't wait to see my groups perform on this stage. The first group to perform would be the chorus, followed by a group from another school, then the band, followed by a group from another school, and then the jazz band. I brought the chorus into the warm-up room and proceeded to prepare them for the performance. When it was time for the group to perform, an assistant came into the room and told me that we had to wait because the judges had not yet arrived. More waiting, finally we were led on stage by the student guides, and the chorus was able to perform. After the chorus performed, I was met by the festival director. The group that was to follow the chorus had a bus breakdown, and would I mind going right into our band performance? I said OK and had the kids set up the stage for the band performance. After the band performance, the festival director came up to me again. The school that was supposed to follow the band performance was also delayed, and would I mind having the jazz band perform immediately? Again, I said OK, and the jazz band set up and performed. So now three groups had performed, all of them from Newfound. The kids didn't seem to mind. It gave them an extra hour in the amusement park. Everyone seemed to have a good time, and except for returning to the school at around 2:30am, everyone appeared to be quite pleased. However, once again, the forgetfulness of my seniors took front and center, as it turned out that the bass player in the jazz band left his new electric bass at the school that we were judged in back in Pennsylvania.

The next school year started out quite normal. The performances in the first part of the year went great, and I was starting to gear the groups up for the State Large group festival. I had experienced a loss of several key seniors to graduation, and as a result, I wasn't confident that they could repeat their Large Group "A" rating performance. With the chorus, however, things were different. Most of the strong singers were back, and I was fairly certain that they could attain another "A" rating. As it turned out, I was right, and it was great to be able to hang another "A" rating plaque on the wall.

THE SMART WAY AND THE STUPID WAY

The Spring Trip that year was somewhat unique. I had kept in touch with many of the teachers in District III, and I had talked to the group that still participated in the concert exchange with Islesboro, which they were still doing each year. I asked if I could bring my students from New Hampshire, and they agreed. In order to do this, the mainland concert and the Islesboro concert needed to be scheduled on back to back days. So on a Thursday, the first day of the trip, we left from Newfound in the early afternoon, and headed for the mainland high school where the first concert would be held. After a late afternoon rehearsal and supper, the combined bands and choirs presented a concert in the evening with the audience consisting mostly of parents of participating students. After the concert, I was amazed at how quickly the Newfound kids managed to pack their equipment on the bus, but then I remembered that I told them earlier not to waste time packing up because that would cut down on their swimming time at the hotel. So we checked in to a hotel not far from where the evening's concert was held. Now, in doing music trips over the years, I have learned that there are generally two ways in which a hotel makes room assignments for our group. The smart way is to assign kids and chaperones to a block of rooms that are all in the same section of the hotel, and as far away from other guests as possible. This allows the adults to closely monitor the kids' activities and be aware of any kids that might want to test the chaperones when it comes to curfew. It works really well. Then, there is the stupid way, where the hotel assigns kids and chaperones to what seems like random rooms throughout the hotel. On the Newfound trip, the hotel decided to assign rooms the stupid way. They had our students and chaperones assigned to rooms all over the hotel, with no apparent pattern to where people were placed. When the Newfound kids arrive at a hotel, usually the first thing they want to do is to go swimming. It is an absolute must that each year, I choose a hotel that has a swimming pool. So, after check-in, kids changed into swim suits, and headed for the pool. Ordinarily, this would not be a problem, but in this case we had a group of students walking the halls from their rooms, all the way across to the other side of the hotel where the pool was. Unfortunately, this meant walking past the hotel bar, and when several twenty-something male bar patrons saw the girls walking past them in swim suits headed for the pool, they immediately left the bar, and tried to pick up the girls. As soon as I found out what was going on, I called hotel security. The issue was resolved before there were any problems, but I couldn't help thinking that the whole situation could have been avoided if only the hotel was smarter about how they assigned rooms to our group. The next morning, we headed to Lincolnville, and the ferry landing for catching the ferry to Islesboro. Unfortunately, the weather did not cooperate very well, and there was a light rain falling for most of the day. Still, the concert was very successful, and the students performed before a significant number of island residents, as well as the student body of the Islesboro School. In the evening, we took the Newfound students to a performance of "Pirates of Penzance", and the trip was an unqualified success. I finished the school year feeling very satisfied, but I noticed that I was feeling very tired. In fact, I think I probably spent most of the first three weeks of summer vacation sleeping.

BUT MR. JUDD, WE DON'T SING

On the first-class day of a new school year, the plan for my classes is fairly straightforward. I spend the first part of the class going over the Music Department Handbook with the students, pointing out important information and performance dates for the new school year. I then go over all the aspects of group warm-ups and exercises that we will use for each class. On this particular first day, I went through my planned activities for my chorus class as normal. At the end of class, I was approached by two freshmen students. One of the girls said "Mr. Judd, there's something you need to know, we don't sing". At first, I thought I heard her wrong. I asked her to repeat what she said, and she replied, "We never sing in chorus." Her partner nodded in agreement. "If that's the case," I said "then what are you doing here? Singing is kind of a central requirement in chorus". There was no reply, only silence. I said, "You were in chorus in middle school, but you never sang?" The girls nodded. Setting aside the issue of how they could possibly go through chorus in middle school without singing, I said "That's not going to work here. If you are not willing to sing in chorus you should probably be in another class." I sent them to the Guidance Office, so they could drop chorus and select another class.

Later in the day, I was having a conversation with the other teachers in my wing, an art teacher, a PE teacher and the Health teacher. I told them what had happened earlier with these two girls in my chorus class. "I couldn't believe it!" I said. "Can you imagine being in chorus through middle school and never singing" The guys shook their heads in agreement. "What you need to do," one of them said "is to think out of the box and create a chorus class where nobody sings." We all had a good laugh, but the following morning, the two freshmen girls walked into the classroom of the Health teacher and presented him with the papers from Guidance transferring them into his class. Having been part of the discussion with me the day before, the teacher immediately knew that these were the girls that I had been talking about. At first, the teacher said nothing, and gathered the materials that the girls would need in his class. As he was handing the materials to the girls, he said "You do realize that we sing in this class, don't you?" I don't know what the reaction of the girls was, not realizing if he was serious or just teasing them.

The rest of the fall went by without incident, but then, one day, about a week after the Winter Concert, I was finishing up my first period band class, when I felt a major wave of dizziness wash over me. I could still get up and walk, but I knew that this needed attention. I went to the school nurse and explained what had happened. She took my blood pressure, which was fairly normal. She then checked my pulse, and then checked it a second time. "We need to call an ambulance for you" she said as she picked up the phone. As it turned out, my pulse was running at nearly 160. It slowed down by the time I got to the hospital, but they kept me overnight for observation.

Since most of my doctors are in Maine, I knew I needed to check with them. I saw my primary doctor, and then a cardiologist. Nobody had an explanation for what had taken place, but we all knew that the situation needed to be monitored.

As the year progressed, an unfortunate development occurred. Marie, my school superintendent, the only superintendent that ever hugged me, passed away from cancer. Part of me felt lost, and the prospect of who would take her place filled me with concern. It had taken me many years to find myself in a successful music program such as Newfound. I would think that a new school superintendent coming into a position would not want to mess with successful programs, but experience has taught me never to assume such things. As the year started winding down, for the Music Department Spring Trip, I decided to make a return to the Music Showcase Festival in New Jersey. We had been so successful in the event four years prior, that I wanted to see how we would fare again. This time, the results were not nearly so spectacular. Newfound competed head to head with two other schools, and although the scores were close, within a fraction of a point, Newfound lost out in both the band and chorus categories, although the kids won awards for best alto section in chorus, and best low brass section in band.

After an uneventful summer, the following school year started out relatively well, but I was still experiencing this fatigue issue. It was especially noticeable at marching band shows. Even though all of my children had graduated from high school, I was still helping out with the marching band at the school they attended, writing the music for their field show, and assisting with instruction where I could. However, when the group attended a marching band show, a good deal of walking was required at most of those events. The warm-up area for bands is usually a fair distance away from the stadium, so that the music from a band that is warming up doesn't interfere with a band that may be performing in the stadium. Not only that, but in most cases, the bus parking area is quite a way from both the warm-up area and the stadium. Most folks can do all the walking with no problem, and it never previously bothered me to walk those distances, but now I was struggling. It took a lot longer for me to get from one place to another, I was walking slower, and getting out of breath a lot easier. I thought that perhaps the congestive heart failure I had experienced a number of years ago had returned. I also brought my band to University of Massachusetts Band Day, which was being held that year in Gillette Stadium where the Patriots play. I thought it would be a great experience for the kids, and indeed it was. At half-time, they were part of a 3,500-piece massed band that performed. However, the day took a toll on me physically with all the walking around that was required.

I went to see the doctor and explained the issue. She put on her stethoscope and listened to my lungs. "No problem there" she said. "It's definitely not congestive heart failure". She then listened to my heart, and paused, and listened some more, and listened a whole lot more, and listened, a very long time, moving the stethoscope around the general area, and I thought "Uh-oh". She then had her assistant bring in an EKG machine and hook me up to it. When I saw the EKG strip, I was shocked. It showed a highly irregular heartbeat. It looked like a child had scribbled a line across the EKG strip. "I need to send you to the cardiologist" the doctor said. The next few months I spent going from test to test, doctor to doctor, frequent blood tests, as well as a great deal of concern from my family. I was able to continue teaching, but I had to spend most of my time sitting down, teaching from a chair, or a stool. I felt physically limited. I had to ask students to do various lifting and moving chores. A few months later, in the spring, they finally gave me a diagnosis. They told me I needed heart surgery. It seems that I had a torn heart valve that needed to be repaired or replaced. The next person I had to visit was the heart surgeon. The surgeon I saw came highly recommended, and after some discussion, he told me he would try to repair the valve, but if that wasn't possible, he would have an artificial one standing by. Just for the heck of it, I asked what would happen if I didn't have the procedure done. "You'll be dead within a year," he said very matter of factly. I needed to set aside three months for the procedure and recovery. Now I had to make a decision since summer vacation is only two months. Would I leave school a month early and use summer vacation for the rest of my recovery, or would I have the procedure done when school let out for the summer and allow the recovery to extend through the rest of the summer and into the first month or so of school. I went and talked to Mike, my principal and told him I wanted to leave school just after the Memorial Day Parade to have the procedure done and miss the final month of school. Mike understood and was very supportive. The next few weeks were filled with decisions about how the music program would function while I was away. Getting a substitute music teacher to finish out the year for me was not an option. There simply were not any folks available with the background and availability to do it. The band had a performance scheduled for graduation, the chorus at the Baccalaureate ceremony held the night before graduation. We went to the middle school band director for help in leading the band during graduation, and a former Newfound music teacher who was now a stay-at-home mom to conduct the chorus at Baccalaureate. Since these two music teachers could not meet with their groups every day, plans had to be made for substitute teachers on days that the music teachers were not available. In addition, a procedure for administering and grading final exams had to be established. It was a lot of work and planning. In the middle of all this, the normal music department events took place. I went into the Spring Concert feeling the students were adequately prepared and expecting the evening to progress without incident. My wife made the trip from Maine, and stationed herself nearby, just in case she was needed. Mike, my principal, paced the floor backstage the entire evening. The kids played well, but what I wasn't counting on was their reaction to my situation. Midway through the band performance, the kids stopped me, and sort of commandeered the stage. They presented me with a huge card, signed by all of them, and then about 30 students came to where I was conducting, and gave me a group hug right in front of the audience. Even my drum section, which had been particularly difficult to manage that year, and not quite familiar with the details of my situation, gave me an even larger hand printed card, saying that they were truly sorry for causing my "heart attack"!

There were other adjustments to make as well. Since October, I had been planning the Music Department Spring trip, this particular year to New York City to see "Phantom of the Opera". Now, my doctor was telling me that I should not do the trip, so we had to find a last-minute replacement for me, and I had to orientate all of the chaperones to be able to function on the trip without me. I also ended up calling the chairman of the Memorial Day Parade, asking if I could ride in a vehicle on the day of the parade. The chairman was very accommodating. I ended up turning the band over to the middle school band director, who was quite capable and by this time had several years' experience doing the parade, but I hated the idea of not being able to march with my band.

I entered the hospital on June 1st, with my surgery taking place the next day. I then spent several days in the hospital, followed by two weeks in an acute care facility, and then the rest of the summer in cardiac rehab. I began the next school year on schedule and looked forward to getting back in class. Mike came in to see me the first day as I was sitting at my podium in my conductor's chair and said, "It's so great to see you in that chair again". That's the thing about Newfound. I don't think I ever felt unsupported. Even though I was back and feeling much better, there were students and staff members constantly asking how I was doing.

A NEW PRINCIPAL

The new year started off fairly well. The music performances all were satisfactory. It was turning out to be a pretty good year. Then, as spring was approaching, Mike announced that he was retiring. I was devastated. I was going to lose the best principal I ever had, the most supportive, the most caring. I had no idea who was going to fill his position, and to what extent the music program would be affected. As the Spring Concert was approaching, I asked Mike, half-jokingly, if he would please consider staying another year so he could continue to introduce the Music Department concerts, especially the Lakes Region Music Festival, an honors festival that Newfound was expected to host the following year. For a few seconds, it really did seem as if he was seriously considering it, although of course, at this time, he was committed to his retirement. By this point, we had a new superintendent, and when she asked the faculty for volunteers to serve on an interview committee for the principal position, I volunteered.

The committee ended up interviewing three candidates for the principal position. The first candidate displayed a shockingly limited knowledge of the issues that the Newfound staff considered high priority. He had no experience as a principal, and when he was asked about Advanced Placement and Running Start courses, such as we offer at Newfound, he had no idea what we were talking about. The second candidate seemed to have a better background and knowledge of issues, but I still wasn't impressed. The third candidate was Paul, the Newfound Assistant Principal. Certainly, being a part of the Newfound staff was an advantage for Paul, and he displayed an understanding of those high priority topics as he shared his vision for the school. Paul had certainly demonstrated his administrative abilities. The previous year, he had been selected as the New Hampshire Assistant Principal of the Year. He was also well liked by the students, and several dozen of them crowded a school board meeting to advocate for Paul to become the new principal, something that I think several of the school board members were impressed with. In the end, Paul succeeded Mike as the Newfound Principal.

When the next school year started, the transition from Mike to Paul was almost seamless. When I started making plans for the Music Department Spring Trip to Boston to attend a performance of the Blue Man Group, Paul asked if he could go along. Mike had gone with me a few years earlier when I took the kids to Maine, so I didn't see a problem. The year continued, and then in January, Newfound hosted the Lakes Region Music Festival, a regional honors festival involving students from several area schools. The festival membership included the music directors from 12 high schools in the Lakes Region of New Hampshire. I had served a two-year term as President of the organization some years before, and I would begin another two-year term again after the conclusion of the festival I was hosting. At first, things were looking good. Everyone was supportive of the hosting effort. But then, difficulties started to arise. First, the school district business office balked at some of the expenses that other host schools had their districts cover as normal procedure. In Newfound's case that would mean that for the transportation of music stands, chairs and choral risers from the middle school, plus a custodial presence on site the day of the festival, the Newfound School District would bill the Music Department. Then, I received the cost estimate from the food service department for the meals that we would the provide. The estimate was way beyond what I had budgeted, and I began to wonder if the music department would see any profit from hosting this event. Plans continued, and the day before festival, the weather forecast was ominous. I started reliving nightmares of the first festival I hosted in Maine, where mother nature threw me an impossible curve ball. Rather than take a chance, we decided to play it safe and postpone the festival for a week. One of the requirements of hosting this festival was that a make-up day be scheduled one week later than the original scheduled event. It was well known by all the directors, and it was written into the contracts of the guest conductors. As it turned out, the weather on the day of what would have been the festival was pretty nasty, with snow and ice most of the day. We certainly had made the right choice in rescheduling the festival. This gave me an additional week of preparation time, although most of the preparations were complete by this time anyway. As soon as school ended on Friday of that week, I began setting up for the festival for the following day. All of the band and chorus student were required to sign up for various jobs necessary, which in the case of the students required help either setting up or cleaning up after the festival was over. I had reserved various rooms of the school for festival rehearsals including the library for the festival jazz band, the music room for the chorus, and the gym for the concert band. The gym would also be the site of the Festival Concert. I certainly would have wanted the concert in Newfound's auditorium, which would be a wonderful space for such an event. However, the fire rated capacity of the auditorium was about 475, and I was expecting more than 600 people at the concert, so I had no choice but to use the gym. Since on this day before the festival, the gym would not be ready for set-up until 5pm, I turned my attention to the other rooms. I had a student crew set up the chairs and music stands for the jazz band in the library, while in the music room, I started setting up chairs for the chorus by myself. I was feeling kind of grumpy because the three students that were assigned to help me set up for the chorus did not show up. As I was setting up the chairs, I said out loud to no one in particular in an empty room "If I start feeling more annoyed than I do now, I'm going to start talking to myself". It was about then that I started to feel something going wrong. Now, with all the things that I had gone through with my heart, having pain was not one of them. I never had pain in the months leading up to my heart surgery, and I wasn't feeling any pain now. However, I knew something was wrong because all of a sudden a huge wave of fatigue swept over me. I had to stop what I was doing and sit down. I kept waiting for the fatigue to pass, but it didn't, and when the set-up crew for the gym came in at 5:00, I was of no help to them at all. The next morning, as the festival began, my son, Greg, arrived from Maine to help me out, and I don't mind saying that without his help I would not have been able to get through the day. In the days after the festival, I made an appointment to see the cardiologist as soon as I could. He told me that my heart had slipped back into "A-Fib", similar to the time before my heart surgery. One again, my heart was again beating irregularly. I had to undergo a procedure called Cardioversion, in which after a mild sedative was given, an electrical shock was applied to my heart to get it to beat in a normal rhythm. After a number of days, I started feeling better, but the fun wasn't over. The local hospital, where I had my heart surgery had just established a new Medication Management department. I had been on the drug Warfarin ever since my heart surgery. As many people in this situation know, Warfarin is blood-thinning drug, used to avoid possible stroke. As a result, the "thinness" of my blood needs to be monitored periodically. Then, based on blood test results, the doctor will tell me to adjust the amount of medication I take. When my case was switched over to the Medication Management department, they decided they did not like my Warfarin level, and started making changes in my daily Warfarin dose.

It didn't take long for problems to develop. One day, as I was in the middle of a band rehearsal, my nose started bleeding. I arranged to have my class covered and went to the nurse's office. After a while the bleeding refused to subside, and the nurse sent me to the Emergency Room. At the Emergency Room, they were not able to stop the bleeding either and decided to put a plug in my nose. They also decided they didn't like my blood test results either and admitted me to the hospital overnight. Eventually, the bleeding stopped, and they released me. When the weekend came, I traveled to Maine as I normally do. Just as I was getting ready to return to New Hampshire on Sunday afternoon, my nose started bleeding again. This time, my wife, the nurse, took me to the Emergency Room where we live, and said to the doctor "This isn't just a nosebleed, it's a hemorrhage." Because of the high dose of Warfarin that I was taking, my blood was very thin, and the nosebleed was inevitable. The doctor put another plug in my nose and ordered me to stay in bed for a week. I was really annoyed at having to miss school for this. It certainly seemed avoidable to me. In the meantime, the bus company that I was planning to use for the Music Department annual Spring Trip, this time to Boston, canceled on me, saying they didn't have enough drivers to do the trip. Just what I needed, a crisis like this while I was flat on my back three hours away. Then something extraordinary and unexpectedly happened. My principal, Paul, who saw the dilemma I was in, took it upon himself to contact local bus companies so that the Boston trip could go on as scheduled. When I returned to school the next week, Paul said to me "I have a surprise for you. I found a bus company to do the Boston trip." I was astounded. Never in my time as a teacher had I ever received such incredible support from an administrator.

THE YEARBOOK VISIT

It was about this time that the yearbook adviser made an unannounced visit to my class and asked if she could take some candid photos of the chorus class that was in progress. I nodded my approval, and she moved around the perimeter of the class, snapping photos. I didn't think much about it and went on with my class. I didn't realize her real reason for coming to the room at that time, but the reason would become obvious a couple of months later.

In May, the Boston trip went off without a hitch, and a couple of weeks later, I took my Jazz Band to a festival at a high school in the area. The students in the Jazz Band would be out of class that day, but the administration had always been supportive. That particular day, we would miss the annual "Spring Fling" at the school. It is a day when time is set aside for various fun activities for the students, and an assembly is held where they present a yearbook to the person who the seniors dedicate the yearbook to, and for the students to acknowledge any retiring staff members.

The jazz festival went fine, and we returned to Newfound just as school was letting out. The students got off the bus first and headed to the music room with their instruments. I followed, and as I arrived at the door to the music room, with students trying to catch their buses streaming past. I heard someone shout my name. I looked around, and Paul, the principal, was walking towards me with the yearbook adviser close behind. Paul was holding a yearbook, and he handed it to me as he got to the music room door. As he handed me the yearbook, I noticed that my name was printed on the cover, and he said "Congratulations, the senior class has dedicated this year's yearbook to you!" I was surprised, honored, and astounded all at once. The irony didn't escape me that I missed the yearbook dedication announcement earlier that day because I was with students performing at a festival. I turned to the dedication page, where there was a dedication message by the senior class. There was also a candid photo of me teaching class from my podium. "Of course" I thought. The day that the yearbook adviser came to my class with her camera, she said she wanted to take candid photos. She didn't say of who, or why. In the meantime, students came up to me to congratulate me, both seniors and underclassmen, the first of an astounding collection of students, teachers, family and friends, even people I didn't know. It seemed surreal. I started wondering if someone had made a mistake. Schools across the country have yearbook dedications to staff members in their schools. It has been my observation that most of the people that receive yearbook dedications are long-time staff members, teachers or other personnel that have dedicated their careers to serving the students of their schools, many of them on the verge of retirement. Many retire never having an honor such as this bestowed on them. I had only been at Newfound for 10 years. It seemed extraordinary that I would be selected for this honor teaching such a comparatively short time in the school. After everyone had left, and I was alone, I called my mother with the news. I felt it was only right that she be the first person I share this with. After all, it was mostly through her that I learned how important it was for students to be successful when they performed, whether it was dance, or music.

FINALE

So, I have continued to teach at Newfound since my yearbook dedication year. As I said before, I don't want to retire unless my health forces me to. I spend a significant amount of time during school vacations going to doctors, who up to now along with my caring wife have been able to keep me going. Since my yearbook dedication year, there have been several things worthy of noting that have taken place.

To begin with, I happened to notice that the students were very interested in the movie "Pitch Perfect", about collegiate a cappella singing groups. When I suggested the idea of forming such a group at Newfound, the idea was met by a large amount of enthusiasm among the choral students, and some band students as well. The group turned out to be spectacularly successful, and for a couple of years, was a highlight of the concerts at Newfound. Then, there was the year that I took the band and chorus to a festival in New Jersey, the same festival that I had taken them to several years before where we received 9 trophies. This time, we came home with 11 trophies, including 1st Place in Concert Band, Jazz Band, Chorus, Select Choir, and a cappella group. I have also continued to take the band and chorus to the New

Hampshire Large Group evaluation Festival. This past year, the band did particularly well, better than they have in several years. To begin with, they went into the sight-reading portion of the festival, and came away with a rating of "Exemplary", the highest rating given. They then went into the public performance of the festival and had an excellent performance. One of the pieces we performed was "Scottish Portrait" by Swearingen. The middle movement of the piece features the tune "Scotland the Brave" which is written in a beautiful chorale treatment and the band played it as well as I possibly could have expected them to. The final portion of the festival is the band clinic, where one of the judges goes into a room with the band and gives the group constructive comments to the group about their performance. So, the judge for this clinic went through the Newfound program selections giving thoughtful comments on what the band did well, and where they could improve. Toward the end of the clinic session, the judge asked if we could play the "Scotland the Brave" movement of the "Scottish Portrait". The band took out the music and we played it once again, and they played it as well as they did in the public performance. When we finished, I put my baton down and waited for the clinical comments from the judge. There were none, all he did was smile and thank the kids for playing. Wouldn't you know it? He wasn't interested in giving us comments about the piece. He just wanted to hear us play it again.

As I look back over all my years in this profession, one question that I will probably have to answer at some point is - which of my students is the most memorable? There are many standout students that I have had over the years, starting with Brent, from my days at Fryeburg Academy. Brent went on to become a music teacher and returned to the academy to teach. Brent put Fryeburg on the jazz map of

Maine so to speak, with his students winning several state jazz titles in Jazz Band and Jazz Choir. There was Scott, my keyboard player in Ansonia. I still have yet to have a student that can improvise on the keyboard as well as Scott could. There were the twins, Brian and Bruce, from my first year at Lisbon. Bruce has gone on to be the professor of jazz studies at a college in Massachusetts, while Brian has gone on to be a professional player and university instructor. There have also been numerous students of mine that went on to become music educators themselves, with many of them doing quite well in their own right. However, I would have to say that the student that I found to be the most memorable and has had the greatest impact on me was Lisa. Lisa was a Japanese exchange student, who came to Newfound in the fall of the year following my yearbook dedication. I actually heard about Lisa before I met her. During the preparation days for the teachers just prior to the students coming in to start the new school year, I had conversations with two or three staff members that apparently had gone to an event where a fiddle band was performing. It seems Lisa was also there, and at some point the fiddle player in the band allowed her to play his violin. This fiddle player, a gentleman who runs a music shop in a nearby town that deals mostly with string instruments, apparently was so impressed with Lisa's playing, that he offered to loan to Lisa a violin from his shop the entire year she was at Newfound, since Lisa was unable to bring hers from Japan. On the first day of school, she came to band class. I explained to her that we had no orchestra at Newfound, and band arrangements usually don't have violin parts. I was kind of embarrassed and apologetic about it. Many high schools in the country have orchestras in their school. However, in New England, most do not. There are a few New England high schools that have band orchestra, and chorus in their music programs, but most of the others, including Newfound, have only band and chorus. I expected that Lisa probably would just change her class schedule and only participate in chorus, which was also on her class schedule. However, I figured I would at least give her some options. I told her that she was welcome to learn any of the other instruments that we have in band and be part of the group. After going over the list of instruments that I had for students to borrow, Lisa decided to try the string bass. Her reasoning was that since she already played a string instrument, the easiest transition for her would be the string bass. She told me she could read bass clef, so I drew up a chart of where the notes were located on the bass and gave her some bass parts from the band music to work on. Lisa picked up the bass very quickly. Within a few days, she was holding her own with the rest of the band kids, and within a couple of weeks, she was fully functioning on the bass in band. It was necessary to order a new bow for the bass for Lisa to use. There are two types of bows that bass players use, the German bow and the French bow. I learned on the German bow, in which the handle of the bow fits squarely in the hand of the player. The French bow is designed like the violin, viola, and cello bows, where the player grips the bow on top of the bow stick. So, I ordered a French bow for Lisa, and when it came in, it was a lot more comfortable for her to use. The only difficulty that Lisa had in playing the bass, is that she was very short, and had a hard time reaching the notes at the top of the fingerboard. The way she would compensate for this was whenever she had a note in the half- position, at the very top of the fingerboard, she would tilt the bass toward her, so that her fingers could reach the note. Lisa also mentioned to me that she was interested in playing with the jazz band, and with jazz practices starting up soon, I thought I might introduce her to the electric bass. Within 30 minutes she was fully functional on the electric bass. Now, I was duly impressed. There were students in the past that came in to learn bass and struggled for nearly an entire academic year to get to the level that Lisa was now playing, and it was only mid-September. It was only the first of many times that she would impress me.

Every year in my chorus class, before we start working on concert music, we work on a piece that explores choral basics. In the first chorus assessment of the year, students have to sing this piece, and I then rank all of the test scores. The top scorers are the students that I invite to be in the Select Choir. Lisa earned a spot in the select choir, no problem. A week or so later, I was working with a section of the sopranos in chorus. I was teaching them a phrase in the music that they were having some difficulty with. I instructed them to try it again and turned to the piano to give the starting pitch. As I was doing this, Lisa started singing the phrase, and did it completely correct. When I pressed the starting note on the piano, it matched her pitch exactly. I stopped what I was doing and turned to her.

"Do you have perfect pitch?" I asked.

"Yes..." was the reply.

"Aaand, you were going to tell me this, when?"

She just smiled and shrugged her shoulders. As time went on, Lisa would come to the music room during lunch period to practice violin. At this point, Lisa asked to participate in the a cappella choir, and thus, was now a member of all five music ensembles that I directed. As I listened to her practice the violin, it certainly seemed that she would make a great candidate for the New Hampshire All-State Orchestra. I proposed the idea to her, and she agreed to try. I ordered the audition music, and she started practicing it. I had no doubt that she would work diligently on it. I asked a couple of other teachers, who were string players, to listen to Lisa. They both agreed that she had a good handle on the audition piece and would make a formidable All-State candidate. About six weeks later, it was time for the All-State auditions. Lisa's host family brought her to the high school in Manchester where the auditions were being held. I met her in the auditions warm-up room, and she seemed nervous. It occurred to me that she may not have ever done an audition before. I told her that she had worked very hard on the piece, and that three of us teachers have heard her play it, and we all felt there was no reason to think that she wouldn't play it well. At this time, a student guide came to take Lisa to the auditions room. I stayed behind, since teachers are not allowed to view student auditions. When I saw Lisa later, she told me she had made a couple of mistakes during the audition, but when I received her score sheet, she received an excellent score, and thus was accepted to the All-State Orchestra. Not only that, but she qualified for the state Chamber Music Festival, in which only the very highest scoring All-State students are accepted.

Lisa was certainly making an impact on me. I've always had students that love music, but there was something different about Lisa, the way she would throw herself into every rehearsal, her incredible work ethic, and her pure enjoyment of the music she was making. I couldn't help but look forward to every day when she would come into my class. It certainly seemed that my room was her favorite place to be. There are always kids who say at the end of a class period "Gee, I wish I could be in this class every period of the day." Lisa would say this too, but I really think she meant it more than the other kids.

A couple of weeks after the All-State auditions, we held the Newfound Winter Concert. After the Winter concert, I then began preparations for three different festivals at once. The Lakes Region Festival, in which Lisa sang in the honors chorus, the State Large Group Evaluation Festival, and the State Solo & Ensemble Festival. In the Solo & Ensemble event, students are judged as soloists, or in small ensembles, duets, trios, quartets, etc. and given a letter rating by the judges. A rating of "A" is considered Superior. A rating of "B" is considered Excellent. A "C" is Good, and a "D", well, I don't talk much about "Ds". Lisa decided she wanted to enter the festival in both the vocal and violin categories. I usually allow students to pick the pieces they want to do, with my guidance, of course. For her vocal entry, she chose a tune from a Broadway show, which is something most of my students do. For her violin entry, she chose the Mozart violin concerto, which is basically a college level piece. I was certain that she would do well with both her solos. Lisa received an "A" for her vocal solo from a fairly tough judge. However, I was astounded by her violin solo score sheet. She received an "A" rating for her violin solo, but almost all the captions on the sheet were perfect scores.

As winter flowed into spring, we had another event at the school that we do every year, "Newfound Jazz Night". We do the event in the cafeteria, doing the best we can to turn the room into a nightclub atmosphere with tablecloths, centerpieces, etc. The concert features performances by three different groups, the middle school jazz band, the high school jazz band, and an adult jazz group. After the adult group performs, all of the students are called up front, and we all play the "C Jam Blues" as a finale with various students taking improvisational solos. As we did this tune, I happened to glance over toward Lisa, who was playing the electric bass. On her face, she was a picture of pure joy, smiling the entire time. She obviously loved what she was doing. I thought maybe I had imagined it, but the adult piano player noticed the same thing, and spoke to me about it. This moment presented a springboard for several conversations that I would have with Lisa in the coming weeks about what she would do when she returned home to Japan. Lisa was unsure about what she wanted to do for a career. I told her it didn't matter what she decided, so long as whatever she ended up doing made her happy like she was on Jazz Night. I told her "If it doesn't make you happy like Jazz Night, then it's wrong for you".

It occurred to me that Lisa would be leaving in a matter of weeks. A pit in my stomach formed each time I would think about it. Having her in my class seemed to be more and more precious each day, but it seemed that time flew by. Before I knew it, Spring Concert had come and gone, and we were in the midst of end of the year activities. One of those end of the year activities is Senior Awards Night, which occurs about a week before graduation. At this event, the senior class gathers in the auditorium, while teachers and other guests present them with scholarships and awards. Each academic department at Newfound has its own set of awards they present to seniors. For the music department, I was to give out four awards, the Outstanding Senior Musician award; the National School Choral award, to the outstanding chorus member; the John Philip Sousa award, to the outstanding band member; and the Directors Award, to the outstanding overall musician. When it was my turn to give out awards, I didn't spend a lot of time presenting the first three awards. Then, it was time to present the Director's Award, which was going to Lisa. At first, I hesitated. Lisa had grown on me so much that she didn't seem like just a student to me. I couldn't help but think of her as a daughter, or at least a daughter I wish I'd had, and now it was time to start saying goodbye.

Just about everyone in the auditorium knew that Lisa was going to get the award, and I started off my presentation by talking about her talents and abilities. I talked about her achievements and her dedication to the music program being a member of band, jazz band, chorus, select choir, and a cappella group. Then, I had to pause, as I was starting to choke up. In a way, it was maddening. I had never choked up before an audience before. I knew I needed to end this, but I had one more thing to say to put my feelings about Lisa into perspective. I said, "Music teachers, and others have a saying. The saying is 'You never get tired of seeing their eyes light up'". At this point, my voice was cracking, but I had to finish. "I see Lisa's eyes light up every time she walks into the music room, and of all the qualities that Lisa has, that's the one thing that I'm going to miss the most". I then called Lisa up to the front to accept her award. The response from the audience was ear splitting, and Lisa came up to the stage in tears. As a rule, I try to never touch students. I sometimes get hugs from kids, but it's not something I ever initiate. I broke that rule when Lisa came to the stage. I gave her a big hug, with both of us crying. After giving her the award, I then needed to leave the stage as quick as I could. It wouldn't do for me to stay in my seat on the stage wiping tears from my eyes while other awards were being given out.

A few days later, Lisa's last day at Newfound, she came into the music room to see me while I was sorting music. This was the moment I had been dreading. It certainly felt like she was a daughter who was now leaving forever. Lisa gave me a gift, a charcoal drawing of a violin she made, that won 1st place at the school art show. I, in turn, gave her a stack of music theory workbooks, just in case she decided to become a music major, and a card, in which I wrote at the bottom "Remember-Happy like Jazz Band". Eventually, it was time for Lisa to leave. That stoic teacher facade that I always tried to portray had faltered before, but now it just came crashing to dust. All I could do was hug her, and cry like a baby.

FINALE – TAKE 2

The first day that I sat down to write this saga, I sat at the computer for about five hours, writing all kinds of things down. There was so much that I wanted to share, the good and the bad, it just kept flowing out of me. I thought "Heck, this is a piece of cake. I should be able to finish this in three or four months." Well, three or four months ended up being nearly three years. So, yes, I wrote down a lot of things, but I tried not to stray from my central precept. I'm just a music teacher, not a great one, certainly not a bad one, but one who has witnessed many incredible things happen, mostly because of what I am. Every so often, a student will relay to me that when they woke up that morning, the last thing they wanted to do was go to school. Perhaps they were having difficulties in some of their classes, or maybe they were not getting along well with some of their teachers. However, once they realized that on that particular day, the band would be working on a really cool sounding piece, they throw off the covers, get out of bed, and start getting ready for school. At my next concert, there may well be a father, who comes to the concert to see his son play with the band. He is concerned about his son, who shows very little motivation, or concern about his future. When he hears his son play a solo in the band performance, he feels better about the situation. After all, if his son can show success with music, then there are probably other things he can succeed in as well. A mother will also come to the concert. She is distraught over the death of a family member, but she comes to the concert anyway to see her daughter perform with the chorus. When the chorus sings the Lacrimosa, from the Mozart Requiem, she becomes overwhelmed, and begins to cry. The music, however, has a therapeutic quality, and even though it doesn't make the pain go away for her, it does help her cope. After the concert, she gives her daughter a big hug before they head to the parking lot. Yes, all of these things have occurred, and more, multiple times, although I'll never know the exact number of times. Students and parents don't always share these things with me. You won't find these types of things happening as much in other classes. Kids doing a chemistry experiment usually won't have much of an audience. Kids in a math class don't usually care about how well all the other kids in the class are doing, nor is it normal practice in that class for kids to work as one group to accomplish a goal. However, in music class, that changes. My attitude when I'm in front of my band or chorus is simple. *We are going to play this piece to the best of our abilities. The most important thing is to portray the intentions of the composer. We will not allow ourselves to be distracted from this goal, and any errors we make, we will try to eliminate the next* time. If all the kids are focused, it's amazing what they can accomplish. Sometimes, when some of these amazing things occur, I have trouble comprehending how I arrived at this place, where I have had these experiences. If we could put some of these experiences into a movie, I can almost imagine a lot of folks saying "It couldn't have happened that way. Things like that don't occur in the real world". And yet, it all happened. It wasn't fiction.

Some may wonder if, after all the years that I have been in education, is there any advice I have for the nation's schools. I could, but education is political enough without me jumping in with my opinion. However, I am concerned about those school boards and administrators in education that devalue music. Music, and the other arts foster creativity more than any of the other subjects in the curriculum. All the STEM classes (Science, Technology, Engineering, Mathematics) in the world won't help a student in the global economy whose creativity is sub-par. You can get kids to memorize all kinds of facts, figures and procedures, but it won't mean anything if they can't create their way out of a wet paper bag.

As I write this, I am sitting alone in my music room. That will change in a matter of minutes when my next class will come in. I gaze across the room at the instrument storage cabinet. On top of the cabinet are more than 40 trophies. When I first arrived at Newfound, there were nine. Soon, the bell will ring, and the students will shuffle into the room in small groups of 2's and 3's. There will be a lot of chatting, usually about whatever is happening at school that day. Eventually, they will all settle into their seats, and with a minor stray thought in the back of my mind, a conversation I had with myself all those years ago on the Garden State Parkway, I'll say "OK class, please take out your music!".

CPSIA information can be obtained
at www.ICGtesting.com
Printed in the USA
JSHW021550240423
40734JS00001B/3